Morningstar® Guide to Mutual Funds

Morningstar® Guide to Mutual Funds

5-Star Strategies for Success

Christine Benz

Peter Di Teresa

Russel Kinnel

John Wiley & Sons, Inc.

Published by John Wiley & Sons, Inc., Hoboken, New Jersey.
Published simultaneously in Canada.

For general information on our other products and services, or technical support, please contact our
Customer Care Department within the United States at 800-762-2974, outside the United States at
317-572-3993 or fax 317-572-4002.

Wiley also publishes its books in a variety of electronic formats. Some content that appears in print may
not be available in electronic books. For more information about Wiley products, visit our web site at
www.wiley.com.

ISBN 0-471-26966-2

Printed in the United States of America.

10 9 8 7 6 5 4 3 2 1

Foreword

WE ALL KNOW that if you invest wisely, you can increase your wealth, but it's easy to overlook the lessons that investing can teach us about ourselves. Money is a difficult subject to discuss. Emotions run deep when it comes to our finances, causing most of us to shy away from deep thoughts on how we save or invest. Sure, we might boast to our friends about a particular stock purchase that went through the roof, or tell tales of an IPO opportunity that got away, but we seldom speak honestly or openly about our overall financial experiences, even with those closest to us. That's unfortunate. Ultimately, to know oneself as an investor goes a long way toward knowing oneself as a person.

I know that's been true for me. I started investing in mutual funds as a teenager. My father bought me 100 shares of the Templeton Growth Fund when I was in my early teens. He showed me the fund's prospectus and annual report and explained that I was now an owner of a little piece of each of the companies listed in the report. It was a wonderful introduction—not only to mutual funds, but also to the world of adult activities. I'm not saying I stopped reading *Boy's Life* the next day and switched to the *Wall Street Journal,* but an introduction had been made. Over time, I read more about investing and particularly about mutual funds. I paid special attention to Sir

John Templeton's advice, reading his annual reports and watching him on his visits to *Wall $treet Week* with Louis Rukeyser. In short, I had started down the path to becoming an investor.

Over time, I've realized that the real lesson from those first few shares of Templeton Growth wasn't how a mutual fund works, but how a responsible adult acts. In effect, my Dad was showing me that investing was something he did to help provide for our family. He wasn't jumping in and out of hot stocks. He was systematically setting a little bit aside each month to build for a better future, and he wanted me to know that I could do the same. He taught me that investing, by its very nature, is a responsible act. It's deferring the instant gratification of consuming today in hopes of providing a more secure future for yourself and for your loved ones. How different that message was from the messages on television (save those of Rukeyser's show) that portrayed investing as something only for the snobbish elite. The same shows that disparaged investing were supported by countless commercials touting the immediate satisfaction to be derived from spending!

Fortunately, our collective attitude toward investing has improved since the days when J. R. Ewing was the only one on television you saw making investments—and doing so to hurt people, I might add! The rise of personal financial journalism, led by *Money* magazine, has opened up investing to a much wider audience. There's never been a time when an individual investor had as many resources at his or her disposal as today. If anything, the challenge has shifted from finding information to making sense of an overload of information!

The 1990s, in particular, saw a surge of interest in the investment markets. Unfortunately, it wasn't always a mature or well-grounded interest. To a large extent, big market returns drove people to trade the instant gratification of consumption for the seemingly instant gratification of investment riches. I had an advantage many investors didn't have in that market: over 20 years of investing experience, albeit almost all of it with very small sums at stake. Nevertheless, I'd seen my shares both rise and fall; I'd weathered a number of down markets and had learned that staying the course paid off in the end. I especially knew from my readings on John Templeton that investing was never as easy as it appeared to be in the heady days of the Internet-led bull market. While Templeton has enjoyed enormous success as an investor, he always stresses the importance of humility, recognizing that even with thorough research there is still a significant chance that your stocks will lose money. He has warned repeatedly that even your best-researched stock pick may well decline in value by 30%, 50%, even 70% or more. Pointedly, he also notes that investors who get rich quickly are usually the same ones who get poor quickly. How truly his words played out after the technology bubble of the late 1990s.

Still, even with the sharp losses of recent years, our generation is making progress as investors. We're learning important lessons not only about investments, but also about how we respond personally to both gains and setbacks. In so doing, we lay the foundation for better results ahead. Bear markets shouldn't cause you to lose faith in the markets. Rather, they should be seen as a part of the inexorable cycle of the market. Sure, they can damage investor portfolios, but they also bring opportunities. The test is whether you have the fortitude to withstand the inevitable downturns and unearth the values they create. How odd it is that many of the same investors who bemoaned being late to the game in the 1990s, but plunged in anyway, later turned their backs on stocks at much more attractive prices. Clearly, the path to investment success requires a discipline that's easier to grasp than to master.

Fortunately, you don't have to go it alone. I learned much about patience and the benefits of weathering bad markets through the lessons of owning the Templeton fund. I've learned even more by working at Morningstar® with a group of people who genuinely like investing and want to learn more. Having smart people to share ideas with is a great benefit during tough markets. Sadly, many investors have no choice but to go it alone, having few friends or colleagues with whom they feel comfortable discussing their finances. That was certainly the case for me prior to joining Morningstar. I didn't find a lot of fellow investors in high school or even in college. I remember long nights in graduate school poring over personal finance magazines trying to make sense of the bewildering world of mutual funds to begin to put together a financial plan for my family. What a joy to join a community of fellow investors.

Now that opportunity is open to everyone. *The Morningstar Guide to Mutual Funds* is an invitation for you to join a community of investors who want to better understand what makes funds tick and what separates the top managers from the rest of the pack. You'll learn from three fine teachers—Christine

Benz, Peter Di Teresa, and Russ Kinnel—each of whom not only offers great insights on funds, but also has a real talent for making investing accessible and fun. You'll learn the lessons we've found most valuable over the years—everything from how to read fund documents to assembling a well-balanced portfolio. In short, you'll get the "on-ramp" introduction you need to get moving along the road to better investment results.

Even if you're a seasoned investor, I think there's much in these pages that will help you hone your skills as an investor. I hope that you'll also become a part of an investing discussion that continues each month in *Morningstar FundInvestor* and daily on Morningstar.com. Among our editors and readers, you'll find a group of independent thinkers who trade ideas in a shared quest to help people make better investment decisions. It's a lively and rewarding discussion, one that's evolving as its participants, both in print and on the Web, have grown. I value what I learn from our writers and readers about investment opportunities, but even more so I admire the spirit and spark they bring to the endeavor. They help me keep my feet on the ground during good markets and my head up during bad ones.

Please join us on this journey toward better investment results and greater financial independence. I think you'll learn a lot about investments and possibly a little about yourself along the way. Maybe you'll even use this book to introduce a young person in your life to the world of investing and set them on their own journey. In any case, I wish you well.

DON PHILLIPS

Acknowledgments

MANY PEOPLE PLAYED important roles in creating this book. Amy Arnott and Erica Moor shepherded this book from start to finish, putting in long hours as they coordinated and edited the work of all of the contributors and kept the process on track. Award-winning Morningstar designer Jason Ackley created the graphics and layout.

Morningstar Mutual Funds editor Scott Cooley and analysts Langdon Healy, Jeffrey Ptak, and Shannon Zimmerman, along with Tricia Rothschild, contributed important content. We were fortunate to be able to draw on Susan Dziubinski's tremendous work in educating investors. Senior analysts Bridget Hughes and Eric Jacobson provided valuable edits. David Pugh, our editor at John Wiley & Sons, gave us vital guidance for completing the book. Not only did Don Phillips write the foreword, as Morningstar's first analyst, he has set high standards for all of us who have come after him.

Morningstar fosters collaborative efforts, and it's fair to say that the hundreds of people who work here deserve a share of the credit for this book. Most important, founder Joe Mansueto set the spirit for Morningstar and for this book by promoting independent, objective analysis that puts investors first.

Contents

XVI CONTENTS

PART ONE

How to Pick Mutual Funds

Know What Your Fund Owns

MOST OF US wouldn't buy a new home just because it looked good from the outside. We would do a thorough walk-through first. We'd examine the furnace, check for a leaky roof, and look for cracks in the foundation.

Mutual fund investing requires the same careful investigation. You need to give a fund more than a surface-level once-over before investing in it. Knowing that the fund has been a good performer in the past isn't enough to warrant risking your money. You need to understand what's inside its portfolio—or how it invests. You must find out what a fund owns to know if it's right for you.

The stocks and bonds in a fund's portfolio are so important that Morningstar analysts spend a lot of their time on the subject; news about what high-profile fund managers are buying is a constant source of e-mail chatter in the office. Our analysts examine fund portfolios of holdings, talk with the managers about their strategies in picking those holdings, and check on recent changes to the lineup. Knowing what a fund owns helps you understand its past behavior, set realistic expectations for what it might do in the future, and figure out how it will work with the other funds you own.

At the most basic level, a fund can own stocks, bonds, cash, or a combination of the three. If it invests in stocks, it could focus on U.S. companies or venture abroad. If the fund owns U.S. companies, it might invest in giants such as General Electric or Microsoft or seek out tiny companies that most of us have never heard of. A manager may focus on fast-growing companies that command high prices or on slow-growth (or no-growth) firms trading at bargain-basement prices. Finally, managers can own anywhere from 20 to hundreds of stocks. How a manager chooses to invest your money has a big impact on performance. For example, if your manager devotes much of the portfolio to a single volatile area such as technology stocks, your fund may generate high returns at times but will also be very risky.

A fund's name doesn't always reveal what a fund owns because funds often have generic handles. Take the intriguingly named State Street Research Aurora and American Century Veedot funds. If you were to skim over only their names, you would be hard-pressed to glean that the former focuses on small companies that are trading cheaply, whereas the latter is a go-anywhere fund that uses computer models to help direct investments. Nor do the objectives that the firm identifies in its prospectus always give you clues about its portfolio. Aegis Value Fund focuses on tiny, budget-priced stocks, whereas Alliance Premier Growth focuses on fast-growing stocks of large companies. The Aegis fund returned 43% in 2001, whereas the Alliance fund lost 25% that year. Yet both funds are classified as "Growth" funds in their prospectuses. To discern their differences, you'd need to dig beneath the funds' stated objectives.

Using the Morningstar® Style Box™

A desire to help investors choose funds based on what they really own—instead of on what funds call themselves or how they've performed recently—was precisely what inspired Morningstar to develop its investment style box in the early 1990s. The style box provides a summary of a given fund's portfolio—it does not tell you about every security the fund owns, but the box gives a quick and clear picture of the portfolio as a whole. (To check out a fund's current style box, go to Morningstar's Web site, www.morningstar.com, and type in a fund's name or ticker.) The style box isolates two key factors that drive a stock fund's performance: the size of the stocks the fund invests in, and

the type of companies it invests in—rapidly growing companies, slow growers, or a combination (see Figure 1.1).

To figure out which square of our stock style box a whole fund portfolio
lands in, we first analyze each and every stock in that portfolio. We look at a
stock's market capitalization (the number of shares outstanding multiplied by
the stock's price), categorizing each holding as small, medium, or large. We
then figure out the portfolio's overall capitalization. The calculation resem-
bles a simple average, except that it takes outliers into account (e.g., large-
company stocks in a mostly small-cap portfolio) without letting them
completely distort the results. A portfolio's capitalization—whether the fund
invests mainly in small, medium-size, or large companies—forms the vertical
axis of the style box.

Once we've pinpointed what size stocks a fund invests in, we plot its investment style on the horizontal axis of the box. We classify stocks as value
(think stodgy dividend payers like Philip Morris), core (steady but not scin-
tillating growers, e.g., Procter & Gamble), or growth (highfliers like eBay or
biotech firm Amgen). We score each stock in several ways ranging from value

Level of Risk		Investment Style			Median Market Capitalization
		Value	Blend	Growth	
Low	○	Large-Cap Value	Large-Cap Blend	Large-Cap Growth	Large
Moderate	◔	Mid-Cap Value	Mid-Cap Blend	Mid-Cap Growth	Medium
High	●	Small-Cap Value	Small-Cap Blend	Small-Cap Growth	Small

Figure 1.1 The Morningstar style box is a nine-square grid that provides a quick and clear picture
of a fund's investment style.

criteria such as dividend yields and price/earnings ratios to growth factors such as earnings and sales growth. This helps us decide whether to classify a stock as growth, value, or core. Once we have classified each stock's investment style, we then classify the entire portfolio, based on which square of our style box most of its stocks land in.

Understanding the difference between a growth stock and a value stock is critical to understanding what makes a fund tick. Growth stocks typically enjoy strong growth in earnings that is often related to a hot new product or service. Because the market expects good things from these fast growers, and earnings growth usually drives a higher share price, investors are willing to pay more for the shares than they will pay for slower growers.

Value stocks, on the other hand, look like growth stocks' less successful cousins. These companies' earnings are usually growing slowly, if at all, and they often operate in industries that are prone to boom-and-bust cycles. So why does anyone bother with these underachievers? The answer is, because they're cheap. Managers who focus on value stocks are willing to put up with unattractive historical earnings growth because they think the market is being overly pessimistic about the company's future. Should things turn out better than the market thinks, the bargain-hunting fund manager stands to profit.

As you might expect, different-style funds tend to behave differently in various market and economic environments, which is why the style box can be so handy. Quickly eyeballing a fund's style box can give you some indication of how it might perform in good markets and in bad. As a rule of thumb, the large-cap value square of Morningstar's style box is considered the safest because large-cap companies typically are more stable than small ones (the high-profile blowups of giants like Worldcom and Enron notwithstanding). And in down markets, when investors are concerned that stock prices could be too high across the board, value funds' budget-priced stocks don't have very far to fall.

Funds that hit the small-growth square of the style box are usually the riskiest. The success of a single product can make or break a small company, and because small-growth stocks often trade at lofty prices, they can take a disastrous tumble if one of the company's products or services fails to take off as the market expects. These funds can deliver glittering riches in upmarkets, though: In 1999, the average small-growth fund returned 58% (for more on the correlation between investment style and risk, see Chapter 3).

Using the Morningstar Categories

Despite the usefulness of the Morningstar style box, it's just a snapshot of the fund's most recent portfolio. When you are selecting a fund to play a particular role, such as adding large-cap value stocks to your portfolio, you want to be confident that it actually has played that role over time. That's what we have in mind when we plug funds into Morningstar categories. We assign funds to categories based on the past three years' worth of style boxes. A single portfolio could reflect a temporary aberration—maybe the fund's holdings have been doing really well, so they have grown from small- to mid-cap as stock prices have gone up. But because a fund's category assignment is based on three years' worth of portfolios, it gives you a better handle on how the fund typically invests.

Our categories are based on the style box with style-specific categories ranging from large value in the upper left corner to small growth in the lower right corner. We also carve out some categories for specialized funds. To name a few, there are categories for high-yield bond funds, Japan funds, and health care funds. Morningstar slots funds into about 50 categories (see Figure 1.2).

As with the style box, Morningstar categories pick up where fund names and prospectus objectives leave off. They help you figure out how a fund actually invests, which in turn lets you know how to use it in your portfolio. If you're looking for a good core stock fund, you might begin your search within the large-blend category. Funds that land there usually invest in the biggest, best established U.S. companies and buy stocks with a mix of growth and value characteristics. Thus, large-blend funds tend to be a decent bet in varied market and economic conditions. Although they may not lead the pack too often, neither are they apt to be left completely behind. (This subject is discussed in detail in Part Two.)

By targeting funds in different categories, you are much more likely to pull together a diversified portfolio than if you rely on funds' prospectus objectives to show you the way. An investor focusing exclusively on prospectus objectives might think he or she had a diversified mix in a portfolio that consisted of Dreyfus Premier Value (with a prospectus objective of Growth),

Domestic Stock	Large Value	Mid-Cap Blend
	Large Blend	Mid-Cap Growth
	Large Growth	Small Value
	Mid-Cap Value	Small Blend
International Stock	Europe Stock	Pacific Stock ex-Japan
	Latin America Stock	Japan Stock
	Diversified Emerging Markets	Foreign Stock
	Pacific Stock	World Stock
Specialty Stock	Communications	Precious Metals
	Financial	Real Estate
	Health	Technology
	Natural Resources	Utilities
Hybrid	Conservative Allocation	Bear
	Moderate Allocation	
Specialty Bond	High-Yield Bond	Emerging Markets Bond
	Multisector Bond	Bank Loan
	International Bond	
General Bond	Long-Term Bond	Short-Term Bond
	Intermediate-Term Bond	Ultrashort Bond
Government Bond	Long-Term Government	Short-Term Government
	Intermediate-Term Gov't	
Municipal Bond	Muni National Long	Muni Ohio
	Muni National Intermediate	Muni Minnesota
	Muni NY Long	Muni Maryland
	Muni NY Intermediate	Muni Single State Long
	Muni CA Long	Muni Single State
	Muni CA Intermediate	Intermediate
	Muni Florida	Muni Short-Term
	Muni Pennsylvania	Muni High-Yield
	Muni New Jersey	

Figure 1.2   Morningstar's category breakdown for the fund universe.

Hancock Sovereign Investors (Growth and Income), and Armada Large Cap Value (Equity-Income). Diversified? Not so fast. According to their Morningstar categories, which take their underlying holdings into account, all three funds are actually large-cap value offerings.

Examining Sector Weightings

Checking a fund's category and style box can go a long way toward helping you know what a fund is all about, but it may not tell the whole story. Not all funds that land in the same style box or even the same category will behave the same way. Both Fidelity OTC and Marsico Growth land in the large-cap growth category. Yet they have tended to own very different kinds of large-growth stocks. In the late 1990s, Fidelity OTC often dedicated more than half of its assets to technology-related stocks—as much as 75% at one point. Marsico Growth also staked a sizable amount on tech, but its position topped out at 40% of the portfolio.

What a difference those two approaches made! A heavy weighting in the tech sector was a boon in 1999, when investors adored technology stocks. Fidelity OTC soared an amazing 73% that year, whereas Marsico Growth gained 53%. A 53% gain is an impressive return in its own right, but if you had put $10,000 in each fund at the start of the year, your Fidelity OTC investment would have been worth $2,000 more than Marsico Growth at the end of 1999. But anything that produces such strong returns can also prove an Achilles' heel, and that's exactly what happened to Fidelity OTC; when tech collapsed in 2000, it lost 26%, whereas Marsico Growth lost 16%. The moral of the story isn't that a technology-heavy fund like Fidelity OTC is automatically a bad idea, but, that people who own it, should limit their investment in it and make sure to diversify with other funds.

Morningstar calculates a fund's sector exposure based on the percentage of its portfolio that is committed to stocks in each of 12 industry groupings. We also cluster those sectors into one of three "supersectors": information, services, and manufacturing (see Figure 1.3). We developed the broader classification system because the sectors within our supersector groupings tend to behave in a similar way in various stock market environments. In the recent market downturn of 2000 through 2002, every sector in our information supersector—hardware, software, telecommunications, and media—incurred

👁 Information Economy	🖥 Service Economy	🏭 Manufacturing Economy
📈 Software	💊 Health Care	🚗 Consumer Goods
💻 Hardware	🛒 Consumer Services	⚙ Industrial Materials
📱 Telecommunications	📄 Business Services	💧 Energy
🎙 Media	$ Financial Services	💡 Utilities

Figure 1.3   Morningstar's sector breakdown. Twelve sectors are divided into three supersectors representing broader economies.

terrible losses. If all the funds in your portfolio heavily concentrate their holdings in a certain supersector, it can be a strong indication that your portfolio needs exposure to other parts of the economy. Similarly, if you have a job in a technology-related field, you will want your portfolio to have plenty of exposure outside the information supersector because much of your economic well-being (through your job) is already tied to that area.

Examining Number of Holdings

To understand what a particular fund is up to, knowing the number of stocks it owns can be just as important as any of the other factors we have discussed. For obvious reasons, whether your fund holds 20 stocks or hundreds of them will make a big difference in its behavior. (Because Securities and Exchange Commission regulations limit the percentage of its assets that a fund can commit to each holding, fund portfolios rarely have fewer than 20 stocks.) Janus Twenty, which divides its portfolio among a small number of stocks, is likely to see a lot more gyrations in its performance—for better and for worse—than one that spreads its money wide like Fidelity Contrafund (it owns more than 400 stocks), even though both are large-growth funds.

Checking Up on the Frequency of Portfolio Changes

In addition to checking categories, style boxes, sectors, and number of holdings (phew!), a fund's turnover rate is another important factor when you're judging a fund's style. Turnover measures how much the portfolio has changed during the past year and shows approximately how long a manager typically holds a stock. For example, a fund with a turnover rate of 100% has a typical holding period of one year; a fund with 25% turnover holds a stock for four years on average.

Turnover is a pretty simple calculation: To figure it out, fund accountants just divide a fund's total investment sales or purchases (whichever is less) by its average monthly assets for the year.

A fund's turnover rate can give you important insights into a manager's style. It can tell you whether a manager tends to buy and hold, picking stocks and sticking with them for the long haul instead of frequently trading in and out of them. To give you a basis for comparison, stock funds on average have turnover rates of 114%. We consider a fund's turnover rate to be notably modest when it's 30% or lower.

Insights about turnover are useful because managers who keep turnover low tend to practice low-risk strategies, whereas high-turnover funds tend to be aggressive and much riskier. That gets back to investment style: As a rule of thumb, the more value-conscious your manager is, the more patient he or she will tend to be with the holdings in the portfolio. Meanwhile, growth-oriented fund managers often employ high-turnover strategies, and as we mentioned, higher-priced stocks often equal more risk.

High turnover can also spell tax consequences for investors. A manager who sells stocks at a profit incurs a taxable gain, which the fund is required to distribute to investors. If you own the fund in a taxable account instead of in a 401(k) or Individual Retirement Account, you'll have to pay taxes on that distribution. If the fund has a high turnover rate, the tax consequences could cut into returns you would otherwise pocket.

As if that weren't enough, high-turnover funds can incur higher trading costs than low-turnover offerings. When we say *trading costs* we're not just referring to the dollars that the fund pays its brokers to execute the trade (though those charges can cut into your returns, too). Rather, we're also referring to the fact that big funds can "move the market" when buying and selling their shares. Say a big fund like Fidelity Contrafund wants to get out of one of its largest positions in a hurry. Because Contrafund is flooding the market with shares, it may have to accept lower and lower prices for those shares as it unloads its position. The more the fund engages in such trading, the less attractive its average purchase and sale prices will be, and the less its shareholders will profit. (We probably shouldn't pick on Contrafund in

Fund Name	Category	Turnover %
Dreyfus Appreciation	Large Blend	5
Mairs & Power Growth	Large Blend	8
Dodge & Cox Stock	Large Value	10
Vanguard Health Care	Health	13
Gabelli Asset	Mid Blend	15
Third Avenue Value	Mid Blend	16
T. Rowe Price Equity-Income	Large Value	17
Longleaf Partners	Mid Value	18
Liberty Acorn	Small Growth	20
Selected American	Large Blend	20

Figure 1.4   Ten great low-turnover funds.

particular—it has been a strong performer, despite its huge asset base and high-turnover approach. But in general, a fund that combines a high-turnover strategy with a big asset base is fighting an uphill battle.)

For all these reasons, we think you greatly improve your portfolio's odds of good long-term performance if you put the bulk of your assets in low-turnover funds. Figure 1.4 provides a list of some of our favorites.

Investor's Checklist: Know What Your Funds Own

▶ Use a fund's Morningstar style box as a visual guide to learn what the fund owns and how it's apt to behave in the future.

▶ When assembling a diversified portfolio, look for funds that land in a variety of Morningstar categories.

▶ Look in Morningstar's large-blend category for core funds that are unlikely to go too far out on a limb. Want something with a little more zip? Growth and/or small-cap categories are a good place to start.

▶ Check a fund's sector weightings relative to its category peers to see if the fund is betting heavily on a given area of the market.

▶ If you're concerned about risk, look for funds that spread their assets over many holdings. Fewer holdings equal more risk.

▶ Put the bulk of your portfolio in low-turnover funds, which are generally less risky and more tax-efficient.

2

Put Performance in Perspective

Now WE CAN move on to the question most investors start with: How much money has the fund made? It's no wonder that this is the first thing people think about. People invest in hopes of making money, and returns tell you what the fund made in the past. Historical returns sell funds—that's why mutual fund ads in financial magazines or newspapers often feature big mountain charts showing the funds' returns.

Yet as hard as it might be to believe, a fund's past returns are not particularly predictive of its future returns. (The best predictor of good returns? Low costs. We talk more about the importance of low expenses in Chapter 5.) Nonetheless, a fund's past history can offer some clues about whether it's worth owning. In this chapter, we discuss where a fund's return numbers come from, and how to check whether a fund's return is satisfactory.

Understanding Total Return

To make sense of the return numbers in advertisements, fund company literature, the newspaper, and on Morningstar.com, the first thing you should know is that these figures are based on important conventions. For starters, the numbers are known as total returns because they reflect two things:

market gains (or losses) in the stocks or bonds the fund owns—the fund's capital return—and income received from those investments. Income comes from the dividends paid by stocks and the interest paid by bonds the fund owns. Together, those capital returns and income returns make up total returns. For example, Vanguard Wellington earned a 4.19% total return in 2001. That was based on a 0.78% capital return (the amount the fund's stock and bond investments appreciated during the year) plus a 3.41% income return (the total of the dividends the fund received from its stocks plus the yield from its bonds for the year).

Total-return numbers for periods longer than one year are typically represented as *annualized* returns. An annualized return is something like an average, except that it takes compounding into account (i.e., it recognizes that if you made gains in the first year that you owned a fund, you have more to invest at the beginning of the next year). At the end of June 2002, Oakmark Select had a three-year annualized return of 12.87%. The fund never actually earned that exact amount in any year. But if you had bought the fund in July 1999 and hung on for the next three years, that's what your per-year earnings would work out to be.

Checking Up on Aftertax Returns

The total-return number is calculated on the assumption that shareholders reinvest any distributions that the fund makes. Mutual funds are required by law to distribute, or pay out, almost all income they receive (from dividend-paying stocks or interest-paying bonds) to their shareholders. They also must distribute any gains they realize by selling stocks or bonds at a profit. If you choose to reinvest those distributions, and most investors do, you will get more fund shares instead of a check in the mail. If you decide to take the money, your returns may be lower than those of someone who reinvested and got more shares.

If you own your funds in a taxable account instead of a retirement plan or Individual Retirement Account, you should know that the total-return figures you typically see don't include the bite taxes can take out of your return. When a fund distributes income or capital gains to shareholders, it's called a *taxable event.* And, of course, paying taxes cuts into the money you made. The difference can be significant. As of June 2002, MFS Value had a five-year annualized return of 10.46%. Van Kampen Comstock had a five-year return of 10.44%, just fractionally behind. But if you take out taxes, the story is completely different. MFS Value had a 7.37% return after taxes, whereas Van Kampen Comstock delivered a much smaller 5.02% aftertax return. If you were investing in a taxable account, neither fund would be a particularly great bet, but the MFS fund would definitely be the better of the two.

The good news is that it's fairly easy to find out how well a fund has shielded investors from taxes. The Securities and Exchange Commission now requires funds to disclose what shareholders would have kept after they paid taxes. If you're buying a fund for a taxable account and not through a 401(k) plan or Individual Retirement Account, seek out the aftertax return numbers, because they'll matter most for you. You can find a fund's aftertax returns in the fund's annual shareholder report, and you can also see these numbers by going to www.morningstar.com and typing in the fund name or ticker. There you'll get a fund's raw aftertax return and also can see how that compares with the fund's Morningstar category peers. Many fund companies now report aftertax performance on their Web sites, too. (Aftertax returns assume the highest income tax rate. If you're in a lower tax bracket, the tax bite on distributions will be less, so your aftertax return will be higher than the reported figures.)

Putting Returns in Perspective

Maybe you're feeling pretty good about your investing prowess—you own a fund that has gained an average of 10% per year for the past three years. Then you chat with a coworker who claims to have a fund that is up 13% per year. Maybe it's time for some serious self-appraisal; after all, you must be a pretty poor fund-picker to lag by about three percentage points per year. Here's hoping you have some other talents to fall back on.

Actually, try not to be too hard on yourself. You may be much better at selecting funds than those numbers might suggest. Without context—unless you know what types of fund you and your coworker have—the numbers are meaningless. You may own a large-cap value fund that has been trouncing its peers. Meanwhile, your coworker owns a fund in the red-hot small-value category. His returns look high, but his fund is actually lagging far behind its small-value competitors.

To know how well a fund is doing, you can't look at returns in isolation: You need to make relevant comparisons. Use an appropriate yardstick such as a stock or bond index or a group of funds investing in the same kind of securities—the Morningstar categories that you read about in Chapter 1.

Using Indexes as Benchmarks

An index is the most common kind of benchmark. When you read a fund's shareholder report, you will always see the fund compared with an index, sometimes more than one. An index is a preselected, widely recognized group of securities, either stocks or bonds.

Ask someone to name a stock market index and odds are good that the answer will be the Dow Jones Industrial Average. You can't escape the Dow—it's the index that usually heads the stock report on the evening news. Although the Dow is familiar, it isn't a great performance benchmark for your mutual funds because it is extremely narrow; it includes just 30 large-company stocks. Most stock funds include many more holdings and do not focus solely on blue chips.

Instead, the index you'll hear about most often in investing circles is the Standard & Poor's 500 index, which includes 500 major U.S. companies. Because S&P chooses the stocks in the index to cover a range of industries, it has greater breadth than the Dow. Thus, it's a reasonable yardstick for many funds that focus on big, name-brand U.S. stocks.

Yet despite widespread use, the S&P 500 has its own drawbacks. Although it encompasses 500 stocks, it's designed so that the companies with the biggest market capitalizations (the total value of their outstanding shares), such as Microsoft and General Electric, take up the greatest percentage of the index. As a result, such names tend to influence the index's performance. On days when these giants do well, so does the S&P 500.

That's why you wouldn't want to compare a fund that focuses mostly on small companies, such as Third Avenue Value, against the S&P 500 index alone. Small-company stocks make up a very small portion of the index, so it would be surprising if the fund performed much like the index at all. In 2000, Third Avenue Value gained nearly 21%, while the S&P 500 lost 9%; in 1998 the fund gained just 4%, while the index was up 21%. Those disparate returns reflect that small and large stocks often go their separate ways. In the late 1990s, large caps scored tremendous gains and small caps made relatively modest ones; then in the early 2000s, large caps ran into a brick wall and small caps came into their own.

Likewise, it makes little sense to compare a foreign-stock fund like Janus Overseas with the S&P 500. That fund owns only a smattering of U.S. stocks, focusing instead on foreign issues. And there's even less reason to judge a bond fund against the S&P 500, which includes only stocks.

So what indexes should you use to make appropriate comparisons? If you're examining a small-company fund, use the Russell 2000 index, which is dedicated to small-capitalization stocks. Use the MSCI EAFE index, which follows international stocks, to judge a foreign fund. And use the Lehman Brothers Aggregate Bond index for most taxable-bond funds. There are dozens of other indexes that segment the stock and bond markets even more. For example, they may focus on inexpensive large-company stocks or fast-moving small companies, regions of the world such as Europe or the Pacific Rim, or technology stocks. Figure 2.1 provides a summary of major indexes and what they track.

Morningstar also has its own line of indexes, which correspond with its U.S. stock style boxes. In addition to a broad market index, the Morningstar U.S. Market Index, we offer indexes for each of the nine squares of the style box (e.g., the Morningstar Mid Cap Value Index), the three investment-style columns (e.g., the Morningstar U.S. Value Index), and the three capitalization rows (e.g., the Morningstar Large Cap Index). You can see the performance of these indexes as well as their components by going to the Markets cover page on Morningstar.com.

Using Peer Groups as Benchmarks

Indexes can be useful, but peer groups such as the Morningstar categories, which we discussed in Chapter 1, are even better because they allow you to compare the fund with other funds that invest in the same way. An index may be a suitable benchmark because it tracks the same kinds of stocks that a fund invests in, an index itself isn't an investment option. Your choice isn't between investing in a fund and an index but between a fund and a fund.

If you're trying to evaluate a fund that invests in large, cheaply priced companies, compare it with other large-value funds. Or compare those that

Dow Jones Industrial Average	Computed by summing the prices of the stocks of 30 companies and then dividing that total by an adjusted value— one which has been adjusted over the years of account for the effects of stock splits on the prices of the 30 companies.
Standard & Poor's 500	A market capitalization-weighted index of 500 widely held stocks often used as a proxy for the stock market. Standard and Poor's chooses the member companies for the 500 based on market size, liquidity and industry group representation. Included are the stocks of industrial, financial, utility, and transportation companies.
Russell 2000	A commonly cited small-cap index that tracks the returns of the smallest 2,000 companies in the Russell 3000 Index.
Lehman Brothers Aggregate	A broad bond-market benchmark that includes government, corporate, mortgage-backed, and asset-backed securities.
Wilshire 5000	This is a market capitalization-weighted index of the most-active U.S. stocks. The Wilshire 5000 measures the performance of the broad domestic market.
MSCI World	The Morgan Stanley Capital International World index measures the performance of stock markets in 23 nations: Australia, Austria, Belgium, Canada, Denmark, Finland, France, Germany, Hong Kong, Ireland, Italy, Japan, Malaysia, the Netherlands, New Zealand, Norway, Portugal, Singapore, Spain, Sweden, Switzerland, the United Kingdom, and the United States.
MSCI EAFE	The Morgan Stanley Capital International Europe, Australasia, and Far East index is widely accepted as a benchmark for international-stock performance. The MSCI EAFE index represents many of the world's major markets outside the U.S. and Canada.

Figure 2.1 Major indexes and what they track.

buy only Latin America stocks with others that invest exclusively in Latin America. To find a fund's category, go to www.morningstar.com and type in the fund's name or ticker, or check its page in *Morningstar Mutual Funds*™ (found in most public libraries).

Armed with information about a fund's true peer group, you're in a much better position to judge its performance. Say you owned Oakmark Select back in 1999. At the end of that year, you might have been disappointed—

sure, your fund made 14.5% for the year, but the S&P 500 was up more than 21%. Alongside that benchmark, your fund was a dog. But the fund looked much better versus its peers: Oakmark Select is a mid-cap value fund, and those funds on average gained 8% for the year.

The fact that Oakmark Select trailed the S&P 500 in 1999 didn't so much reflect the fund's quality as it did the relatively weak performance of mid-cap value stocks that year. Those stocks couldn't keep up with the fast-moving technology stocks that were driving the index's gains. Like Oakmark Select, most mid-cap value funds own few or no large, growth-oriented stocks. And, like that fund, they do own mostly midsize, value-priced securities. Looking at the index gave you no insight into how your fund really did, but comparing the fund with its category told you that it did just fine.

The Perils of Return Chasing

It can be frustrating when your fund is in the red or lagging other categories, even if it's doing well relative to its peer group. That frustration can lead to the investors most common and costly mistake investors make—chasing returns. They buy hot-performing funds in hot-performing categories, and when one fund turns cold, they sell it and jump into another hot fund. The catch is that by the time you've noticed the hot fund category and decided to make a switch, that category could be ready to cool off. Meanwhile, your once-lagging fund could be poised for an upturn. Simply put, there are never clear signals that it's time to buy one fund type or swap into another. Jumping around, therefore, often spells missed opportunities. Studies using data from major online brokers indicate that investors who buy and hold for the long haul gain several percentage points more per year on average than do fast traders.

Morningstar's own studies give another perspective on this. By tracking new money flowing into funds and fund sales, we have found that investors often buy or sell at just the wrong time. When everyone is buying a particular kind of fund, that is often a sign that the category is due for a fall. Tech funds skyrocketed in 1999, and investors were tossing in new money hand over fist. The funds then crashed in 2000. On the other hand, investors had little interest in value funds in 1999, but those funds came to the fore in 2000.

Instead of switching among funds, we recommend building a portfolio of varied funds. That way, whatever the market is doing, at least some portion of your portfolio is likely to be doing well. It's not sexy, it's not a hot tip, but we know of no better way to improve your odds of being a successful long-term fund investor. (In Part Two, we explain how to build a portfolio that suits your goals and is also less likely to be tossed around by changes in the market.)

Return History: The Longer the Better

You can check a fund's returns versus its category in a publication such as *Morningstar FundInvestor, Morningstar Mutual Funds* (many public libraries subscribe to these products), or in the free portion of Morningstar.com. But which returns should you consider? How the fund did for the past 3 months, the past 10 years, or some period in between?

Because studies show that trading in and out of funds doesn't work, be a long-term investor and focus on a fund's returns for the past 3, 5, and 10 years. Compare those returns with those of other funds in the category to get a clear view of performance. Although we wouldn't rule out a fund that was below par for one of those periods, there's little reason to buy a fund that's inferior for most periods.

Take a look at the fund's calendar-year returns versus its category, too. That's a handy way to identify a fund that may look good because of a couple of strong recent years but has little to recommend it overall. Many so-called bear funds (funds that short stocks)—soared to the top of the charts during the decidedly bearish market of 2000–2002. But a look at year-to-year calendar returns revealed that prior to their recent winning streak, the funds had been terrible place to invest.

Finally, ask how long the fund's current manager has been aboard the fund. Maybe the fund sports terrific long-term returns over every period, but the person who helped deliver those great returns has retired or moved on to another fund. In that case, the fund's long-term record may have little bearing on how it will perform in the future.

Investor's Checklist: Put Performance in Perspective

▶ See how a fund's return stacks up relative to an appropriate yardstick—either a peer group of funds with a similar investment style or an index—to determine whether its returns are good or bad.

▶ Pay attention to a fund's aftertax returns—available in its annual shareholder report—if you're buying a fund for a taxable account.

▶ Employ a buy-and-hold strategy instead of chasing hot-performing funds.

▶ Check a fund's performance over several time periods—the longer the better.

▶ Eyeball a fund's year-to-year returns to see how consistent its performance has been.

▶ Make sure that the manager who built a fund's past return record is still on board before buying in.

3

Understand the Risks

THERE'S AN OLD saying that investors are driven by two emotions: greed and fear. We covered greed in Chapter 2. Now it's time to explore the fear of losing money. Regrettably, most investors have had to confront that fear head-on in recent years.

In the later years of the 1990s, when the stock market seemed unstoppable, it was difficult for investors to believe that there could be a downside. Many investors who knew that their funds might run into trouble figured that they could just grit their teeth through the rough patches. During the 1990s, after all, downmarkets typically only lasted a quarter or two, and then it was off to the races again.

Although many market watchers warned that certain sectors of the market—notably technology and telecommunications stocks—were ridiculously overpriced, few investors were prepared for the viciousness of the market downturn. You would have to go back to the 1970s to find a market as brutal as that of 2000, 2001, and 2002. From its March 2000 peak through September 2002, the broad market was down 38.2%, and more daring fund categories suffered much worse losses. A $10,000 investment in the average large-cap growth fund in March 2000 would have shrunk to $4,393, while the typical tech-fund investor saw a $10,000 investment shrivel to just $1,680. Ouch!

It's easy enough to say that those are just paper losses—you don't really lose the money until you sell. But such paper losses can keep investors up nights and often lead them to sell when their funds are losing money. They worry about how much worse things might get and whether they might lose everything. Investors know that in the past the markets have recovered, but it can be hard to keep that in mind in the thick of things. As a result, people often sell at the worst time, turning their paper losses into losses in fact.

Remember, funds that make big short-term gains tend to incur big losses. You can't get big returns without taking on a lot of risk—witness the Internet-focused funds that flew high in the late 1990s and then came crashing down. Taking a close look at the fund's portfolio—using some of the tools discussed in Chapter 1—can help you know if a fund harbors risks that haven't yet been realized. Measures of a fund's past volatility—standard deviation, Morningstar Risk, and the Morningstar Rating™ (the star rating)—also can provide insight into how risky a fund is apt to become.

Evaluating Future Risks

In Chapter 1, we discussed the tools you can use to analyze a fund's investments: Morningstar style boxes and categories, sectors, and concentration. These are key factors to focus on when judging the kinds of risks a fund is taking on and whether it's right for you.

Investment-Style Risk

As noted in Chapter 1, the Morningstar style box is a great way to find out how risky a fund is apt to be. Over the long term, large-value stock funds, which land in the upper left-hand corner of the Morningstar style box, tend to be the least volatile—they have fewer performance swings than other stock mutual funds. On the opposite end of the spectrum, funds that fall in the small-growth square are typically the most volatile group (see Figure 3.1).

A fund such as Van Wagoner Emerging Growth, which owns small, growth-leaning stocks, is likely to experience more dramatic ups and downs than one holding large, budget-priced stocks, like Vanguard Wellington. Van Wagoner Emerging Growth might deliver higher returns over the long haul, but its performance will tend to be much more erratic. Investors may have to go on a pretty wild ride to get those returns.

Three-Year Standard Deviation
U.S. Stock Funds

Investment Style

Value	Blend	Growth	
			Market Cap
14.93	16.60	23.44	Large
17.30	19.47	34.11	Med
18.67	22.63	36.53	Small

Three-Year Standard Deviation
Taxable Bond Funds

Duration

Long	Med	Short	
			Quality
2.18	3.83	5.53	High
2.61	4.47	5.51	Med
8.40	9.07	10.09	Low

Figure 3.1   Standard deviation, a measure of volatility, shows which investment styles have been the most (and least) risky over the past three years. The higher the number, the more volatile the funds in a given style box have been.

Similarly, our bond style box shows how risky your fixed-income fund is apt to be. Generally speaking, the safest square of the bond style box is the top-left square—home to funds with limited interest-rate sensitivity and high credit qualities. Such funds won't see their bonds drop in value too much if interest rates go up, and they focus on government and high-quality corporate bonds, meaning that there's little risk that the issuers will fail to keep up with their bonds' interest payments. Funds that fall into this square of the style box are often just a notch riskier than money-market funds. Meanwhile, the riskiest square is the upper right-hand corner of the box. Happily, few funds occupy it—bond funds tend to take on credit or interest-rate risk, usually not both.

You can also use the style box to get a handle on whether a fund is likely to be more or less risky than its category peers. If you're looking at a technology fund that lands in the small-growth bin of the style box, you know it's likely to be more volatile than a fund that falls in the large-cap row. Or if you're looking for a bond fund that focuses on mortgage-backed bonds, you know that a fund with a long duration (a measure of interest-rate sensitivity) is apt to post more losses if interest rates go up than a fund with an intermediate-term duration.

Sector Risk

In addition to the fund's investment style its sector concentration can also indicate how vulnerable it is to a downturn in a certain part of the market. Investors who paid attention to sectors back in 1999 did themselves a huge favor. They could see that even though, Fidelity OTC, a large-growth fund, had higher returns than Marsico Growth, another large-growth fund, it was also much more vulnerable to a downturn in just one stock sector.

As described in Chapter 1, Bob Bertelson, manager of Fidelity OTC, made a big bet on technology stocks that was abundantly rewarded in 1999, then punished later on. Bertelson couldn't control how the market would feel about tech stocks, but he could decide how much sector-specific risk was acceptable for the fund. A fund that bets a lot on a single sector is likely to display high volatility, with dramatic ups and downs. As long as the manager's strategy doesn't change, that volatility will continue. Sometimes the fund will make money and sometimes it will be down, but its volatility will remain high, reminding investors that even though the fund may currently be making a lot of money, it also has the potential to fall dramatically.

Although there are no rules of thumb for how much is "too much" in a given sector, you'll do yourself a big favor if you compare your fund's sector weightings with other funds that practice a similar style as well as with a broad-market index fund such as Vanguard 500 Index or Vanguard Total Stock Market Index. This is not to suggest that you should automatically avoid a fund with a big wager on an individual sector; in fact, some of the most successful investors are biased toward a market sector or two. (Exhibit A: Warren Buffett, whose Berkshire Hathaway is heavily skewed toward financials stocks, particularly insurers.) But you'll need to balance that fund with holdings that emphasize other parts of the market.

Concentration Risk

Just as a fund that clusters all its holdings in a sector or two is bound to be more risky than a broadly diversified portfolio, so funds that hold relatively few securities are riskier than those that commit a tiny percentage of assets to each stock. As mentioned, Janus Twenty has just 21 holdings, whereas Fidelity Contrafund had nearly 400 stocks as of its last portfolio. If a few of Janus Twenty's holdings run into trouble, they can do a lot more damage to performance than a few of Contrafund's can. If Janus Twenty had its money spread equally among 20 stocks, each would count for 5% of the portfolio, but a single stock would account for just 0.25% of Contrafund's holdings. If one of Janus Twenty's picks were to go bankrupt, it would take a far bigger bite out of returns than if Contrafund got caught with the same bum stock. (For similar reasons, concentration should also be a consideration when evaluating bond funds, particularly those that focus on junk bonds.)

Because managers almost never spread the fund's money equally across every holding, along with checking a fund's total number of holdings, it's a good idea to check a fund's top 10 holdings to see what percentage of the assets are concentrated there. Even though a fund has 100 holdings, if the manager has committed half of the fund to the top 10, that fund could be a lot more volatile than one with the same number of holdings but less concentration at the top. Sentinel Common Stock and California Investment NASDAQ 100 each own 100 stocks, but Sentinel has 27% of its assets in its top 10 holdings, whereas California Investment has 53% parked at the top. Simply because they make up so much more of its portfolio, California Investment is going to suffer a lot more if its top holdings run into trouble.

Assessing Past Volatility

Although conducting a fundamental analysis of a fund—checking its investment style and concentration in sectors and individual stocks—is one of the best ways to assess an offering's riskiness, past volatility is also a fairly accurate indicator of future risk. If a fund has seen lots of ups and downs in the past, it's apt to continue to have herky-jerky returns. It's like playing poker: If you bet at the $10-dollar table, you don't know how much you'll win, but you have a pretty good idea how much you could lose. Play at a higher-stakes table and you could win more money more quickly, and you could also lose a lot more. Morningstar studies show that funds with high volatility in one time period usually exhibit similar volatility in subsequent time periods. Meanwhile, even-keeled funds continue to exhibit low volatility.

The Gut Check

If you want to make sure that you're going to be comfortable with a fund you're considering, do a simple check to see whether you can tolerate those periods when the fund is in the red. Look at how much the fund has lost in the past and ask yourself if you could hold on during those periods. (You can find this information in an individual fund's Quicktake® report on Morningstar.com, or in the pages of *Morningstar Mutual Funds*.) Take a look at the years and quarters in which the fund has lost the most money. For example, if you had $10,000 in Janus Twenty at the beginning of 2000, your stake would be down to $6,758 by year-end (the fund lost 32.42% for the year). The fund's worst quarter in recent years was a 24.6% loss in the first quarter of 2001. A $10,000 investment at the beginning of the quarter would have been worth $7,540 at the end. What would you do if you didn't know when the fund would come back or whether it might go on to lose as much in the next quarter or year?

In principle, long-term investors can ignore such downturns. If you don't need the money for a decade or more, the downside should be less important. What matters is what you have at the end, not how you got there; and many rewarding funds have taken their shareholders on relatively wild rides. That's all fine in theory, but owning such a fund can spell unnecessary stress. Uncertainty is a problem for many investors. They would rather bail out than hang around to see what happens next. If such losses would cause you to sell the investment, it's probably not the fund for you. And even if you believe you could stick it out, would you suffer too much stress worrying about the fund? Then don't buy it. Look for something steadier. Successful investing means not only making money but also being comfortable in the process.

Standard Deviation

But what if you want to quickly shop among a group of funds to figure out which is the least risky? Standard deviation is probably the most commonly used gauge of a fund's past volatility, and it enables quick comparisons among funds. Morningstar analysts like standard deviation because it tells investors just how much a fund's returns have fluctuated during a particular time period. Morningstar calculates standard deviations every month, based on a fund's monthly returns for the preceding three years. Standard deviation represents the degree to which a fund's returns have varied from its 3-year average annual return, known as the mean. By definition, a fund's returns have historically fallen within one standard deviation of its mean 68% of the time. As of mid-2002, Needham Growth had a mean of 20.20% and a standard deviation of 43.47 for the trailing 3-year period. Those numbers tell you that about two-thirds (68%) of the time, the fund's annualized return was within 43.47 percentage points of 20.20%. That's a huge range of returns, from a 23.27% loss to a 63.67% gain. If you're a cautious investor, you would not get anywhere near that fund, despite its compelling return numbers. You would be much happier with a fund that had a much lower standard deviation, even though its returns were lower.

The catch is, standard deviation doesn't tell you much when you look at it in isolation. A fund that has a standard deviation of 25 for the past 3 years is meaningless until you start making comparisons. Just like returns, a fund's standard deviation requires context to be useful. If you're looking at a fund with a standard deviation of 15 for the same period, you know that the fund with the standard deviation of 25 is substantially more volatile.

An index can be a useful benchmark for a fund's volatility as well as for its returns. Say the two funds in our example land in Morningstar's large-cap blend category. The S&P 500 index is a good benchmark for that group, because it emphasizes large companies with a variety of investment styles—growth, value, and everything in between. At the end of June 2002, the S&P 500 index's 3-year standard deviation was 15.56. You can tell that the fund with a standard deviation of 25 has taken investors on a much wilder ride than the index. Unless it also has much higher returns to compensate for the stress of owning it, buying that fund would make little sense.

You can also compare a fund's standard deviation with that of other funds that invest in the same way, such as those in its Morningstar category. If the two funds in our example are both large-cap blend offerings, then the one with the standard deviation of 25 is apt to drop a lot further than the one with a standard deviation of 15 when large-blend funds are down. Unless the more volatile fund has substantially better long-term returns than the less volatile fund, there's no point in buying it.

As with returns, you can also check a fund's volatility level by comparing its standard deviation with the average for its category. (You can find category-average statistics, including standard deviation, in *Morningstar Mutual Funds*.) In 1999, Janus Olympus had a standard deviation of 31.91 while the typical large-growth fund had a standard deviation of 24.19. Janus Olympus also had much better returns than the average, but its high standard deviation indicated that it had been about 30% more volatile than its typical competitor. This was a warning sign that the fund could also lose a lot more than the average if things were to turn ugly. When large-growth funds fell an average of 14.6% in 2000, Janus Olympus dropped 21.6%. It dropped an additional 33% in 2001, versus a 23% loss for the typical large-growth fund.

Morningstar's Risk Rating

Standard deviation is useful because it tells you about the fund's past performance swings, and big swings usually beget more big swings. But standard deviation doesn't tell you whether the fund's swings were gains or losses, and that's an important distinction for most investors. Theoretically, a fund with extremely high returns year in and year out could have a standard deviation just as high as one that had posted fairly steep losses. Consider two small-cap value funds: In 2002, Wasatch Small Cap Value had a standard deviation of 25.72, and ICM/Isabelle Small Cap Value's standard deviation was 25.68. Yet the Wasatch fund's return for the past three years averaged 35% per year, whereas ICM/Isabelle's return averaged 17.7%. During that period, Wasatch's worst three-month loss was 10.8%. ICM/Isabelle lost as much as 29.1% in three months. The Wasatch fund had, hands down, the better risk/reward profile, but standard deviation wouldn't have helped you choose it over the other fund.

That example illustrates why investors should look at the whole picture, not simply returns and standard deviation. Just as we want to know how successful a fund manager has been at making money for shareholders, we want to know how successful he or she has been at protecting them from losses. That's why Morningstar's risk rating not only looks at all variations in a fund's returns—just like standard deviation—but also emphasizes a fund's losses relative to its category peers. The formulas driving Morningstar's risk rating are complicated, but the underlying idea is straightforward: As investors, we don't like losing money! (You can find a fund's risk rating by going to Morningstar.com and typing in its name or its ticker.)

Morningstar's risk rating looks at funds' performance over a variety of time periods. We don't rate funds that are younger than 3 years old because shorter periods just don't give an adequate picture of a fund's performance. If a fund is 3 years old, its Morningstar risk rating will be based entirely on that 3-year period. For a 5-year-old fund, 60% of its risk rating is based on the past 5 years and 40% on the past 3 years. A 10-year-old fund's 10-year record will count for 50% of its risk rating, while the 5- and 3-year periods count for another 30% and 20%, respectively (see Figure 3.2). Morningstar looks at this combination of periods because we think long-term investing is important, but we also want to be sure that funds don't earn good ratings just on the strength of success years ago. We assign funds new risk scores every month.

Because we measure a fund's risk relative to its category, it's easy to compare funds that invest in the same way. The least risky 10% of funds in a category earn the "Low" risk designation, the next safest 22.5% are considered to have "Below-Average" risk, and the middle 35% are deemed to have "Average" risk. The next 22.5% are deemed to have "Above-Average" risk, while the final 10% are considered "High" risk. If you're contemplating a large-cap value fund with High Morningstar risk, you know that it has exhibited more volatility (including real losses) than 90% of large-value offerings.

The Morningstar Rating (The Star Rating)

Because investors are extremely concerned with risk, a fund's risk rating counts for fully one half of its overall Morningstar Rating (better known as the star rating). The other half of the Morningstar Rating looks at a fund's return rating relative to other funds in its category.

Age of Fund	Morningstar Rating Based on:
At least 3 years, but less than 5	100% 3-year rating
At least 5 years, but less than 10	60% 5-year rating 40% 3-year rating
At least 10 years	50% 10-year rating 30% 5-year rating 20% 3-year rating

Figure 3.2 How a fund's age factors into its Morningstar rating.

We calculate a fund's Morningstar return rating in much the same way as we do the risk rating. We use the same combination of time periods (3-, 5-, and 10-year returns go into the calculation). We also adjust a fund's returns for any sales charges to better reflect what real investors would have made (discussed in Chapter 6). And as with the risk rating, funds that rank in the top 10% of their categories on the return front earn a return rating of "High"; the next-best, 22.5% earn a return rating of "Above Average," and so on. We repeat the process every month.

Once we have both a risk rating and a return rating for a fund, we put them together into an overall rating calculation. By combining Morningstar risk and return, we come up with a risk-adjusted return score for each fund in a category. We then rank the funds according to their scores. The highest-scoring 10% of funds within each category earn five stars, the next 22.5% get four stars, the middle 35% get three stars, the next 22.5% two stars, and the worst 10% receive a single star (see Figure 3.3).

How to Use the Star Rating

The list of funds available, at 6,000 and counting, is overwhelming. The star rating allows you to skim over that huge number and arrive at those funds that have done a good job of balancing risk and return. You can use it to weed out funds that have been too risky for too little gain and, focus your search on the better funds. You can also use the star rating to monitor your holdings. In general, if your fund's star rating drops below 3, that's a good reason to do some due diligence on your holding. It may well be that your manager's style has simply been out of favor in the market and is due for an upswing, but it may also indicate a more fundamental problem.

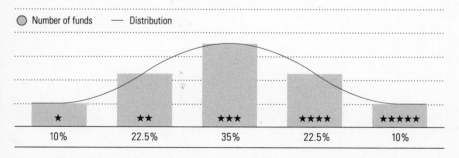

Figure 3.3 Here's the distribution of star ratings within a category in the Morningstar rating system.

But before you start using the star rating there are a couple of important things to note about it. One is that it's purely quantitative. As much as we might enjoy the power to do so, Morningstar analysts don't award stars to funds they like or yank them off funds they dislike. (Fund managers sometimes ask our analysts what they can do to get more stars. We always tell them, make more money for your shareholders and give them a smoother ride.)

You should also know that if a management change occurs, the rating stays with the fund—it doesn't travel with the manager to a new fund. That means a fund's rating could be based mostly on the success of a manager who is no longer there. It's also worth noting that the star rating it's based on how the fund did in the past. It won't predict short-term winners. (As Morningstar's Managing Director Don Phillips likes to say, "The star rating is an achievement test, not an aptitude test.") That said, funds that have done a poor job in the past tend to be poor performers in the future and historically superior funds tend to earn above-average ratings in the future, too.

Finally, to use the star rating effectively, you need to first establish the kind of fund you want. The star rating will tell you whether one technology fund is better than another, but it won't tell you whether you should even be buying a technology fund or how much of your portfolio you should commit to it. (Later chapters of this book are devoted to building a portfolio and identifying the categories of funds you should invest in.) Because we award 5-star ratings in every category, funds that are inappropriate for most investors can earn the highest star ratings. Kinetics Internet Fund garnered 5 stars as of mid-2002—it notched spectacular returns during the dot-com boom and made a well-timed shift out of Internet stocks in time to save it from the sector's eventual collapse. Yet most investors simply don't need a fund that focuses specifically on the technology and telecom sectors.

The star rating is a great first screen, but it's not the only piece of information you should consider when assessing a fund. Before buying a fund, instead of just asking, "Does it get 5 stars?" you should ask yourself the following six questions: What does the fund own? How has the fund performed? How risky has the fund been? Who runs the fund? What's the fund family like? And finally: What does the fund cost? We've covered the first three in Chapters 1 through 3; the rest are covered in Chapters 4 and 5.

Investor's Checklist: Understanding the Risks

▶ Use a fund's style-box placement as a rough gauge of its risk level. Large-value funds are typically the least risky, and small-growth funds are often the most risky.

▶ If you're seeking a tame fund, steer clear of offerings with big weightings in individual sectors.

▶ Scan a fund's number of holdings, as well as the percentage of assets it holds in its top 10 positions, to see how much company-specific risk it harbors.

▶ Get a handle on whether a fund is appropriate for you by checking its worst historical return period. If you would not be able to hang on through that type of loss, steer clear.

▶ Use backward-looking volatility measures, including standard deviation and the Morningstar risk rating, to visualize a fund's future volatility level.

▶ Check the Morningstar rating (a.k.a. the star rating) to get a quick look at a fund's historical risk/reward profile.

4

Get to Know Your Fund Manager

LET'S SAY YOU followed the first three chapters of this book and have found a fund with a mix of good returns without too much risk. You also understand exactly the role it's supposed to play in your portfolio. But if the manager who earned that great record is gone, you could be in for an unpleasant surprise.

Because managers are vital to a fund's success or failure, Morningstar analysts spend a lot of time talking with them, either on the phone or in person. Every time we write a fund analysis, and sometimes in between analyses, we try to talk to the manager.

The manager can shed light on strong or poor performance and give us insight into why the fund's portfolio looks the way it does. Maybe the manager expects the economy to take a turn for the better and is emphasizing the sectors that will benefit most. That tells you that the fund could be poised for a strong run or could run into trouble if the economy slows.

By interviewing many managers with similar investment strategies, we can also ferret out the best investment arguments and build a level of confidence in a particular manager's investment rationale. If we hear five different managers all talking about the latest trendy stock—and it happens more often than you might think—we get skeptical about any claims they make about uncovering values others have overlooked. We're also wary of fund companies that always try to put a positive spin on performance, or hype up their strategies to make them sound better than they are. Over the years, we have noticed that managers of better-performing funds are typically the most straightforward about what is and is not working in their portfolios.

Understanding Types of Fund Management

Before you can judge the quality of your manager, you need to know the three types of fund management (and one subtype; see Figure 4.1). The most straightforward way is the single-manager approach. These are the managers who, like Fidelity's Peter Lynch, become the stars of the fund industry. A manager like Lynch or Robert Stansky, who holds Lynch's old post at Fidelity Magellan, is listed as the fund's sole manager. Of course, even a sole manager seldom works in total isolation. Stansky gets plenty of market research and stock ideas from Fidelity's stock analyst staff. But Stansky is the one who picks the stocks that go into Magellan's portfolio and who decides when to cut them loose. He's the key decision maker.

Solo Management	Describes a fund that is managed day-to-day by just one person. That person is responsible for all key decisions affecting the fund's assets.
Management Team	Describes a fund that is managed jointly by two or more persons. Also can be used to describe a fund that strongly promotes its team-managed aspect or team culture.
Multiple Managers	Describes a fund that is managed independently by two or more two persons. Often, this term is used to describe funds that have divided net assets in set amounts among the individual managers. In most cases, multiple managers are employed at different subadvisors or investment firms.
Subadvisor	Describes cases in which the fund company employs another company, called the subadvisor, to handle the fund's day-to-day management. In these instances, the portfolio manager generally works for the fund's subadvisor, and not the fund company.

Figure 4.1 The various management arrangements a fund can have.

Then there's the management team, popularized by fund companies like American Century and Putnam. The team may consist of two or more co-managers who work together to select the fund's portfolio holdings. Some-times one manager will make the final call on what to buy or sell, or each manager may have greater say about investments that land in his or her area of specialization. In other cases, the process is more democratic and each manager has equal say.

Finally, and much less common than the other two, is the multiple-manager system. In this system, a fund's assets are divided among a number of managers who work independently of each other. American Funds is the group best known for using this approach. The multimanager approach is be-coming more common because of so-called all-star funds such as those of-fered under the Managers and Masters' Select names. Those funds hire name-brand managers from different fund groups and portion out assets among them. These hired guns are known as subadvisors.

Although we have been impressed with American Funds and a few other companies that favor team management or multiple-manager approaches, we generally favor the single-manager approach. Naming a single manager makes it clear who's ultimately accountable for managing shareholders' money. It's also easier for investors to get information about an individual than about a nameless, faceless committee. On the flip side, team-managed and multimanager funds are likely to have greater continuity, which can help smooth transitions if one manager leaves.

Assessing Management

When savvy investors such as pension managers and consultants visit money managers, they focus their examination of the company on personnel. They look at the backgrounds of managers and analysts, examine the hiring pro-cess, dig into the way analysts and managers work together, and examine compensation systems.

With limited time and access, it's not practical for most individual in-vestors to go through the same due-diligence process, but you can learn most of what you need to know without flying out to visit management. Evaluating management—either of a company or a fund—is the point at which investing becomes more art than science. You won't find management skill neatly summed up in a data point; you must use your judgment. By looking at a few key criteria, you can improve your portfolio's performance, find managers who will stick around, and feel more comfortable about the funds in your portfolio.

Quality and Quantity of Experience

There's no reason to settle for an inexperienced manager when there are hundreds of funds with skilled, seasoned management. Although you'll often hear the claim that most fund managers are under the age of 30, the average manager is actually about 10 or 15 years older than that. In fact, most investors do have experienced managers working for them. In a past study, we looked at the 25 largest funds, which represent about one fourth of all mutual fund assets, and found that the typical big fund boasts a veteran team with more than eight years' tenure at the fund. That figure significantly understates management's experience, because it usually represents only the time a manager has spent at the fund, not the manager's total years in money management.

You can find a manager's tenure at a fund on Morningstar.com or a fund company's Web site. Our one-page fund report (found in print and online) also contains information on other funds the manager runs. Check to see when and where the manager's career in investing began and when he or she began managing money. A good rule of thumb is to search out managers who have logged at least 10 years as an analyst or manager and 5 years as a portfolio manager. If the fund manager previously ran other funds, take a good look at the records of those funds to see how they fared against others in their peer group.

Experience is not the only thing that matters, though. Where a fund manager learned about investing is as important as total tenure. Look for managers who learned to invest from great managers, or who cut their teeth at firms with lots of great funds. The manager might have come up through the ranks at a giant, high-quality firm like Fidelity or American Funds, a high-quality boutique like Longleaf or Davis/Selected, or somewhere in between, such as Mutual Series. We'll take a manager with 5 years of experience at the top-notch American Funds group over one with 15 years at an unimpressive shop anytime.

Ownership of the Fund

One of the best ways to find a manager whose interests are aligned with yours is to find a fellow shareholder. Most managers have money in their funds, but they also have a lot at stake in their bonuses. A typical manager might have $1 million invested in his or her fund, but stands to pocket a $2 million bonus if it crushes its peer group. Naturally, that manager has a big incentive to take the risks necessary to produce big returns. Meanwhile, the manager probably doesn't even know what his or her fund's tax position is because the firm's bonus system is based on pretax returns.

Now consider a less common example: A manager has $75 million of his own money invested in his fund. With a king's ransom in the fund, that manager has a powerful incentive to stay focused on long-term returns and capital preservation. A bonus can't sway that. In addition, the chances are pretty low that the manager will be tempted to jump ship. On top of that, he'll be very tax conscious because capital gains distributions would cost him millions in taxes. Not many managers have that kind of loot in their funds, but it's worth the effort to track a couple of them down.

Finding out how much a manager has invested in the fund can be tricky. When it comes to their investments, fund managers don't have to tell you a thing. You won't get a peep out of the ones who have only a token investment in their funds, but the ones with fortunes in their funds are generally happy to share that information (see Figure 4.2).

Great Shareholder Reports

You can learn a lot about managers by reading their shareholder reports. A good shareholder report is long on insight and short on spin. You want managers who can explain the rationale for their actions in plain English. Good managers will own up to their mistakes and share the lessons they have learned. When they describe their investments, look to see if they have original insights or are simply repeating trendy investment banker's jargon.

Finding great shareholder reports isn't just a sign that you've found a smart manager—great reports are a sign of respect for shareholders. If a manager

---

Tweedy Browne Global Value

Selected American

Longleaf Partners

Third Avenue Value

Figure 4.2   Firms where managers have $75 million or more of their own money invested.

considers you a fellow owner, he or she will share important information that you're entitled to know. Some of our favorite shareholder reports are from Oakmark Select, Tweedy Browne funds, Davis/Selected funds, Clipper, and Third Avenue funds. See if your funds' reports stand up to the best. For more information on how to read a fund's shareholder report, see the Frequently Asked Questions (FAQs) section at the end of this book.

A nice side benefit to scrutinizing the shareholder reports is that you'll know the fund better and be able to make better use of it. When you look at it closely, you might find that you're not comfortable with a manager's strategy. On the other hand, if you like and understand your fund's strategy, you'll be more likely to stick with the fund if it runs into trouble.

Dealing with Management Changes

Knowing who runs your fund is important, but what happens if your manager leaves? Is your fund an automatic sell candidate? Maybe in some cases. Back in the mid-1990s, Oppenheimer Mainstreet Growth & Income was an alluring fund. Its returns since launching in 1988 were among the very best in the entire fund universe, and lots of people bought the fund that year. Yet John Wallace, who had earned that record, left in the middle of 1995, and the fund wasn't the same after he left. It fell far behind its competitors during subsequent years. (Oppenheimer brought in a new manager in 1998 who helped get the fund back on track.) Investors who bought the fund because of its great record, without knowing that the manager who had earned it was no longer there, were sorely disappointed.

Most of the time, a management change is not cause for panic. A Morningstar study found that strong-performing funds generally stay ahead of the pack after a management change, whereas weak performers tend to keep lagging. When Peter Lynch left Fidelity Magellan back in 1990, many investors worried that the fund would fall apart. In fact, the three managers who have run the fund post-Lynch have acquitted themselves well.

That's why we generally recommend that investors adopt a wait-and-see attitude when a fund undergoes a change. We don't think current shareholders should follow the manager out the door, especially if they hold the fund in a taxable account and have earned capital gains in the fund. You could be sticking yourself with a big tax bill for no good reason. If you switch your money to another fund, it has to perform significantly better than the old one to make up for any tax hit you've incurred. And it may turn out that the new manager is a worthy successor to the old one.

When a Management Change Isn't Cause for Concern—and When It Is

Based on what we've learned over the years, here are some examples of when investors generally should sit tight following a management change:

▶ *If you own a fund from a category with modest variation in returns.* Successfully managing a bond fund is a matter of gaining fractions of a percentage point in returns. Returns within a category of bond funds usually don't vary much. For example, in 2001, short-term government bond funds gained an average of 7.24%. Two-thirds of the funds in that group had returns between 6% and 8%. Unless your manager is so exceptionally good or bad as to reliably deliver returns outside that mass, a management change isn't likely to mean much.

▶ *If a fund family has a strong bench.* When a fund manager leaves Fidelity, Morningstar analysts usually don't get too worked up about it. Why not? Fidelity has scores of talented managers and analysts who can take up the slack.

▶ *If your fund uses a team-managed or multiple manager approach.* Team-managed and multimanager funds where the team really did work democratically are least likely to be affected by the departure of a single individual.

▶ *If your fund's new manager has racked up a strong record elsewhere.* In this case, you want to be sure that the firm has also brought aboard the new manager's whole staff—not just one individual. That might sound odd, but it happens frequently when fund companies hire outside money-management firms called subadvisors instead of hiring their own investment professionals directly. When Vanguard brought aboard an entirely new team to run Vanguard Capital Opportunity, we were enthusiastic because the same team had done an outstanding job at Vanguard Primecap.

Although selling immediately is usually not the best course of action, keep a close eye on manager changes in the following situations:

- ▶ If your fund hails from a firm that has just a handful of funds. Replacing the departing manager may stretch resources pretty thin.
- ▶ If your fund happens to be the one good one among a group of poor ones. This holds true whatever the fund family's size.
- ▶ If your fund is run by a single manager. This is particularly a concern for funds at smaller shops.
- ▶ If your manager's skill at selecting stocks has been key to the fund's performance.
- ▶ If your fund resides in a category such as small-cap growth or emerging markets, where the range of returns is broad.

Assessing Fund Companies

As touched on in the preceding section, managers are not lone wolves, and whether a fund succeeds or fails depends on the quality of its analysts and traders as well as its manager. Every sizable fund is the product of all three groups working together. There are three elements to focus on when assessing a fund company: research capabilities, corporate strategy, and ownership.

Research Capabilities

Fund giants like Fidelity and Putnam employ hundreds of analysts and scores of portfolio managers. Other firms have very little analyst support and the managers rely heavily on research produced by big Wall Street brokerage firms. The problem with relying on Wall Street is that it's almost impossible to outsmart the market using widely available research reports.

A few managers can do it, but that's not the norm. It can be tricky to get a handle on the depth of a firm's research bench, but many fund companies will provide the number of analysts at the firm or even biographies of those analysts. Quantity isn't the same as quality, but it does at least let you know that there's a complete organization behind the manager.

But the key way to get a handle on the quality of a manager's support team is to look at the records of funds from the same firm. If you're considering buying a growth fund, be sure to check out all the growth funds managed by a family to see if the firm excels at growth investing. You might find that the fund you're considering is a gem but it's surrounded by mediocrity. That's a sign that the fund is just getting by on the strength of a good manager (or luck) and will deteriorate if the manager leaves. The Legg Mason funds run by Bill Miller have always stood out above the rest of the firm's funds. This is not luck—it reflects that Miller is head and shoulders above his colleagues, and if he were to leave that would be a cause for concern. The best firms have great investors throughout the organization—whether they are analysts, managers, or chief investment officers.

Corporate Strategy

Analyzing a fund company's corporate strategy might sound like consultant-speak, but a company's strategy translates into real differences in investment results. Some firms apply rigorous risk controls to all their funds, while others give their managers a lot more leeway—for better and for worse. We would put T. Rowe Price in the former camp and Janus in the latter. Some firms are divvied up into fiefdoms, whereas others have universal analyst pools that share information with all fund managers. In addition, each fund company strikes a different balance between its own desire to boost corporate profits and the need to do what's best for fundholders.

You can gauge a fund company's priorities by asking a few key questions. Does it close funds to new investment to preserve good returns for current fundholders, or does it have a history of letting funds get too big for their own good? Does it roll out trendy funds that can bring in a lot of assets, without considering whether such funds make good investment sense, or does it run a disciplined lineup based on what its managers do best? Can it retain managers and analysts, or does the firm have a history of seeing managers go elsewhere?

Ownership

The main thing to look for here is stability. Whether a firm is privately held or public, one of the key issues is how likely it is that the firm will merge into another entity. A fund operation that isn't garnering asset growth commensurate with its performance or that doesn't fit in with the parent company's priorities is more likely to become a merger candidate. After a merger, fund companies will often shuffle their management teams and merge funds for reasons that make internal business sense but simply create confusion for fundholders. In addition, mergers have been known to spur key managers to hit the road. When Dreyfus bought Founders Funds in the late 1990s, two of Founders' best managers promptly left. It's not an accident that nearly all the best firms have chosen to grow organically instead of pursuing mergers.

Investor's Checklist: Get to Know Your Fund Manager

▶ Remember that evaluating fund managers can be as much art as science. You won't find quality of management summed up in a single data point.

▶ Look for a manager with experience. A rule of thumb is to stick with managers who have at least 10 years of experience as a manager or analyst and 5 years running a fund. Also, favor managers who have learned from some of the best or cut their teeth at high-quality firms.

▶ Find a manager who is investing along with you. If the manager has a big stake in the fund, that's even better.

▶ Look for a manager who takes the time to write great shareholder reports. A detailed shareholder report will help you understand the fund's strategy and it is a sign that the management team considers you a fellow owner.

▶ Find out who is behind the manager. A fund manager needs a strong support staff for research and trading.

▶ Make sure you understand the company's research capabilities, corporate strategy, and ownership.

▶ Try to stick with fund companies that have continued to grow organically instead of merging with other companies. Mergers can be disruptive to fund shareholders and often cause managers to head out the door.

▶ Check out a wide range of funds at the firm to see if they are successful across the board. Be wary of fund companies that have only one star fund surrounded by mediocre offerings.

▶ Avoid firms that dump trendy funds on unsuspecting investors.

5

Keep a Lid on Costs

ASK YOUR NEIGHBOR how much she pays for cable television service every month and she can probably tell you within a dollar. Ask her how much she pays for money management and she might not have any idea. Yet, she's probably paying five times more for money management than for cable. If you figure a 1% fee for a $150,000 portfolio, that's $1,500 a year. And if an advisor is managing her money, she might be paying another $3,000 to $5,000. After your home, your money management fees may well rank among your top household expenses along with your car payments and food budget.

The tendency of investors to lose track of such a big figure is why money management is such a great business to be in. The fees are spread out over the year so that you hardly notice them. In any single year, your portfolio's appreciation or depreciation before costs is sure to be greater than the expense bill, so you're more likely to focus on that. The catch is that, with compounding interest, those fees can add up to a small fortune from the time you buy your first stock or fund to the time you make your last sale.

Avoiding the Rearview Mirror Trap

If all funds cost the same or paying more assured better management, costs wouldn't matter. Fund expense ratios cut a wide swath, however, and high-cost funds don't have better managers than low-cost funds. Investors too often ignore costs because they make the mistake of driving while looking through the rearview mirror. Investors look at a performance chart and reason that the fund at the top managed to overcome its expense ratio in the past, so why should it be a hurdle in the future? The problem is that for every high-risk, high-cost fund that hits it big, there are 10 more that fail. You seldom notice the ones that fail because they generate little coverage for the same reason that television news reports on lottery jackpot winners do not give equal time to the millions of people who failed to win any money. High-cost funds that made big losing bets often are merged away. That reduces the number of high-expense failures.

Looking through the windshield rather than the rearview mirror, you can see that expense ratios are the clearest thing ahead. You can't know which sectors will perform well or whether your fund manager will jump ship, but you have a very good idea what a fund's expense ratio will be. In general, expense ratios show little change year over year. For example, Janus Twenty soared to a 73% return in 1998 only to swoon to a 32% loss in 2000, but its expense ratio hardly changed. Expenses are the easiest part of fund returns to predict and control.

If the difference between a cheap and an expensive fund only added up to a few dollars after 20 years, no one would care. However, the power of compounding interest makes small sums grow very large over time. Compare the results of the supercheap Vanguard 500 Index, which costs 0.18%, with the reasonably priced Janus Twenty at 0.84%, and rather pricey Van Wagoner Mid Growth at 1.95% (see Figure 5.1). If you were to invest $10,000 in each fund and each produces 10% annualized returns *before taxes* over a 20-year

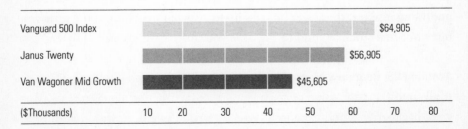

Figure 5.1 Hypothetical growth of a $10,000 investment after 20 years. This example assumes that each fund generated a 10% return before expenses.

period, you would end up spending a little over $1,000 in fees for Vanguard 500, $4,500 for Janus Twenty, and $9,100 for Van Wagoner Mid Growth. The gap in final dollar values would be even greater because the money that would have been withdrawn to pay fees would still be compounding in the cheaper funds. Thus, a $10,000 investment in Vanguard 500 would have grown to $64,905 while Van Wagoner Mid Growth would have grown that sum to $45,605—a gap of $19,300! If you had invested $100,000, you could add a zero to that figure ($190,000) and if you had $1 million in the fund, you would be talking about a $1.9 million gap.

This hypothetical scenario works in practice, too. In a 2002 study published in *Morningstar Mutual Funds,* our colleague Scott Cooley broke funds into quartiles, ranging them from the highest to lowest cost. He found that in all categories, low-cost funds outperformed high-cost funds. He did this by going back to funds' 1996 expense ratios and tracking their performance for the subsequent five-year period. For small-growth funds, the cheapest group produced annualized five-year returns of 8.47% between 1996 and 2001, whereas the highest-cost quartile produced returns of 6.97% over that five-year stretch. For large-blend funds, the advantage was a narrower—but still significant—1.2% a year.

Scott made the case by going one step further. Because investors who choose high-cost funds often do so because these offerings produced strong past performance, Scott took a closer look at this subset. He compared funds with high expenses but top-quartile returns for the five-year period ending December 1996 with low-cost funds that landed in their category's bottom quartile over the same period. Over the ensuing five years, the cheap funds with lousy track records whipped the high-cost funds with strong trailing records.

People often assume that paying more means you get higher quality. It's a pretty good bet that a Lexus is a better car than a Hyundai, even though you may not think it's worth the additional cost. In the fund world, however, the outstanding managers at American Funds Fundamental Investors can be hired for a mere 0.64% a year. Vanguard Primecap's brilliant crew charges a mere 0.50%. You can hire two-time bond fund manager of the year Bill Gross for only 0.56% at Harbor Bond. When you're considering a fund with higher expenses, make sure that its management can do a better job than great managers like these. Figure 5.2 provides a survey of expenses for each type of fund.

Category	Average Expense Ratio %
Large Value	1.41
Large Growth	1.50
Large Blend	1.24
Mid-Cap Value	1.43
Mid-Cap Growth	1.60
Mid-Cap Blend	1.40
Small Value	1.51
Small Growth	1.64
Small Blend	1.53
Conservative Allocation, Moderate Allocation	1.26
Foreign, Europe, Japan and World	1.75
Emerging Markets (including Latin America and Pacific/Asia)	2.19
All Sector Funds	1.72
Bond	1.04
High Yield	1.28
Emerging Markets, Multisector and International Bond	1.39

Figure 5.2   Expenses for each fund type.

Understanding Sales Charges

If you invest through a broker, you'll have to pay sales charges in addition to the fund's expense ratio. A sales charge that you pay when you buy a fund, is known as a front-end load. A sales charge when you sell is a back-end load. (These charges are taken out automatically; you will not be writing a check to cover them, so you might not even realize that you're paying them or know how large they are.) If you own a fund that charges a back-end load, and hang on for a certain number of years, that load may phase out after several years if you don't sell. Alternatively, you might pay a level load, or a percentage of your return each year, for a period of years.

Fund companies often identify the different cost structures available as A, B, and C shares. Although the alphabet soup can be inconsistent from family to family, here are some of the more common types of loads.

Front-end loads are usually called A shares. The fund's sales charge is simply taken out of your initial investment up front. So if you put $10,000 into one of Hancock funds' A share classes, which carry a 4.50% load, you will pay $450 in commissions and invest $9,550 in the fund. Front loads typically range from 3% to 5.75%. If the fund's annual expenses are relatively low, A shares are often the best deal for long-term investors who are buying through a broker or advisor.

B shares usually carry deferred loads. With these shares, you will not pay sales charges until you sell the fund. The charges also decline each year. Federated charges 5.50% if you sell one of it's B-share funds in the first year. Sell in the sixth year, and it will cost you just 1.0%. After six years, you can sell at no cost at all.

Don't expect to get a deal if you hang on for the long haul, though. B shares also include a stiff annual 12b-1 fee. (12b-1 refers to a fee that fund companies are allowed to charge to cover the costs of marketing and distributing their funds.) Long-term investors should therefore look for back-load shares with conversion features. In this type of fund, the back-load shares effectively become front-load shares for investors who have owned the fund for a certain number of years, and front-load shares almost always have lower 12b-1 fees.

Funds with level loads are usually called C shares. They have no initial sales charge (or a relatively modest one of 1% or 2%). However, these funds further compensate the broker who sells you the fund by charging an annual fee (typically about 1%) each year you stay in the fund. That means higher annual costs for shareholders.

Scudder funds' C shares don't have an initial sales charge, but they carry heavier annual expenses than the firm's A and B shares. Level-load shares are thus particularly bad choices for long-term investors. Simply, it's better to pay one lump sum up front than to have your return eaten away each year by higher expenses.

There's no single best cost structure. What works for you will depend on three variables: the size of the loads, the fund's annual expenses, and how long you plan to own the fund.

There is absolutely no reason to pay a load if you're picking your own funds. For nearly any load fund out there, you can find a reasonable no-load alternative. And given the bite a sales charge takes out of your investment, you can often get better returns even if the no-load fund isn't quite as good as the load one.

Investor's Checklist: Keep a Lid on Costs

▶ Be a cheapskate. When you look for funds, focus on low costs. Look for bond funds that charge less than 0.80% and stock funds that charge less than 1.25%.

▶ Check out the expense ratios of the funds you already own. If some are steep, see if you can switch to lower cost options.

▶ If you're working with a broker, find out how much you're paying and make sure the advice you are getting is worth the price.

▶ If you plan to buy a load fund and hold on for the long haul, funds with front-end loads (often referred to as A shares) are generally the best deal.

PART TWO

How to Build a Portfolio

6

Match Your Portfolio to Your Goals

Now that you've made your way through the first five chapters of this book, you've learned a lot about how to pick great funds. The next step is to figure out how they can work together in a portfolio.

You want to own funds that will prosper in different markets. You need one that will do well when large-cap stocks thrive, another that can reap the rewards of a strong market for small caps, one that benefits when foreign stocks are booming, and a bond fund to provide stability when stocks are suffering.

The right mix of those funds will help you meet your goals and keep your portfolio on a relatively even keel. This chapter covers the first steps of identifying your goals and targeting a suitable mix of funds for meeting them. In later chapters, we'll dig deeper into constructing a portfolio.

Defining Your Goals

Maybe you're investing for retirement, for your child's education, or for a vacation home. Your goal determines how long you'll be investing (also called your time horizon), and how much of your investment you can put at risk. The closer your goal, the less you can afford to lose and the more you should focus on preserving what you have made instead of on generating additional gains. As we've all seen in recent years, it's possible for the stock market to bleed red for several years at a time. Extended bear markets are rare, but you don't want to be caught in one when you need to draw on a portfolio full of stock funds.

You'll also want to figure out how much money your goal requires. Because most of us have no idea what our goals will cost, we tend to squirrel away money without knowing whether we're saving enough to meet a specific need. For example, some financial-planning experts say we need 80% of our preretirement income to live comfortably once we stop working. In reality, many thrifty retirees make do on less. Others, meanwhile, spend their retirements traveling or taking up expensive hobbies. (Golf, anyone?) They spend *more* in retirement than they did while working.

Next, you need to project how long you'll be paying for your goal. Say your goal is sending your child through college. Will that expense stretch out over four years? Or do you see postgraduate study in the future, too?

The length of time you will need the money matters even more for retirement planning. When do you want to bid the working world farewell? Have you dreamed of an early retirement, or do you find not working at least part time unimaginable? Finally, as unpleasant as it is, you'll need to project when you'll bid the world adieu. When it comes to life expectancy, think long. Although most of us will not become centenarians (a person who retires in 2010 at age 65 could expect to live another 17 to 18 years, according to the Social Security Administration), it's better to err on the side of longevity. Better to have money to pass on to your heirs than to run out.

Finally, be sure to account for inflation. Based on historical inflation rates, you'll actually need $161,270 in 10 years to have the same buying power that you get with $120,000 today. If you forget to allow for inflation, you may be taking up panhandling, not pottery, during your retirement. When it comes to retirement planning, many advisors use a 2%, 3%, or 4% inflation rate. College costs, however, have been growing well ahead of inflation. Some advisors assume that college costs will continue to rise by about 10% per year.

If you suspect that coming up with one portfolio to meet all these goals would be an incredibly complicated task, you're right. It makes much more sense—and is a whole lot easier—to treat each of your goals separately. After all, they each need different amounts of money, have different time horizons, and will require you to draw on your investments for different time periods. Each deserves a distinct portfolio. As you assemble your portfolios, treat each goal independently of the others.

Setting Your Asset Allocation

So you have an idea of what you're saving for, and how much you will need. The challenge is ensuring that you can get from here to there. Before you begin choosing individual mutual funds and/or stocks, think about what the big picture should look like. You need to consider your portfolio's blend of stocks, bonds, and cash—also known as your asset allocation.

As we'll cover in greater detail later, each of these groups will thrive in a different environment. Stocks delivered great returns in the 1990s, but bonds did much better when the market slumped in 2000, 2001, and 2002. There can be significant differences within groups, too. Big, well-known growth stocks drove most of the stock market's strength in the late 1990s. They fell into a bear market starting in early 2000, but smaller, value-oriented stocks, which had lagged in the 1990s, did great.

The ideal would be to own only whatever group is doing well: Hold nothing but large caps when they are strong, switch to small caps when they have their day in the sun, and rotate into bonds when stocks are hopeless. Unfortunately, such a strategy is all but impossible to pull off. Studies by Morningstar and academic researchers have shown over and over again that so-called market-timing is not effective—telling the future is hard.

An interesting piece in the February 2001 issue of *Financial Analysts' Journal* studied the difference between buy-and-hold and market-timing strategies from 1926 through 1999. Essentially, what the authors did was to map all the possible market-timing variations between 1926 and 1999, with different switching frequencies. They assumed that for any given month, an investor could either be in T-bills or in stocks, and then calculated the returns that would have resulted from all the possible combinations of those switches. Then they compared the results of a buy-and-hold strategy with all the possible market-timing strategies to see what percentage of the timing combinations produced a return greater than simply buying and holding.

Only about a third of the possible monthly market-timing combinations beat the buy-and-hold strategy. When the authors looked at quarterly switching over five-year periods, the results got even worse for the timers: Only one fourth of the timing strategies beat buy-and-hold strategies. Annual results were even more grim: One fifth of annual timing strategies beat buy-and-hold strategies.

If you try to time the market, the odds are stacked against you, especially when you consider the effect of trading costs. What's more, the bulk of the returns (positive and negative) from any given year come from relatively few days in that year. This means the risk of not being in the market is also high for anyone looking to build wealth over a long period of time.

Instead of getting caught up in market-timing, it's better to hold an assortment of asset classes tailored to meet your needs. By diversifying among investments with different behaviors, you can get the returns you need to meet your goals and keep volatility in check. No matter what the market, odds will be good that at least some part of your portfolio is doing relatively well and may even be prospering.

That's why we think that finding the best asset mix is crucial if you want to meet your goals. In fact, it can be just about as important as choosing great funds.

Stocks offer the prospect of greater returns over the long haul than bonds and cash, but they also carry a lot more risk. If you have a long time horizon, say more than 10 years, you will probably want to dedicate the majority of your portfolio to stocks. If you're saving to purchase a house within a few years, you'll probably want to tilt your portfolio more toward bonds, which can provide income while protecting your principal.

Also, consider what stage of the investing life cycle you're in. A person who recently started working and is putting money away a 401(k) plan is in the accumulating stage, and will probably want to stash at least 80% of assets in stocks. Middle-aged investors should take a more conservative stance if saving for retirement. A mix of 60% stocks to 40% bonds would be a reasonable choice for a 50-year-old with a fair amount of risk tolerance. Finally, retirees should focus on keeping the wealth they have built and will want to limit their stock exposure to about 20% to 40% of assets. These are just general guidelines, and you might need a different mix to meet your specific goals. (Part Five of this book outlines three more detailed model asset allocations. You can use them as guidelines and adjust the mix depending on your willingness to take on more or less risk.)

Although setting the appropriate asset allocation can be challenging, you can now make use of online calculators and tools that make this task easier than ever.

A lot of great tools are available online, including some at www.vanguard .com and www.troweprice.com. Morningstar's version of this planning software is called Asset Allocator. It helps you figure out how likely you are to meet your goal given the amount of money you have to invest and your time horizon. For example, if you want to save $35,000 to put down on a house purchase within the next five years, the program will tell you how likely you are to reach that goal if you save $200, $300, or $400 per month. More important, it will also give you specific information about your portfolio's ideal mix of large and small U.S. stocks, foreign stocks, bonds, and cash.

The mix and the odds of reaching your goal are determined on the basis of historical rates of return and risk for each asset class. It's possible that your portfolio would actually do better, but it's wise to be conservative and err on the side of caution in making projections.

Targeting Your Goal

No matter which asset-allocation tool you use, you'll need to gather some information first.

1. The number of years you have to reach your goal.
2. How much money you need for your goal. (In most programs, you have the option of treating this in terms of how much money you need per year and over how many years.)
3. How much money you can invest right now.
4. How much money you can contribute each month.

Making Up for Shortfalls

Figuring out what your portfolio should look like is just a matter of plugging in the appropriate information, but you may find that your chances of meeting your goal are slim. Time to give up? Not at all. You can do four things to improve your chances.

Invest More Now: In general, the more you invest up front, the more you can make over the long haul (assuming you don't put your lump sum to work right before the market drops). The bigger your initial investment, the faster you will reach your target.

Increase Your Monthly Contributions: Investing a small amount more each month will move you more quickly to your goal.

Extend the Number of Years to Your Goal: If you can't put in more money, maybe you can wait a few more years before drawing on your portfolio. A longer time horizon creates the opportunity for additional compounding of your returns.

Become More Aggressive: If you can't invest more money or time, try changing your portfolio mix by making it lighter in cash and bonds and heavier in stocks. Do so with care, however. In recent years, many soon-to-be retirees have paid a steep price for having too much in stocks.

Diversifying Your Portfolio

After you've determined your goals and your target asset mix, your next job is to try to maximize your return within each asset class by choosing the right investments. That means not only good funds, but also ones that will work well together so that your portfolio, as a whole, does well (see Figure 6.1). Certain types of investments will do well at certain times while others won't.

Some investors think that if they own a lot of funds, they automatically have a lot of diversification. Not necessarily. Back in 1999, we talked with an investor who wanted to know if her portfolio of six funds had enough variety in it. She rattled off a list of names: Janus Twenty, Janus Fund, Janus Overseas, Janus Mercury, Janus Olympus, and American Century Ultra. We were stunned—the investor had picked six funds and had almost no variety in her portfolio. Janus Overseas at least owned foreign stocks, but like

↓ Category Correlation →	①	②	③	④	⑤	⑥	⑦	⑧	⑨
① Large Blend	1.00								
② Large Growth	0.86								
③ Large Value	0.74	0.38							
④ Mid-Cap Blend	0.89	0.84	0.63						
⑤ Mid-Cap Growth	0.61	0.88	0.19	0.76					
⑥ Mid-Cap Value	0.71	0.38	0.95	0.69	0.22				
⑦ Small-Cap Blend	0.64	0.69	0.40	0.89	0.76	0.52			
⑧ Small-Cap Growth	0.54	0.80	0.16	0.74	0.97	0.21	0.83		
⑨ Small-Cap Value	0.58	0.45	0.59	0.79	0.42	0.76	0.86	0.49	1.00

Figure 6.1 Morningstar Category Correlations based on 3-year R-squareds as of 9-30-02. The higher the number, the stronger the correlation.

the other funds, it was laden with growth stocks, mostly in the technology sector. On top of that, the funds tended to focus on large-cap stocks. The problem wasn't that she was loyal to the Janus brand (American Century Ultra shared the same characteristics) but that the group of funds she had picked were all thriving at the same time. Naturally, they were investing in the same way. We urged her to add greater variety to her portfolio. Here's hoping that she did: Those funds lost an average of 21.7% in 2000 and went on to fall even further in 2001.

You don't want to be tipped off that your funds are all similar because they all lost money when the stock market turned ugly. That's why you need to know how your funds invest. Say that you buy a value fund that owns a lot of financials stocks, which tend to do well when interest rates are declining. If that were your only fund, your returns wouldn't look very healthy during a period of spiking interest rates. So you decide to diversify by finding a fund heavy in food and drug-company stocks, which aren't sensitive to interest-rate movements. By owning the second fund, you limit your losses in a period of rising interest rates. That is the beauty of diversification.

Ways to Diversify

Diversification can occur at several different levels of your portfolio. For mutual fund investors, some levels are more important than others.

Diversifying Across Investments: By investing in funds instead of in stocks, you're already ahead of the game here. Say you owned stock in a single company. If the company flourished, so would your investment. But should the company go bankrupt, you could lose a large sum of money. If you own several stocks, your portfolio won't suffer as much if one of your holdings sours. By investing in a mutual fund, you're getting this same protection, but it is spread among even more companies (even the most concentrated mutual funds own about 20 stocks).

Diversifying by Asset Class: The three main classes or groups of assets are stocks, bonds, and cash. Investors treat these as distinct groups because they have distinctive behaviors. Stocks offer higher long-term returns but also carry greater risk. Cash earns tiny returns (think of your savings or money market account), but with virtually no risk. Bonds land in between. These groups will even behave differently during the same time period.

Some financial advisors contend that foreign stocks, real-estate investment trusts, emerging-markets stocks, and the like are also asset classes; but the stocks, bonds, and cash division is the most widely accepted. Adding bonds and cash to a stock-heavy portfolio lowers your overall volatility. Adding stocks to a bond- or cash-heavy portfolio increases your potential returns. For most investors, a mix of all three is the best choice. How you determine that mix depends on your goals and the length of time you plan to invest.

Diversifying by Subasset Classes: Within two of the three main asset classes—stocks and bonds—investors can choose several flavors of investment. With stocks, you may distinguish between U.S. stocks, foreign developed-market stocks, and emerging-markets stocks. Furthermore, within your U.S. stock allocation, you can have large-growth, large-value, small-growth, or small-value investments. You can also make investments in particular sectors of the market, such as real estate or technology. The possibilities for classification are endless and often overwhelming, even to experienced investors.

So what's the bottom line on diversification? Diversifying across investments and by asset class is crucial, and subasset class diversification can be useful. But not everyone needs to own a high-yield bond fund, a foreign fund, a small-cap fund, a real-estate fund, and so on. Nor must everyone have exposure to value and growth styles. You should nonetheless consider the ways that such investments might add variety to your portfolio and allow you to rest a little easier.

Investing for Goals That Are Close at Hand

So far, you have read a lot about long-term goals such as retirement or a child's college education. As an investor, you probably have the most money tied up in those goals, and successfully meeting them (or not) will have the greatest effect on your future. But you may also be saving for a short-term goal such as a major trip or a down payment on a home. Here are some guidelines for effectively targeting those goals.

Investing for Short-Term Goals

Sometimes, the hardest task is choosing investments for goals that are within spitting distance. Figuring out the best way to save money to pay for a home addition in three years or to stash away enough to take a European jaunt in a year or two is not easy. In general, we'd steer clear of stocks for short-term goals because stocks could be down significantly in such a short period, cutting into your stake instead of increasing it. Instead of running that risk, you'll want to put your money somewhere safe, but where it can also grow a bit.

If you put your money in a money market or savings account, you would have easy access, the money would be safe, and you would earn modest interest. But it's possible to do better without putting your money at risk.

Certificates of deposit (CDs) are often popular with short-term investors because, like bank accounts, your principal won't decline in value. This is not the case with the other options we'll discuss. The drawback of CDs, is that you are required to hold it for a set period. If you cash in sooner, you will pay a substantial early withdrawal penalty.

Ultrashort-bond funds invest mainly in short-term Treasury, mortgage-backed, and corporate bonds. With an average duration (a measure that indicates how much a fund is likely to be affected should interest rates change) of just six months, they don't feel much pain when interest rates rise. Money markets, by contrast, carry durations much closer to zero, but offer lower returns. If you don't want to put your principal at risk but would like to eke out a little more return, ultrashort funds are a good first step away from money-market funds.

If you're willing to take on a little more risk, consider investing in a short-term bond fund. Just be aware that you could lose money if interest rates rise: In 1994, the average short-term bond fund lost 0.70%. You'll also want to steer clear of short-term bond funds that take on excessive credit risk. Many short-term bond funds rely on mid-quality corporates (rated A or BBB) to boost their distributed yields. But that can hurt their returns when investors become wary of companies with dicier balance sheets, as they did in 2002.

Investing for Intermediate-Term Goals

Perhaps your daughter will leave for college in six years and you're only beginning to invest for the big event now. Or you know you'll need a new Jaguar in seven years to help cope with the midlife crisis you're anticipating. Here's how to invest for a goal that's 5 to 10 years away.

Many advisors recommend that intermediate-term investors put 25% of the money in a safety net of a short-term bond fund or cash and the remaining 75% in stock funds. Those worried about risk might want to place 35% of their portfolio in bonds or cash. From there, you'll want to shift more into your bond funds as you get closer to your goal.

Large-cap blend funds make the most sense for the stock portion of an intermediate-term investor's portfolio. Large-blend funds invest in the core of the U.S. market and include value and growth stocks among their holdings, making them steadier than most stock funds when the market hits a rough patch. Large-blend funds also tend to be less risky than other U.S. stock funds. In the past 15 years ending in mid-2002, the mid-cap categories have lost as much as 36% of their value in a 12-month period. Small caps have lost 31%. Technology-focused funds suffered even more, going into a 45% tailspin for 12 months. Large-blend funds, on the other hand, were down as much as 19% over a 12-month period.

Balanced funds, also referred to as hybrid funds, are another option for intermediate-term investors. They earn the "balanced" moniker by keeping a steady mix between stocks and bonds, usually placing about 60% of their assets in stocks and 40% in bonds. These funds offer simplicity, but the downside can be costs. You can often buy a short-term bond fund and a large-blend fund and pay less in annual expenses than if you had just bought a balanced fund.

Furthermore, maintaining your own stock/bond mix enables you to shift relatively more into bonds and cash as you near your goal.

When you're within a few years of your goal, you'll want to shift to the short-term strategy discussed earlier because at that point the risk required for bigger gains is too great. You need to preserve what you have made rather than run the risk of having to draw on your portfolio when it's down.

Investor's Checklist: Match Your Portfolio to Your Goals

▶ To build a diversified portfolio, make sure you combine funds that can prosper in different markets.

▶ When you're mapping out your investment goals, consider the impact of inflation on future costs. Also take into account your personal hopes and dreams; for example, if you envision a retirement filled with golf or travel, make sure to build that into your budget.

▶ Don't get caught up in the loser's game of trying to time the market. Instead, pick the right mix of assets to meet your needs and stick with a disciplined investment plan.

▶ Remember that buying a lot of funds doesn't guarantee a well-diversified portfolio. To minimize overlap, select funds with different investment styles and make sure they don't all have big positions in the same top holdings.

▶ Balanced funds can provide instant diversification and allow you to plan for intermediate-term goals. But keep an eye on the costs—they tend to be higher than those for an all-stock or all-bond fund.

▶ To make sure your portfolio is on track, monitor performance on a regular basis and rebalance to make sure your mix is still on target.

7

Put Your Portfolio Plan in Action

CONGRATULATIONS! YOU'RE making good progress on your construction project. You've created a plan for your portfolio by identifying your goal and the kinds of investments that will help you achieve it. In that phase, you were like an architect, sketching out ideas, then drafting plans. Now you're the builder turning those plans into reality.

This chapter covers key elements of that process, including building a solid foundation for your portfolio, determining how many funds you need (and avoiding excess), and simplifying your investment life. If you haven't tried designing your own portfolio, we present a simple, effective portfolio to get you started.

Building Your Portfolio's Foundation

The idea behind core funds is that they're relatively stable funds and tend to be reliable year-in and year-out. They aren't the kinds of funds that will have great years, but they aren't likely to be terrible, either. That makes them easier to stick with during rough times, and they'll help shore up your portfolio when your other funds are struggling. In short, they will provide your portfolio with a solid foundation.

What Makes a Core Mutual Fund?

For longer-term portfolios, most advisors recommend large-cap U.S. stock funds for your core, because those stocks represent the heart of the domestic economy. Large-cap stocks make up about 70% of the dollar value of all U.S. stocks, and they tend to be more stable than small-company shares.

Although it's widely held that small-cap stocks produce better returns over extremely long periods (think multiple decades), we're not convinced that the "small-cap effect" is really that strong. Many of the studies showing a performance edge for small-cap stocks have focused on tiny companies with little trading volume. That makes it tough for an average investor to duplicate the study results in the real world. Most of these studies also ignore trading costs, which can be a big drag on returns over time. Small-cap names also tend to have more protracted down periods than large caps—not a good thing when you're getting close to needing your money. For example, small-cap stocks lagged during most of the 1990s. So does that mean you should skip small-cap stocks? No. We think they're still worth owning: Just make them a smaller portion of your portfolio and be sure to rebalance periodically so you can reap their rewards without leaving too much of your portfolio vulnerable to a downturn. In general, we'd recommend limiting your small-cap exposure to less than 20% of your stock portfolio's assets.

If you're going to make large-cap funds the core of your portfolio, the question is, What kind? Large-cap blend funds, which own big companies that tend to show both growth and value traits, are core stalwarts. Large-blend funds usually don't lead performance lists, but they're even less likely to bring up the rear. They're boring, which makes them ideal core choices.

For cautious investors, large-value funds used to be the preferred core holdings. These funds invest in big, well-established companies with stocks that are cheap relative to those of other large caps. Historically, their focus on slow-growing, generally steady companies earned large-value funds the lowest volatility of any of the Morningstar style categories. But that apparent tranquillity can be deceiving. In recessionary times like 1990, value-oriented funds can lose more money than their blend counterparts. More aggressive investors might want to tilt their portfolios toward large growth. Just make sure to balance that with a value fund to offset some of the risk. (In the following chapter, we'll take a closer look at different types of core stock funds.)

You might want to include a global stock fund as a core holding, too, so that you aren't staking everything on the U.S. market. The fund should focus on the world's developed markets, investing in leading companies, just as your core U.S. funds do. (Before investing in a foreign fund, be sure to check out Chapter 9, which includes a section on international investing.)

If you're building a portfolio for short- or intermediate-term goals, a bond fund might make a good core holding. Stick with bond funds that invest in high-quality securities and focus on those that favor bonds with intermediate-term maturities. (These are easy to find—they are in Morningstar's intermediate bond fund categories.) These funds make good core holdings because funds that focus on lower-quality bonds tend to be riskier. Funds that focus on short-term bonds can be stable, but at the cost of lower returns than you might get otherwise. On the other hand, funds with lots of long-term bonds can deliver higher long-term returns, but they also tend to be volatile. You can capture much of the return of a long-maturity fund with an intermediate-maturity fund, but with a lot less volatility.

If you're in a high tax bracket, consider a municipal-bond fund—the income you get can be exempt from both federal and state income taxes. Focus on the options that favor high-quality intermediate-term bonds and carry low expenses; there is no need to take on extra interest-rate or credit-quality risk for a shot at a modestly higher return. If taxes aren't a concern, consider government-bond or general-bond funds. Here, too, focus on low-cost, intermediate-term choices. Chapter 10 provides more information on selecting a good bond fund.

How Big Should Your Core Be?

Core holdings take up 100% of some portfolios. In others, these investments account for 70% to 80% of assets. There's no hard-and-fast rule for how large your core ought to be. But you'll probably want to put at least 50% of your portfolio in core holdings. After all, these are the solid, long-term investments you're relying on to help you reach your goals. If you're close to your goal, or if you're in retirement and drawing on your nest egg, you may want to commit all—or at least a large portion—of your portfolio to core hold-ings. After all, you want to avoid any unpleasant surprises.

So where do the rest of your assets go? Into noncore investments. There are two kinds of noncore investments: supporting players and specialty funds. (If you look up a fund's Analyst Report on Morningstar.com, you'll see whether we classify the fund as core, supporting, or specialty.) Supporting players are not as stable as core funds, but they can add variety to your over-all portfolio, enhancing returns and helping to temper the overall volatility. These are offerings such as mid-cap funds and small-cap funds that tend to be consistent compared with their competitors. These funds aren't absolutely essential, but they contribute to a well-rounded portfolio. Use such invest-ments for diversification and growth potential. For example, if your core is made up exclusively of U.S. large-cap stocks, you might want to add small- or mid-cap U.S. stocks and a foreign fund to the noncore portion of your portfolio for diversification (see Figure 7.1).

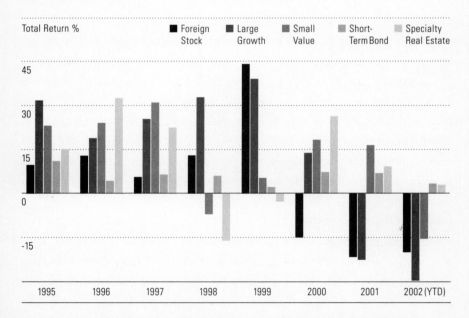

Figure 7.1   By diversifying among a variety of funds, you can prosper in good markets and gain some protection in bad ones.

Specialty funds are the feast-or-famine investments that may juice up returns. They include funds that invest in just one sector and funds run by managers who make large bets on particular holdings or on certain parts of the market. Among foreign funds, those investing in emerging markets or just one part of the world are specialty offerings. On the bond side, this usually means high-yield, or junk, bond funds.

Although you probably wouldn't want to put a significant portion of your portfolio in any one of these investments, they allow for the possibility of extraordinary returns. Of course, they also generally carry a higher level of risk. But as long as you limit the size of the riskier portion of your portfolio, you aren't likely to threaten the bulk of your nest egg, and your investing will be more adventurous. Just be sure to put together a reliable core first. You don't want more thrills than your portfolio can stand. Figure 7.2 provides a list of fund roles within a portfolio.

Core Role	Supporting Role	Specialty Role
Conservative Allocation	Convertibles	Diversified Pacific/Asia
Foreign Stock	Diversified Emerging Mkts	Emerging Markets Bond
Interm-Term Bond	Europe Stock	International Bond
Intermediate Government	High Yield Bond	Japan Stock
Large Blend	International Hybrid	Latin America Stock
Large Growth	Long Government	Pacific/Asia ex-Japan Stk
Large Value	Long-Term Bond	Specialty-Communications
Moderate Allocation	Mid-Cap Blend	Specialty-Financial
Muni California Interm	Mid-Cap Growth	Specialty-Health
Muni California Long	Mid-Cap Value	Specialty-Natural Res
Muni National Interm	Multisector Bond	Specialty-Precious Metals
Muni National Long	Muni Short	Specialty-Real Estate
Muni New York Interm	Short Government	Specialty-Technology
Muni New York Long	Short-Term Bond	Specialty-Utilities
Muni Single State Interm	Small Blend	
Muni Single State Long	Small Growth	
World Stock	Small Value	
	Ultrashort Bond	

Figure 7.2 The role of different fund categories in your portfolio.

Knowing How Many Funds Are Enough

Most of us collect something. For some, it's wine. For others, it's baseball cards. Still others collect clothes. Some people collect investments. They may own a dozen funds in their 401(k) plan, another half dozen or more funds outside it, and 25 or so stocks. That's a lot of investments, and some investors go even further. At the Los Angeles Times Investing Conference a few years ago, we gave a presentation on building a portfolio. We polled the audience to see who owned the most funds and one attendee had 66!

The problem with owning too many funds and stocks is that you can easily lose sight of the financial forest for the trees. You wind up owning funds because they looked appealing when you bought them, but you may not be clear on how they're contributing to your goals. That investor with 66 mutual funds would face a monumental task just remembering all those names, never mind figuring out why he owns them and how they all work together.

If 66 funds is too many, it's natural enough to wonder what the ideal number is. Given that the idea behind a portfolio is to keep volatility in check, how many mutual funds do you need to do that? Morningstar studied just this topic. We constructed hypothetical portfolios ranging from 1 to 30 funds, using every possible permutation of funds. For example, the 30-fund portfolios consisted of every 30-fund combination we could come up with. (We have a lot of computing power to draw on!) We then calculated 5-year standard deviations for each of those portfolios. As you learned in Chapter 3, higher standard deviation can spell bigger gains or losses, whereas a lower number indicates a less volatile portfolio. We found that single-fund portfolios had the highest standard deviation, delivering either the biggest gains or the heaviest losses. So owning just one fund can be a risky bet. Add a fund and the standard deviation drops significantly. Returns are lower, but the downside is less severe, too (see Figure 7.3).

After 4 funds, the effect of adding another fund diminished. It's still noticeable, but not so dramatic. After 7 funds, things have mostly leveled out and after 10 funds, a portfolio's standard deviation stays nearly the same regardless of how many funds you add. Thus, once you own between 7 and 10 funds, there may be no need for more. In fact, the more funds you own, the more likely you are to own at least a couple that do practically the same thing. That could be a drag on your returns because if you have multiple

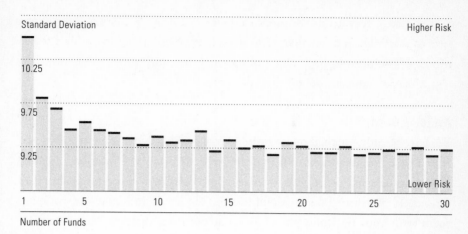

Figure 7.3   How the number of funds in a portfolio affects standard deviation.

funds doing the same thing, one is likely to be better than the others. Focus on the superior fund and you'll get better returns.

What You Really Need: Diversification

We aren't saying that just because you own just a few or a dozen funds, you're in trouble. You need to dig a little deeper to determine if you have the right number for you. That means taking a look at what the funds actually own.

The number of funds you own is less important than how diverse those securities are. Owning seven large-growth funds won't diversify your portfolio the same way that owning one large-blend fund and one small-value fund and one small-growth fund would. As discussed in Chapter 6, it's what your funds own that matters most.

When you're analyzing your portfolio, you'll be looking for two things: funds that invest in the same way and holes in your portfolio compared with your asset-allocation plan. More than one large-growth fund, for example, will add little to your portfolio. If you find that you own multiple investments that are doing the same thing, think about selling some of them to focus on the best choice. And, remember that you can have overlap even though you own just a small number of funds. Conversely, even if you own many investments, you could still have gaps in your portfolio. If you find that you have very little exposure to a major sector of the market or no exposure to asset classes other than U.S. stocks, think about adding a fund to fill the gap. The bottom line: Don't obsess over the number of funds that you own. Instead, concentrate on their diversity.

Avoiding Overlap

We have already touched on one problem of having overlapping stock funds. If you have two or more funds that do the same thing, the inferior funds are a drag on returns. Yet another overlap-related problem could be much more serious. If you don't take a careful look at the funds you own and compare them with your portfolio plan, you could find out that you have taken on much more risk than you intended. Say it's late 1999 and you own a dozen funds. Your portfolio could be well diversified, but three of those funds may invest in large-cap growth stocks. When the bear market started in early 2000, such funds fell off a cliff and continued to struggle. Many investors suffered from a surprise hit. Likewise, many had much more exposure to

Top 15 Holdings for Fidelity Magellan (% Net Assets as of 3-31-02)		Top 15 Holdings for Fidelity Growth & Income (% Net Assets as of 1-31-02)	
Citigroup	4.47	Microsoft	4.17
❶ General Electric	4.37	❶ General Electric	3.66
Microsoft	2.98	❺ Pfizer	3.59
Viacom Cl A	2.83	SLM	3.45
❷ American Intl Group	2.71	❽ Fannie Mae	3.40
❸ ExxonMobil	2.56	❹ Wal-Mart Stores	2.93
❹ Wal-Mart Stores	2.41	❼ Philip Morris	2.93
❺ Pfizer	2.38	❸ ExxonMobil	2.55
❻ Home Depot	1.83	Citigroup	2.04
❼ Philip Morris	1.81	Freddie Mac	1.88
❽ Fannie Mae	1.76	❷ American Intl Group	1.78
Intel	1.66	❻ Home Depot	1.48
ChevronTexaco	1.60	IBM	1.38
Wells Fargo	1.58	BellSouth	1.28
❾ Tyco International	1.49	❾ Tyco International	1.25

Figure 7.4   Nine of the top 15 holdings are the same in these two funds.

particular market sectors, including technology stocks, without realizing it—until those stocks started to tumble.

Your portfolio could also be vulnerable to stock-specific problems. A big advantage of mutual funds over investing directly in stocks is that a fund gives you exposure to a large number of stocks. But what if two or more of your funds are focused on the same stocks? Imagine if, in early 2002, you owned two or three funds that each had a significant percentage of their money in Enron. Without realizing it, you might have had significant exposure to the biggest corporate bankruptcy in history. It's entirely possible that more than one of your funds will own the same stock. Consider this: In 2002, the top 15 holdings of Fidelity Magellan and Fidelity Growth & Income had 9 stocks in common (see Figure 7.4). Janus Twenty and Janus Mercury had 3 stocks in common within their top 15 holdings (see Figure 7.5). If something goes wrong in one of those stocks, more than just one of your funds would be affected. Likewise, if you own individual stocks (such as company stock in

Top 15 Holdings for Janus Twenty (% Net Assets as of 04-30-02)		Top 15 Holdings for Janus Mercury (% Net Assets as of 04-30-02)	
Microsoft	7.69	❶ Citigroup	4.73
ExxonMobil	6.85	❷ Nokia Cl A	4.36
AOL Time Warner	6.55	Liberty Media	3.92
Viacom Cl B	6.42	❸ Pfizer	3.60
American Intl Group	5.42	Berkshire Hathaway	2.95
❶ Citigroup	4.84	Tenet Healthcare	2.49
Home Depot	4.64	Electronic Arts	2.43
Goldman Sachs	4.40	Laboratory Corp of Am	2.35
❷ Nokia Cl A ADR	3.63	Analog Devices	2.33
Eli Lilly	2.86	Fannie Mae	2.14
General Electric	2.45	ACE	2.00
EBAY	2.30	Viacom Cl B	1.99
UnitedHealth Grp	1.86	McKesson HBOC	1.93
❸ Pfizer	1.71	Wyeth	1.86
Coca-Cola	1.45	Celestica	1.85

Figure 7.5   Three of the top 15 holdings are the same in these two funds.

your retirement plan), be alert to your funds also owning those stocks—it could spell additional risk.

If you're worried about duplication of investment styles, sectors, or individual stocks, remember these tips when building your portfolio.

Don't Buy Multiple Funds Run by the Same Manager

Zebras don't change their stripes, and managers rarely change their strategies. Fund managers have ingrained investment habits that they apply to every pool of money they run—you won't find a manager buying growth stocks for one fund he runs and value stocks for another. So if you buy two funds by Famous Manager A, chances are you'll own two of the same thing.

Don't Overload on One Boutique's Funds

Some fund families, such as Fidelity, T. Rowe Price, and Vanguard, offer a lineup of funds that span several investment styles. Other shops, often called boutiques, prefer to specialize in a particular style. Janus is a growth specialist; Oakmark means value; Wasatch operates in small-cap territory. Boutique families are often excellent at what they do, but it's doubtful whether owning three funds from the same boutique will give you anything more than you would get with one.

Watch for Overlap in Your Large-Cap Holdings

Large-cap stocks and funds make great core holdings, but they're perhaps the greatest source of overlap in many portfolios. Why? The pool of large companies is relatively shallow. Only about 250 of all U.S. stocks can be classified as large cap. The remaining thousands of stocks qualify as mid- or small-cap issues. So if you own multiple large-company funds, there's a high possibility of overlap. That's also true if you hold both individual large-cap stocks and large-cap funds. It's hard to think of any justification for owning more than one large-blend fund. Once you have picked up a large-value and a large-growth fund—or a single large-blend fund—start looking at other options.

Take the Four Corners Approach

The Morningstar style box can be a diversifier's best friend. Not only will the style box tell you whether your manager focuses on large-value stocks, you can also use it to identify funds that bear little resemblance to one another. Owning funds in each corner of the box (large value, large growth, small value, and small growth) can be a straightforward way to diversify your portfolio. Morningstar studies show that these fund categories have low correlations with each other: The four corners can all behave differently over the same time period. When the broad market tumbled in 2000 and 2001, large-growth funds suffered most, losing a cumulative 35% for the two years. Small growth dropped 12%, while large value eked out a 2% gain and small value zoomed 39%. Each group has led or faltered during other periods. If you own a large-value fund from your favorite fund company, choose its large-growth, small-value, or small-growth offerings to add something new.

Pay Attention to Your Portfolio's Sector Weightings

Even if you find that you do not have a lot of overlap in individual stock names, you may still be overexposed to one or two sectors of the market. Be sure to check your total exposure to each market sector. For example, if your funds own different health care stocks, the sector still tends to move as a whole. There's no strict rule on how much exposure to a single sector is too much, but more than 30% of your overall portfolio is too much for most people—roughly one third of your portfolio would be vulnerable to weakness in the sector.

Give Your Portfolio a Thorough Examination

Say that you have followed these tips and have put together a portfolio of investments or possible investments. To test for overlap, you could enter all the investments—both the stocks you've bought directly and every stock that your mutual funds own—into a spreadsheet such as Microsoft Excel and sort by stock name. But that's a lot of work.

You can use Morningstar.com's Portfolio Manager to get a quick and easy read on your portfolio's makeup, which will enable you to identify gaps, funds that invest in the same way, overall sector weightings, and stocks that crop up in multiple funds. You can enter all your fund holdings (and any stocks you own, such as company stock in your retirement plan) and then click on Portfolio X-Ray. It will show you how your portfolio is distributed across each square of the Morningstar style box, across sectors, and among cash, bonds, U.S. stocks, and foreign stocks. Finally, select the Stock Inter-section view and you'll see your portfolio's largest stock positions, based on each of your fund's holdings and any individual stocks you have entered into the portfolio.

Simplifying Your Investment Life

The simple things in life can bring great joy, and good investing doesn't have to be complicated. In fact, simplification may lead to better investment re-sults. A simple portfolio can be easier to stick with because you know exactly what you're investing in and why. It's certainly easier to track, and you avoid outsmarting yourself.

Consolidate Your Investments

By investing with only one supermarket or fund family, you eliminate excess complexity, cutting back on paperwork and filing. And the consolidated state-ments you'll receive can make tax time much easier, too. Instead of pulling to-gether taxable distributions and gains from different statements, you'll have them all in one place.

If you want to stick with just one fund family, consider one of the big ones, such as Fidelity, Vanguard, or T. Rowe Price. These no-load families are all relatively low-cost, with Vanguard being the cheapskate champion, and each offers a diverse lineup of mutual funds. If you would rather pick and choose among fund families, then a mutual fund supermarket might be your best option. Fund supermarkets bring together funds from a variety of fund groups.

Jot Down Why You Own Each Investment

Simplification gurus preach that writing down our goals helps us organize our lives to meet those goals. The same can be said for investing: By writing down why you made an investment in the first place, you're more likely to make sure that the investment meets its original goal. If it isn't doing what you expected by sticking with a specific investment style and producing com-petitive long-term returns, you'll be ready to cut it loose. Noting why you bought the fund—to get large-cap growth exposure and consistently above-average returns from a manager who has been in charge for several years, and so on—will help to instill discipline and eliminate some of the emotion that so often gets in the way of smart investing.

Say you bought T. Rowe Price Mid-Cap Growth to cover the costs of your daughter's education in 15 years. You chose the fund because it earned a Morningstar Rating of 5, reflecting a good combination of returns and risk; its expenses were lower than the category average; and the fund didn't risk a lot on the technology stocks that so many other growth funds were feasting on. Those are all good reasons. So you shouldn't even consider selling the fund unless it falls short on these points.

To take the opposite case, maybe you bought Scudder International Equity because you wanted some international exposure and you were attracted by its long-tenured management and consistent performance. But since 1999, the fund's performance has been a lot less impressive and it has also undergone a management change. The fund lagged the foreign-stock group in both 2000 and 2001. Since the fund is no longer meeting your main reasons for buying it, selling would be a reasonable choice. Other legitimate reasons to sell would be that a fund has hiked its expense ratio, or assets have gotten so bloated that performance starts to suffer.

Index, Index, Index

Perhaps the easiest way to reduce investment stress is to accept the market's return rather than trying to beat it. Stop hunting high and low for fund managers who can consistently outdo their competitors—just buy some index funds and go golfing.

With index funds, you don't have to worry about manager changes. Or strategy changes. You always know how the fund is investing, no matter who is in charge. Many investors find indexing boring, especially the mutual-fund hobbyists out there. But even fund junkies admit that index funds are the lowest-maintenance investments around. The real work with indexing comes at the start, when you're choosing the funds that make up your portfolio. Before doing so, check out Chapter 8, which includes a section on index funds.

Put Your Investments on Autopilot

You may pay your electric and water bills automatically—why not invest the same way? You won't have to send a check out every month, every quarter, or every year. There's an added benefit to investing relatively small amounts on a regular basis (also called dollar-cost averaging): You may actually invest more than you would if you plunked down a lump sum, and at more opportune times. When you're dollar-cost averaging, you're putting dollars to work no matter what's going on in the market. You have effectively put on blinders against short-term market swings: Whether the market is going up or going down, $100 is going into your fund every month no matter what. *That's* discipline. Would you be able to write a check for $100 if your fund had lost 15% the previous month? Probably not. But that would mean $100 less working for you when your investments rebounded.

Figure 7.6 shows how automatic investing can enable you to buy cheaper shares on average, which will spell stronger returns. An investor who put in $600 up front in January would have gotten 60 shares at $10 per share. Those shares were worth $12 in June, so her investment was worth $720. If she had dollar-cost averaged her investment, putting in $100 per month, she would have purchased some of her shares on the cheap and wound up with 62.1 shares in June. At $12 per share, she would have had $745.20, $25 more than if she had invested a lump sum at the beginning.

Building a Simple Portfolio

Choosing investments doesn't have to be complicated. Here's a quick, simple example to guide you through the decision-making task. Selecting your

Month	Investment ($)	NAV ($)	Shares Purchased
January	100	10	10
February	100	9	11.1
March	100	11	9.1
April	100	8	12.5
May	100	9	11.1
June	100	12	8.3
Total Result of Investment	600 →	12 ×	62.1 = $745.20

Figure 7.6 How dollar-cost averaging works.

funds, creating a portfolio, and checking that against your allocation model will be exactly the same as the process we use for our hypothetical example.

Say that you have $100,000 to invest, and you want to retire in 25 years. After tinkering with an online asset allocation tool like Morningstar.com's Asset Allocator, you decide that your asset allocation should be 0% bonds, 70% large-cap U.S. stocks, 10% small-cap U.S. stocks, and 20% foreign stocks.

Next, look over Morningstar.com's Fund Analyst Picks for some ideas. (For each Morningstar category, analysts pick the best funds in each category that are open to new investors.) You might decide to put $70,000 (or 70% of your portfolio) in Vanguard 500 Index to cover the large-cap allocation, $10,000 in T. Rowe Price Small-Cap Stock, and $20,000 in Harbor International to cover the foreign position.

You can check to see if this combination matches up with your allocation model by going back to Asset Allocator. As of mid-2002, this portfolio had about 60% in large caps and 20% in small. That's because of two factors: Vanguard 500 Index doesn't own exclusively large-cap stocks and Asset Allocator groups mid-cap issues with small caps. Put half as much into T. Rowe Price Small-Cap Stock and transfer the rest to Vanguard 500 Index and you'll nicely match your target.

Investor's Checklist: Put Your Portfolio Plan in Action

▶ Build a solid foundation for your portfolio by investing in reliable core funds.

▶ After you've established a strong base, consider investing a smaller percentage of your assets in more specialized funds such as small-cap funds, mid-cap funds, or foreign-stock funds.

▶ Don't obsess about the number of funds you own. But if you own a lot of funds, make sure they don't overlap too much. If you own two or more funds that are doing the same thing, consider selling one to focus on the stronger choice (especially if it has lower annual expenses).

▶ Whenever you make an investment, write down why you bought it. If it no longer fits your reasons for buying, it's probably a good candidate for selling.

▶ Simplify your life by buying some index funds or setting up an automatic-investment plan. Dollar-cost averaging takes the emotion out of investing and should produce better returns over time than buying and selling erratically.

Finding Ideas for Your Portfolio

8

Find the Right Core Stock Fund for You

You now know the essentials of creating a portfolio, from determining your asset allocation to selecting the funds to fill out that framework. Don't stick this book on the shelf just yet, though. By learning more, you can invest even more effectively.

The chapters in Part Three cover strategies for getting the most out of stock and bond funds. That means understanding the nuances. This chapter focuses on the various shades of value and growth investing, assessing the pluses and minuses of style-specific versus flexible funds, and how to choose between index funds and their actively managed competitors. In Chapter 9, we address key issues of choosing a fund for foreign exposure, along with how you might use funds to play narrow roles in your portfolio. Chapter 10 is devoted to how bond funds work and how to select the right ones for your portfolio. Finally, Chapter 11 provides guidance in choosing a fund family.

Understanding Value Funds

One of the key choices to make when selecting a stock fund is deciding between those that favor value stocks, growth stocks, or something in the middle.

(For more details on how we define investment style and why we think it's important, see Chapter 1.)

Not all value funds (or growth funds, for that matter) are created equally. Different people have different definitions of what's a *great value.* Maybe you call your shoes a deal because you paid only $14.99 for them at a discount store. Your friend, meanwhile, says her designer shoes, at $125, are a value buy because she got them for less than full price. Fund managers who buy value stocks express similar differences of opinion. All value managers buy stocks that they believe are worth significantly more than the current price, but they'll argue about just what makes a good value, about why those stocks are worth more than their current prices. How a manager defines value will determine what the portfolio includes and how the fund performs.

Why Shadings Matter

A pair of sibling funds offers a great example of why investors need to understand how their fund managers define value. Vanguard Windsor and Vanguard Windsor II are both large-cap value funds, but their performance in recent years could hardly have been more different. In 2001's value rally, Windsor gained 5.7%, while Windsor II lost 3.4%. But the tables turned in 2002: Through the first half of the year, Windsor dropped 12.5% while Windsor II lost about half as much, notching a 5% loss.

What made the difference? Slightly different definitions of value. Windsor's managers focus on beaten-down industries they believe are due for a rebound, and they buy stocks with price ratios that are the cheapest of the cheap. What's more, lead manager Chuck Freeman isn't afraid to add to struggling issues on further weakness or to build sizable positions in troubled companies. Freeman's interest in beaten-up names has really stung at times. The fund entered 2002 with a 3% stake in WorldCom and nearly a 2% stake in Adelphia Communications, and he added to both names on weakness early in the year. Those stocks proved extremely painful in 2002 as both plunged in response to concerns about off-balance-sheet debt and their eventual bankruptcies. In the past, the fund has gotten burned by plays on downtrodden real-estate investment trusts, which dragged on returns in 1998. Windsor II, meanwhile, also emphasizes cheap stocks, but its managers pay more attention to the companies' profitability. As a result, the fund holds fewer deeply out-of-favor investments than Windsor does. That strategy hurt

Top 10 Holdings for Vanguard Windsor II (Portfolio Date: 03-31-02)   % of Net Assets

Philip Morris	3.20
Entergy	2.71
Allstate	2.65
Citigroup	2.61
Bank of America	2.54
Sears Roebuck	2.48
Cendant	2.47
American Elec Power	2.34
Occidental Petroleum	2.27
Boeing	2.16

Top 10 Holdings for Vanguard Windsor (Portfolio Date: 03-31-02)   % of Net Assets

Citigroup	5.53
ALCOA	4.09
Washington Mutual	3.01
TJX	2.71
Pharmacia	2.64
Cigna	2.38
IBM	2.35
Total Stk Mkt VIPER	2.27
Tyco Intl	2.19
Eaton	1.80

Figure 8.1   Different definitions of value have led these funds to different portfolios.

Windsor II in 2001 but helped it in 2002. For a closer look at how two funds can implement value strategies in different ways, check out the top 10 portfolio holdings for the two funds in Figure 8.1. Few of the names are the same.

Value strategies divide (roughly) into the relative-value and absolute-value camps. There are variations within each camp; in fact, Vanguard Windsor and Vanguard Windsor II both practice relative-value strategies.

Relative Value Funds

Fund managers practicing relative-value strategies favor stocks that look cheap relative to some benchmark. In other words, value is relative. These benchmarks can include one or more of the following measures.

The Stock's Historical Price Ratios (price/earnings, price/book value, or price/sales): Companies selling for lower ratios than usual can be attractive buys for value managers. Often, these companies' prices are lower due to some type of "bad news," to which the market often overreacts. When AOL Time Warner collapsed in 2002, a few value managers, such as T. Rowe Price Equity-Income's Brian Rogers, saw the plunge as a buying opportunity since the stock's valuations were lower than they had been in many years.

The Company's Industry or Subsector: A manager may believe that a company is undeservedly cheap compared with its competitors. Managers Chris Davis and Ken Feinberg, stock-pickers at the Davis Financial Fund, bought shares in AIG, one of the few beaten-down names in the insurance industry in mid-2002.

The Market: In this case, a solid company may be dragged down because it operates in an out-of-favor industry. This scenario is common with cyclical sectors, such as energy. Schlumberger, is one of the dominant oil-services companies, but when its industry is out of favor, it will be dragged down, too. Value managers will jump on the opportunity; when investors were down on drug stocks in 2002, Oakmark Select manager Bill Nygren and Vanguard Windsor II's Jim Barrow bought shares in Merck, one of the major players in the industry (see Figure 8.2 for a selection of relative-value funds).

In general, relative-value funds are more likely to participate in different market environments than other value funds. The downside is that they might also have more exposure to volatile growth stocks.

Vanguard Windsor	Berger Small Cap Value
Vanguard Windsor II	Selected American Shares
Vanguard Growth and Income	Davis NY Venture
Dodge & Cox Stock	Putnam Classic Value
American Funds Washington Mutual	

Figure 8.2 Funds that follow relative value strategies.

Absolute Value Funds

Managers such as FPA Capital's Bob Rodriguez, Third Avenue Value's Marty Whitman, and the team at Longleaf Partners follow absolute-value strategies, and are typically considered stricter value practitioners than the relative-value set. They don't compare a stock's price ratios to those of other companies or the market. Instead, they try to figure out what a company is worth in absolute terms, and they want to pay less than that figure for the stock. Absolute-value managers determine a company's worth using several factors, including the company's assets, balance sheet, and growth prospects. They also study what private buyers have paid for similar companies. Private market value is a key tool for Bill Nygren, who's made Oakmark Select and the Oakmark Fund among the most compelling funds for value investors.

Although some of these funds stick with traditional value sectors, such as manufacturers and financials, funds like FPA Capital and Third Avenue Value have also been willing to load up on down-and-out tech names when the sector is out of favor. Third Avenue's Marty Whitman loaded up on semiconductor stocks in the wake of the 1997 Asian economic crisis. Whitman has also been known to invest in distressed debt securities if they're priced cheaply enough.

Absolute-value managers are often willing to make more dramatic sector bets than their relative value counterparts. Most absolute-value funds avoided tech stocks during the late 1990s, which meant they missed out on that sector's huge runup. At the same time, some absolute value managers, such as Scudder-Dreman High Return Equity's David Dreman, the team at Clipper Fund, and former Oakmark Fund manager Robert Sanborn, have often loaded up on tobacco stocks like Philip Morris. The funds got clobbered when Philip Morris lost more than half its value in 1999. Some absolute-value managers have also piled assets into cheap stocks that stay depressed because of weak fundamentals. That problem—also known as the "value trap"—illustrates one of the key dangers of investing in cheap stocks: You might be buying cheap stocks that just get cheaper.

In general, if you own an absolute-value fund, be prepared to wait out some dry spells. Managers who follow strict value strategies tend to be a determined lot, and they're generally not swayed by market fads. It can take a while for an extremely undervalued stock to pay off, particularly if it's in a segment of the market that's badly out of favor (for a selection of absolute-value funds, see Figure 8.3).

Other Types of Value Funds

Some value managers are tough to pigeonhole. When examining a company's growth prospects, Legg Mason Value Trust's Bill Miller is more forward-looking than many of his peers. Thus, you'll find more high-growth stocks, such as on-line retailer Amazon.com and computer makers Dell and Gateway, in Miller's portfolio than you would in the portfolios of absolute-value managers including the portfolio of Longleaf Partners, which generally avoids tech stocks. That difference mattered quite a bit when tech stocks collapsed in 2002: Longleaf Partners lost just 1.6% for the first six months of the year, whereas Legg Mason Value dropped almost 17%.

Other funds, such as Vanguard Growth & Income and Selected American, have also had significant exposure to growth sectors over the years. Rather than loading up on cheap stocks with weak fundamentals, such as thrifts and regional banks, Selected American has tended to favor somewhat more expensive but faster-growing financials such as Citigroup and Morgan Stanley. Neuberger Berman Focus follows a more concentrated growth path to value and has generated exceptional long-term returns while holding just 30 to 35 stocks, including a lot of tech issues.

Weitz Partners Value is another fund that takes a creative approach to value investing. Instead of focusing on traditional value measures like price/earnings and price/book ratios, manager Wally Weitz looks for companies generating

Third Avenue Value	Kemper-Dreman High Return
Longleaf Partners	FPA Capital
Oakmark	Babson Value
Oakmark Select	Tweedy, Browne American Value
Mutual Shares	Harbor Value
Mutual Qualified	Clipper
Mutual Beacon	

Figure 8.3 Funds that follow absolute-value strategies.

strong free cash flows. If he can't find what he likes, he'll sit on cash until the market bids down prices on his favored stocks. Over the years, Weitz has been a big player in media and telecommunications stocks. Gabelli Asset follows a similar tack and also favors media and communications stocks. The fund has a low turnover ratio and doesn't change much over time. Although its favored sectors can wax and wane, the market usually gets around to seeing things the way Gabelli does.

When Value Managers Sell

There are two chief reasons value managers will sell a stock: It stops being a value, or they realize that they just made a bad stock pick. Stocks stop being good values when they become what managers call *fairly valued,* that is, the stock is no longer cheap by whatever value measure the manager uses. For relative-value managers, that could mean the stock has gained so much that its price/book ratio is now in line with that of its industry. For an absolute-value manager, that could mean the stock's price currently reflects the absolute worth the manager has placed on the company.

A manager may also sell a stock because it looks less promising than it did initially. In particular, new developments may lead to a less favorable evaluation of the company. And we often hear from value managers who admit they were overly optimistic about a company's ability to rebound.

When Value Investing Works—And When It Doesn't

Although value investing makes a lot of intuitive sense (it is a chance to buy cheap stocks instead of pricey ones) it doesn't pay off all the time. Both value and growth stocks can be subject to major performance swings. Although value strategies fared well in the early 1990s as companies climbed out of the recession, growth stocks dominated the market in the last few years of the decade. Value-oriented investors did so badly in 1998 and 1999 that some commentators proclaimed the death of value investing. While tech stocks and other growth issues were on a tear, cheaper industrials, durables, tobacco stocks, and weaker financial issues got left out in the cold. All those predictions of the end of value investing led to dramatic shakeups in the fund industry. Market watchers can point to spring 2000 as the value capitulation that marked the bottom for value. Hedge-fund manager Julian Robertson folded up his shop. Oakmark Fund's value stalwart, Robert Sanborn, was nudged aside, and Fidelity's dean of money managers, George Vanderheiden, retired.

In fact, anyone who predicted the death of value investing was dead wrong. Just when it seemed as if things could not get much worse, value managers got the last laugh. After badly lagging growth funds in 1998 and 1999, value funds held up much better when the market dropped, starting in 2000. For the three years ending in July 2002, the typical large-value fund lost about half as much as its large-growth counterpart. In general, value funds fare better after prolonged periods of economic weakness or when investors are skittish about market valuations.

Although value funds generally show less volatility than growth funds, that doesn't guarantee safety. In many previous market downturns, such as the cyclicals/financials decline of 1990, the utilities debacle of 1994, the Asian crisis of summer 1998, and the Federal Reserve Board's interest-rate crusade in 1999, value funds lost as much or more money than growth funds. See Figure 8.4 and Figure 8.5 for our favorite value funds.

Understanding Growth Funds

Value and growth are often considered opposites in investing, and for good reason. Most growth managers are more interested in a company's earnings or revenues and a stock's potential for price appreciation than they are in finding a bargain. In general, growth funds will have much higher price ratios than value funds, because growth managers are willing to pay more for a company's future prospects. Value managers want to buy stocks that are cheap relative to the company's current worth. Growth-fund managers practice different styles, and those styles will affect how the fund performs—and how risky it is.

Earnings-Driven Funds

The majority of growth managers use earnings-driven strategies, which means they use a company's earnings as their yardstick for growth. If a company isn't growing significantly faster than the average (which may be based on the stock's sector or for the market), these managers aren't interested. Within this earnings-driven bunch, earnings-momentum managers are by far the most daring. You might say their mantra is "Buy high, sell higher."

American Funds Washington Mutual A	This fund offers just about everything a value fund should: good long-term returns; little downside risk; decent tax efficiency; and a low expense ratio.
Clipper	This fund's management team has built a superb record by purchasing companies that are trading at 30% or greater discounts to their estimates of intrinsic value. That valuation discipline held back the fund in the late-1990s, go-go growth market, but it has held it in good stead over time.
Dodge & Cox Stock	Management typically looks for companies that have good growth prospects but are cheap based on traditional measures such as P/Es. The fund is run in a conservative manner by a deep, experienced group.
ICAP Select Equity	Manager Rob Lyon uses a concentrated approach here, loading up on 20 companies with reasonable valuations, steady to increasing earning growth, and a catalyst for future growth. Although Lyon has had peer-trumping longer-term returns, he concentrates heavily, exposing the fund to plenty of stock-specific risk, and he trades rapidly, which may make this a more-appropriate holding for a tax-advantaged account (though it has been fairly tax-efficient thus far).
Oakmark I	Bill Nygren, Morningstar's Domestic-Stock Manager of the Year in 2001, has done a great job of identifying companies priced at 40% or greater discounts to their intrinsic values. This fund invests in a mix of mid- and large-caps.
T. Rowe Price Equity-Income	This is another fund that has held up well in the recent bear market. Manager Brian Rogers' penchant for cheap, dividend-paying stocks hurt the fund in the go-go markets of 1998 and 1999, but his conserva-tive approach has kept the fund out of trouble in recent years.

Figure 8.4   Our favorite large value funds.

Berger Mid Cap Value	Tom Perkins seeks out companies trading at or near their historic lows. He eschews companies with high debt or low cash flows but loves fallen growth stocks. The fund's expense ratio has been falling and we expect this to continue, as its asset base has been growing rapidly.
Longleaf Partners	The fund's managers try to ferret out stocks trading at discounts of at least 40% to their intrinsic values and won't hesitate to let cash build if they can't find anything that meets their criteria. The fund's concentrated format can hurt it on occasion, but over time the co-managers' focus on value has helped keep volatility here fairly mild. The fund owns companies of all sizes.
T. Rowe Price Mid-Cap Value	This is a relatively pure mid-cap offering with a conservative strategy. It should remain a relatively steady performer with few surprises.
Tweedy, Browne American Value	This fund has suffered through a couple of below-average years recently, but its true-blue value approach has made it a long-term winner. The fund's since-inception return is still strong, its volatility is low relative to its peers, and managers Christopher and William Browne and John Spears bring a wealth of experience to the table.
Weitz Value	This fund can require patience, but we think it's well worth the wait. Manager Wally Weitz is fond of loading up on sectors where he's finding values, and the cable and telecom arenas are often among his favorite hunting grounds. Although the fund can invest in companies of any size, it has heavily emphasized mid-caps and large caps in recent years.

Figure 8.5   Our favorite mid-cap value funds.

Momentum investors buy rapidly growing companies they believe are capable of delivering an earnings surprise such as higher-than-expected earnings or other favorable news that will drive the stock's price higher. These managers will likely sell a stock when its earnings growth (based on earnings that are reported every quarter) slows. That can be the harbinger of a later earnings disappointment—a negative earnings surprise—that will drive the stock's price down.

Momentum managers typically pay little heed to the price of a stock. Instead, they focus on trying to identify companies with accelerating earnings, as well as catching upswings in stocks that have already shown price gains. Their funds, therefore, can feature a lot of expensive stocks as long as earnings continue to grow at a rapid rate. That behavior is commonly known as price risk. The risk is that if bad earnings news or some other event makes other stockholders jump ship, the stock's price can plunge dramatically. Thus, these funds tend to display significant short-term drops.

One of the best-known proponents of this style is American Century. Founder Jim Stowers II began running the family's funds with an earnings-momentum style in 1971. Other prominent momentum players are Garrett Van Wagoner, manager of Van Wagoner Emerging Growth, and the fund companies AIM Turner and PBHG. These funds have delivered impressive returns in friendly markets: Van Wagoner Emerging Growth gained a stunning 291% in 1999. Since then, though, it has been bleeding red ink. The fund lost 20.9% in 2000, another 59.7% in 2001, and another 69% for the first nine months of 2002. Such funds have the potential to be rewarding long-term investments, but most investors have trouble sticking out the rough stretches. Because of poorly timed purchases and sales, the typical dollar in PBHG Growth lost an average of 3.17% annually over the 10 years ended September 30, 2002, compared with a gain of 9.06% per year for an investment made at the beginning of the period and held for the duration. When we studied other momentum funds, the pattern was the same. In 9 out of 10 major momentum funds, investors' actual returns were significantly lower than reported performance figures would suggest. If you're going to buy a momentum fund, make sure you can stomach significant downturns. Following a disciplined dollar-cost averaging strategy is one way to smooth out some of the bumps that come with the momentum territory. For a selection of momentum funds, see Figure 8.6.

Some managers seek earnings growth in a different way. Instead of searching for stocks with the potential to deliver accelerating earnings, these managers seek stocks that boast high annual earnings-growth rates—generally between 15% and 25%. The basic idea is that if these stocks can continue

PBHG Growth	AIM Constellation
PBHG Emerging Growth	AIM Select Growth
American Century Ultra	AIM Summit
American Century Giftrust	Mainstay Capital Appreciation
American Century Growth	Van Wagoner Emerging Growth
American Century Select	Oberweis Emerging Growth
American Century Vista	Brandywine
AIM Aggressive Growth	Turner Mid-Growth

Figure 8.6 Funds that follow momentum strategies.

to grow at such a rate, they will inevitably command much higher prices in the future. Like momentum investors, managers who employ this strategy typically ignore stock prices, so their funds also carry a great deal of price risk. Alger Capital Appreciation follows this strategy, buying stocks with 20% and higher annual growth rates and featuring high price multiples. The gains it produces can be impressive, but the downside is also dramatic. Although this strategy is different in principle from momentum investing, the results are often similar.

More moderate earnings-growth-oriented managers look for stocks growing in a slow but steady fashion. The slow-and-steady group has historically included such blue-chip stocks as Wal-Mart and Gillette. As long as these stocks continue to post decent earnings, the managers tend to hold on to them. Steady-growth funds often have more modest price ratios than their peers, and often fare relatively well in slow economic environments because they favor companies that aren't dependent on economic growth for their success. But when reliable growers take the lead, as they did in 1998, these funds endure as much price risk as the more aggressive funds. Funds known for following this moderate-earnings-growth strategy include John Hancock U.S. Global Leaders Growth and Dreyfus Appreciation.

Another great example of the slow-and-steady style is Smith Barney Aggressive Growth. Manager Richie Freeman looks for companies with good product pipelines, high insider ownership, and positions in dynamic industries. Once he finds these companies, he hangs on to them: The fund's average holding period is nearly 10 years, and some of the fund's biggest long-term winners have been in the portfolio for well over a decade. Although Smith Barney Aggressive Growth has much longer holding periods than the average growth fund, many of the most successful growth managers let their winners ride. We often hear portfolio managers say that taking profits too early is one of the biggest mistakes growth investors can make.

Revenue-Driven Funds

Not all growth stocks have earnings. In particular, stocks of younger companies—often those in the technology and biotechnology areas—may not produce earnings for years. Some growth managers will buy companies without earnings if the companies generate strong revenues. (Revenues are simply a company's sales; earnings are profits after costs are covered.) Because there is no guarantee when firms without earnings will turn a profit or if they ever will (think of the many Internet companies that went under in 2000), this approach can be risky. Janus funds, for example, owned some stocks with no earnings in the late 1990s. They earned stunning returns when the market was still bullish, but they lost more than many competitors when the market turned ugly in 2000 and 2001. Many managers who focused on companies' revenue growth in the late 1990s have since abandoned their strategies, because many of the stocks in their portfolios imploded in the dot-com bust.

Growth at a Reasonable Price Funds

Managers who seek growth at a reasonable price (GARP) try to strike a balance between strong earnings and good value. Some managers in this group find moderately priced growth stocks by buying stocks momentum investors have rejected; often, these companies have reported disappointing earnings or other bad news and their stock prices may have dropped excessively as investors overreacted by dumping shares. GARP managers also look for companies that Wall Street analysts and other investors have ignored or overlooked and that are therefore still selling cheaply. As with value investors, GARP investors try to find companies that are only temporarily down-and-out and that have some sort of factor in the works (commonly called a catalyst) that seems likely to spark future growth.

Thanks to GARP managers' sensitivity to price, this group of growth funds often features lower-than-average price multiples compared with other growth offerings; as a result, these funds often land in the blend column of the Morningstar style box. Prominent funds with GARP strategies include T. Rowe Price Blue Chip Growth, Fidelity Magellan, and Gabelli Growth. Funds that follow the GARP strategy are listed in Figure 8.7.

Mixing It Up

Few managers follow only one of these growth strategies. Instead, most growth investors blend their stock-picking approaches. Invesco Dynamics buys both core stocks—companies that grow reliably—and faster-moving momentum names. Fidelity Large Cap Stock primarily invests in GARP-type stocks, but it also owns a few names that don't have earnings. Thanks to their diverse mix of growth holdings, these funds may do better when certain growth stocks are out of favor.

When Growth Investing Works

Growth-style strategies generally work better when investors are concerned about economic weakness. Manufacturing and basic-material stocks will suffer when economic growth slumps, but companies with steadier growth generally hold up better. Growth stocks fared far better than value stocks in 1990 and 1991, when investors were wary of companies with weak balance sheets or unsteady results. Growth also came to the fore in the great bull market at the end of the 1990s. Thanks largely to the implosion in tech stocks, however, growth stocks fell far behind their cheaper counterparts in 2000, 2001, and 2002. For a listing of our favorite large-cap growth funds, see Figure 8.8. Our favorite mid-cap growth funds are listed in Figure 8.9.

T. Rowe Price Blue Chip Growth
Fidelity Fund
Gabelli Growth
Fidelity Magellan

Figure 8.7   Funds that follow GARP strategies.

ABN AMRO/Montag & Caldwell Growth N	Manager Ron Canakaris mixes macroeconomic analysis with fundamental research. He sticks to the large-cap names, favoring those with earnings-growth rates of at least 10%. He's not willing to pay through the nose, however, and will consider selling a stock when it reaches a 20% premium to his calculation of its intrinsic value.
Janus Mercury	Manager Warren Lammert has traditionally sought rapid growers that are dominating their niches, without a lot of regard for their price tags.
Harbor Capital Appreciation	This fund buys large-cap companies that are growing revenues faster than the S&P 500 and that boast traits such as strong research and development and defensible franchises. Manager Sig Segalas also prefers to see strong unit-sales growth, which he thinks is key to sustaining of a firm's growth rate.
Marsico Focus	Tom Marsico combines top-down analysis with bottom-up stock-picking. He fills the bulk of the portfolio with steady-growth stocks that he intends to hold for the long haul, but he also has owned more-explosive growth names in the tech and telecom areas.
Vanguard Growth Equity	The fund's managers combine quantitative screens with fundamental analysis and technical analysis to pick stocks. They believe that earnings expectations drive stock prices and pay close attention to earnings revisions and surprises.
America Funds Growth Fund of America	The team of managers, which boasts an average of 25 years of experience, seeks growth stocks selling at reasonable prices and maintains a broadly diversified portfolio.

Figure 8.8   Our favorite large-growth funds.

Deciding between Style-Specific and Flexible Funds

If he were still running a fund today, legendary manager Peter Lynch might get pulled over by the style police. That's not a slight on Lynch's taste in clothing—it's a point about his investing style. The former head of Fidelity Magellan was an opportunist. Sometimes he liked growth stocks. Other times, value

Calamos Growth A	The fund performs solidly in both market rallies and downturns thanks to its managers' strong stock-picking ability. Using quantitative models, John Calamos and his son, John Calamos Jr., look for stocks trading cheaply. They are quick to sell a stock if it reaches their price target or if its fundamentals weaken.
RS MidCap Opportunities	This fund buys fast-growing mid-cap firms that its manager thinks can double in price in two to three years. The risks here are substantial, but so is the potential for strong returns.
T. Rowe Price Mid-Cap Growth	Manager Brian Berghuis looks for companies with sound business models that are growing rapidly. But unlike some other mid-growth managers, he has more than a passing interest in valuations; indeed, the fund's average P/E is well below its typical rival's.
Turner Midcap Growth	Like other Turner funds, this one hunts for stocks that exhibit accelerating earnings growth and positive price trends. Management will pay a premium for its high-momentum picks. That leads it to high-P/E stocks in racy areas, such as tech and telecom.

Figure 8.9   Our favorite mid-cap growth funds.

investments held more allure. Large companies struck his fancy, but occasionally so did smaller firms. Today, financial advisors, investors, and the media look down on such flexible managers. They would rather have managers who stick to one part of the Morningstar style box: They want style-specific managers.

At first glance, Morningstar may appear to be on the side of the style police. After all, we categorize funds by narrow investment styles, such as large growth or small value. But that doesn't mean we only like funds that tend to stay in the same part of the style box year-in and year-out. Style-specific funds have their charms, but flexible funds also have advantages. Neither one is inherently better than the other. There are great and terrible funds in both camps. It's up to you to decide how to use each style in your portfolio.

Flexibility's Charm, Purity's Power

Lynch isn't the only fund-industry luminary who has insisted on having the freedom to pursue his best ideas, wherever they might lead him. Take celebrated First Eagle SoGen Global manager Jean Marie Eveillard: He wouldn't be half the manager he is if he couldn't pluck any type of security from any corner of the world. And even with U.S. funds, some of the best managers, including another Fidelity star, Contrafund's Will Danoff, are drifters who refuse to tether themselves to any one section of the Morningstar style box. The positive aspect of this approach is that your fund will have the potential to thrive in all sorts of market environments. But flexible funds have their downside: They can make building a portfolio tricky. After all, if a fund is a small-cap fund one month and has large-company tendencies the next, how can investors be sure that their portfolios are really diversified? No wonder advisors, investors, and the media are wary of flexible funds.

Style-specific funds, meanwhile, tend to cleave to one bin of our style box. They always invest in, say, small-value stocks, or mid-cap growth stocks. Index funds relentlessly stick to one part of the style box, and families like Putnam and T. Rowe Price offer actively managed funds that tend to stay put. It is much easier to build and monitor a portfolio of style-pure funds. If you select four funds precisely because they invest in different ways, you want to be confident that they will continue to invest that way. Thus, you're always sure that you're diversified.

Using Flexible Funds

Yet writing off flexible funds can mean tossing aside some great funds and fund managers. Here's how even style-specific devotees might work flexible funds into a portfolio:

▶ *Give away some but not all control.* Consider using style-specific funds at the core of your portfolio. If you treat them as building blocks to meet your asset-allocation goals, but save a portion of assets for flexible funds, your overall asset allocation will not get too far out of line.

▶ *Because change is a given, monitor flexible funds carefully.* Keep an eye on where and why your flexible fund's manager is moving. And if you choose to devote significant assets to more than one flexible fund, keep track of how much you have in each investment style. If all your flexible-fund managers are favoring large-growth stocks, you may want to assume they know more than you do and let them ride. But perhaps you should temper that bet somewhat by cutting back there and adding to other parts of your portfolio.

The Indexing versus Active Management Debate

It's the $64,000 question of mutual-fund investing: Are actively managed funds better or worse investments than index funds? The pro-indexing argument usually comes down to this: Most actively managed funds don't beat their index-fund competitors, so your odds of investing in a superior fund are much better if you just buy an index offering. The argument for active management is that some funds do beat the index options: Why not go for the best returns you can get?

Both arguments are correct. We aren't being wishy-washy—it's a matter of where index investing and active management are most effective. Morningstar's managing director, Don Phillips, often advises investors to think of indexing and active management as two ends of a horseshoe. On one end, use index funds to give your portfolio low-cost exposure to the large stocks that dominate the market. On the other end, you can find excellent actively managed funds. You can build great portfolios by buying the best of either group.

Morningstar studies show that indexing tends to be more effective in some investment styles than in others (see Figure 8.10). If you're running a fund focused on large-cap U.S. stocks, you are investing in the most closely watched stocks in the world. It's pretty much impossible for you to know anything about Microsoft or General Electric that hordes of Wall Street analysts and other fund managers don't also know. That's why index funds are so hard to beat—they go along for the ride, while many active managers can end up outsmarting themselves. Low costs are also a huge help. Index funds don't have to hire a bunch of analysts to dig through financial statements or visit factories. Vanguard 500 Index, for example, charges shareholders just 0.18% per year (that's 18 cents for every 100 dollars you have in the fund), whereas the typical large-blend fund costs 1.22% per year. That means every year Vanguard 500 Index has roughly a one percentage point edge on most of

Fund Category vs. Index	Fund Category Return +/- Index			
	1-Year	3-Year	5-Year	10-Year
Large Growth vs. Russell 1000 Growth	1.39	2.94	0.98	-0.09
Large Blend vs. Russell 1000	0.52	0.61	-0.99	-1.18
Large Blend vs. S&P 500	1.58	1.37	-0.91	-1.16
Large Value vs. Russell 1000 Value	-1.47	-0.65	-2.11	-2.09
Mid-Cap Growth vs. Russell Mid-Cap Growth	-1.40	2.65	0.84	0.31
Mid-Cap Blend vs. Russell Mid-Cap	-0.31	-0.24	-0.86	-0.14
Mid-Cap Value vs. Russell Mid-Cap Value	-2.85	-0.43	-0.78	-1.23
Small Growth vs. Russell 2000 Growth	2.70	8.69	6.18	4.60
Small Blend vs. Russell 2000	4.18	6.72	2.63	0.51
Small Value vs. Russell 2000 Value	0.36	0.50	-0.44	-0.79
Foreign Stock vs. MSCI EAFE	1.84	1.90	0.87	1.27
World Stock vs. MSWI	3.53	4.37	0.76	-0.35

Figure 8.10   How fund categories have performed versus appropriate indexes. Data as of 9-30-02.

its rivals. It can make a bit less than the average before expenses and still come out ahead after subtracting costs.

Funds that venture outside the large-cap arena have many more stocks to choose from. Managers have more than 700 U.S. mid-cap stocks and more than 4,000 small caps to pick over. Being an active manager who can pick and choose can be a real advantage over the index. Many small-cap managers tell us that they earn their keep by avoiding stocks that they believe could turn into disasters, and investing more heavily in upstarts they think have great long-term prospects. Index funds don't have the luxury of choice—they match their benchmarks. Likewise, foreign-fund managers have thousands of foreign stocks to choose among. They can even decide to avoid investing in some countries entirely. But if the index includes a struggling market, the index fund has to invest there. For example, Japan struggled through much of the 1990s. If you were a foreign-fund manager, an easy way to stay ahead of the major foreign indexes and index funds was simply not to invest in Japan. That said, the long-term data on foreign indexing is scant.

Although a lot of us at Morningstar tend to invest at least part of our portfolios in actively managed funds, an all-index-fund portfolio is a reasonable strategy for people who don't want to make a full-time job out of analyzing funds. You could certainly do much worse. By opting for an index fund, you are generally assured that the fund will be competitive over the long haul, even if it doesn't dominate its category. You also don't have to worry much about your fund manager leaving. After all, he or she isn't picking the fund's holdings. And if you're paying close attention to your portfolio's asset mix, you can be confident that your fund won't suddenly change its style when you look away.

If you want to invest in actively managed funds, focus your search efforts on fund categories where active managers can add to performance. For your large-cap exposure, you may well be better off going with an index fund. And whatever portfolio slot you're trying to fill, always compare your actively managed options with index funds that track the same stock arena. If the active funds aren't doing better, there's no reason to choose them over an index option.

Choosing an index fund isn't necessarily a snap, though. More than 200 index funds ply their trade in 24 different investment categories. To complicate matters, some investment categories (such as large blend) have multiple index funds, each locked to a different benchmark. The following suggestions will help you choose an index fund that meets your needs.

Know What Index Your Fund Follows

Vanguard 500 Index, Fidelity Spartan Total Market Index, TIAA-CREF Equity Index, Domini Social Equity, and Schwab 1000 all land in the large-cap blend category. But they each track different indexes: the S&P 500, the Wilshire 5000, the Russell 3000, the Domini Social Equity Index, and the Schwab 1000 Index, respectively.

The differences can be significant. Domini Social Equity tracks a custom-made benchmark. It focuses only on what it deems to be socially responsible firms in the S&P 500, then adds about 150 companies that aren't in the index. Knowing what index a fund tracks gives you a handle on the risks and returns you can expect and how they differ from other index funds. If you are buying Domini's fund, you had better be a fan of Microsoft. It constituted about 6% of assets and was the fund's largest holding in early 2002. Meanwhile, Microsoft was a relatively measly 3.4% of Vanguard 500 Index and was the second-largest position (General Electric was the largest). Microsoft was a smaller portion of the other index funds. Thanks to big positions in Microsoft and in growth sectors such as technology, services, and retail, Social Equity outpaced Vanguard 500 Index and other large-blend index options during the bull market of the late 1990s. But it has been more volatile, too, and lost a lot more in 2000 and 2001.

Know Your Options

Thanks to the variety of index funds, you have much more flexibility than a decade ago, when tracking the S&P 500 was about your only option. Today, you can build a well-balanced portfolio made up entirely of index funds. Figure 8.11 lists some common indexes that funds track.

Know the Tax Effects

One of the most common myths about indexing is that all index funds are tax-efficient. After paying taxes on income and capital gains distributions, even investors in the highest tax bracket get to keep a significant portion of

Index	What it Tracks	Index Funds
S&P 500	500 of the largest U.S. stocks.	Vanguard 500 Index Fidelity Spartan 500 Index Schwab S&P 500 Select T. Rowe Price Equity Index 500
S&P Midcap 400	400 mid-cap stocks that are too small to make the S&P 500.	Vanguard Mid Capitalization Index Dreyfus MidCap Index Federated Mid-Cap Index
Russell 2000	2000 small-cap stocks that are too small to make the Russell 1000.	Vanguard Small Capitalization Index
Lehman Brothers Aggregate Index	Broad bond market index that includes government bonds, corporate bonds, mortgage-backed securities, and asset-backed securities.	Vanguard Total Bond Market Index Merrill Lynch Aggregate Bond Index

Figure 8.11 Major indexes and index funds that track them.

their pretax returns. Funds that buy the biggest stocks, such as Vanguard 500, do boast terrific tax efficiency; as of July 2002, Vanguard 500 Index's shareholders kept about 92% of their pretax earnings for the past 5 and 10 years. That's impressive, given that large-blend investors on average kept about 76% of their pretax earnings.

Vanguard 500 Index tends to be tax efficient because it only has to sell stocks when they drop out of the index. Stocks that leave the index usually are small players (most companies drop out of the index precisely because they have become too small)—no stock after number 231 accounts for more than 0.10% of the S&P 500 index. When S&P 500 index funds sell these smaller positions, they don't reap sizable taxable gains. Also, the taxable income distributed by the fund tends to be modest—in early 2002, Vanguard 500 Index's latest income distribution figure (known as its yield) for the past 12 months was just 1.25%.

Don't expect tax efficiency from funds tracking other indexes, though. Shareholders of Vanguard Small Cap Index, for example, kept an average of 83% of their pretax returns over the trailing 10 years ending June 30, 2002. The challenge for this and other small-cap index funds is that stocks grow too large to be considered small caps and are removed from the index. The index fund has to sell that stock. That spells a taxable gain: For the stock to have grown too big for the index, it has to have gone up in price—the fund will be selling the stock for more than it paid. The fund is required to distribute that profit to shareholders, who then have to pay taxes on it.

Know the Costs

Another common assumption about indexing is that all index funds are cheap. Because they don't demand the resources of active management, they certainly ought to be. But some index funds charge surprisingly high annual expenses. Consider this: Devcap Shared Return, a socially screened index fund, takes a 1.75% bite out of your investment every year. That's huge when you consider that the average large-blend index fund's expense ratio is 0.41%.

Using Exchange-Traded Funds As an Index Fund Alternative

Another passively managed investment option began to create a buzz a few years back: exchange-traded funds, or ETFs. Giant asset managers such as

Barclays Global Investors rolled out scores of new offerings in 2000, and Vanguard launched its own version (called VIPERs). Like mutual funds, ETFs are baskets of securities. Like stocks, ETFs trade on an exchange. Unlike mutual funds, which investors can only buy or sell at the price at the close of the day, ETFs trade like stocks—investors can buy and sell them throughout the trading day. Investors can also sell ETFs short and buy them on margin. Anything you might do with a stock, you can do with an ETF.

There are a number of ETFs on the market (Figure 8.12), with nicknames including Qubes, SPDRs ("spiders"), HOLDRs, iShares, and Diamonds. These ETFs track sector-specific, country-specific, or broad-market indexes. Although investors have been slow to embrace more than a couple ETFs, they can be worthwhile investments. Here are the pluses and minuses of ETFs for determining if these options are right for you.

The Advantages of Exchange-Traded Funds
ETFs have some clear advantages over traditional mutual funds.

Greater Flexibility: These funds trade throughout the day, so you can buy and sell them when you want and can easily switch from one to another. When you buy a mutual fund, on the other hand, you're buying at the end-of-day NAV (or share price), no matter what time of day you place your order.

Exchange-Traded Fund Name	Index It Tracks
SPDRs	S&P 500
NASDAQ 100 Trust Shares	NASDAQ 100
Midcap SPDRs	S&P Midcap 400
iShares S&P 500 Index	S&P 500
Diamonds Trust, Series 1	Dow Jones Industrial Average
iShares Russell 2000 Index	Russell 2000
Vanguard Total Stock Market VIPRs	Wilshire 5000
iShares Russell 3000 Index	Russell 3000
Technology Select Sector SPDR	Components of S&P 500
iShares S&P Smallcap 600 Index	S&P Smallcap 600

Figure 8.12   The largest ETFs and the indexes they track.

The Potential for Lower Expenses: The iShares S&P 500 Index, for example, has an expense ratio of just 0.09%.

On a $10,000 investment, you would save $9 a year by choosing iShares S&P 500 Index over Vanguard 500 Index. The latter charges just 0.18% per year for its services but Vanguard also levies an annual fee of $10 for smaller account holders, which increases the iShares' edge.

Tax-Friendly Structure: With a regular mutual fund, investor selling can force managers to sell stocks to meet redemptions, which can result in taxable capital-gains distributions being paid to shareholders who stay on board. But when you buy or sell an ETF, you're often buying or selling existing shares in an exchange with another investor. That shields the fund from the need to sell stocks to meet redemptions. This should make ETFs more tax-efficient than most mutual funds, and they may therefore hold a special attraction for investors in taxable accounts. Keep in mind, however, that ETFs can and do make capital-gains distributions, because they must still buy and sell stocks to adjust for changes to their underlying indexes.

The Disadvantages of ETFs

Your Fund May Not Trade in Line with Its NAV: Because ETFs trade like stocks, there can sometimes be a brief discrepancy between the share price of an ETF and the value of its holdings. ETFs use a method known as arbitrage to correct such discrepancies, however. Heavily traded issues such as SPDRs (which track the S&P 500) and QQQs (which track the NASDAQ 100 index) should trade right around the value of their underlying securities.

Trading Costs: The expense advantage of ETFs may also prove to be more mirage than fact for many investors. Because ETFs trade like stocks, you have to pay a broker's commission whenever you buy or sell an ETF, just as with a stock. If you plan on making a single, lump-sum investment that you hold for years, then it may pay to choose an ETF. However, even assuming a low commission of $8 per trade, a single lump-sum investment of $10,000 in the iShares S&P 500 Index would need to be held for nearly two years to beat Vanguard 500 Index's total costs over the same period.

The companies offering ETFs tout low expenses as one of their key benefits. But if, like most of us, you dollar-cost average and invest regular sums of money, brokerage costs mean you could actually end up paying far more for investing in an ETF than in a comparable mutual fund. Also, investors who want to trade frequently would save money with a regular mutual fund versus an ETF. (For your information only—we still don't think frequent trading makes any sense.)

The bottom line: ETFs' cost advantages aren't always as large as they might seem, and trading costs can quickly add up. If you are in the market for a fund that tracks a broad index such as the S&P 500, or want to invest regular sums of money, it's tough to make a case for choosing an ETF over one of the existing low-cost mutual-fund options.

Investor's Checklist: Find the Right Core Fund for You

▶ All value managers buy stocks that they think are worth more than the current price, but they often take different routes toward that goal. When you buy a value fund, make sure you understand where it lands on the value spectrum and how it fits in with the rest of your portfolio.

▶ Not all growth funds are created equal. Some fund managers focus on companies with improving earnings growth, while others specialize in momentum, revenue growth, or growth-at-a-reasonable price (GARP) strategies.

▶ Don't rule out using flexible funds that roam into different areas of the style box. Although they can be tricky to slot neatly into a portfolio, flexibility can be an advantage for a talented manager.

▶ Remember that the choice between indexing and active management doesn't have to be either/or. You can create a successful portfolio using either strategy, or by combining the best of both worlds.

▶ If you have a lot of money to work with and plan to invest a lump sum, ETFs can be cheaper and more tax-efficient than index mutual funds. But since you have to pay a commission to trade them, they're not the best choice if you have a small portfolio or like to invest at regular intervals.

9

Move Beyond the Core

In this chapter, we focus on funds that can play specific roles in your portfolio. Some, such as the sector funds, can add some spice, boosting your returns. Others, such as real-estate or foreign-stock funds, can add greater variety to your mix, providing more stability when the stock market goes through rough patches. You'll read about each type of fund, what it can contribute to your portfolio, and how to use it.

Using Sector Funds Wisely

If you ever played with a magnifying glass on a sunny day, you know how powerful focusing can be. In fact, it's the principle behind sector funds, mutual funds that invest in a specific industry. How powerful can sector investing be? In July 2002, of the 10 funds with the best 10-year returns, seven were sector funds of various stripes and the other funds had big weightings in a few sectors. That's a common pattern—for most periods, sector-focused funds tend to have the highest returns. The sectors will change but the leaders will usually have relied on just one or two industries to help them build their impressive return records.

Stellar returns lead investors to flock to particular sectors, such as technology during the late 1990s or financials in the mid-1990s. Although sector investing offers great potential, it offers great risk, too. The standard deviation (the variation of a fund's monthly returns for the preceding 36 months around its average monthly return for the period) of the typical technology fund is double that of the S&P 500. At the end of 1999, 9 of the 10 funds with the best 10-year returns were technology funds. By early 2002, only 2 remained in the top 10 and other tech funds had fallen far off the pace. Investors drawn to sector funds can be like moths to a flame. The allure is hard to resist, but you could get severely burned. Sector funds can be great investments, but be sure to use them carefully, as part of a broadly diversified portfolio. You'll read below about the variety of sector funds, smart ways you can use them, and what to look for when buying a sector fund.

The Many Flavors of Sector-Fund Investing

Investors have more than 300 sector funds to choose from, spanning eight Morningstar categories: communications, financials, health care, natural resources, precious metals, real estate, technology, and utilities. Some sector funds focus more narrowly, honing in on a particular subsector of an industry. John Hancock Regional Bank fund is a financials fund but, as the name indicates, it invests exclusively in banks. Then there's Fidelity Select Medical Delivery, a health care fund that focuses entirely on medical services such as HMOs, hospitals, and physicians' groups. Other health care funds focus exclusively on biotechnology companies. Their concentrated focus often makes these funds more volatile than the typical sector fund. When a narrow subsector like Internet stocks falls out of the market's favor, investors in these funds are particularly exposed to losses.

Do You Need a Sector Fund?

This is an easy question to answer: No one *needs* a sector fund. "You could go your entire life without ever owning a sector fund and probably never miss it." So said John Bogle, founder of the Vanguard fund group. (Never mind that Vanguard offers sector funds such as Vanguard Health Care and Vanguard Energy. Both are terrific performers but Bogle now says that he thinks launching them was a mistake.)

You also need to be prepared for potentially disastrous results—that's why we say to keep your sector plays small. After peaking in March 2000, most technology funds took only about a year to slip from leading the mutual-fund pack to lying overturned in the ditch. You don't want to expose much of your portfolio to such extreme performance.

Furthermore, many investors warm up to funds that focus on a certain sector at the very time that area is about to cool off. Investors chasing such hot funds can wind up losing money when the funds tank. From 1991 through 1993, Fidelity Select Automotive gained 163%, nearly triple the S&P 500 index's return for that period. But investors didn't start buying the fund until 1993, and new investments flowing into the fund peaked just in time for the fund's 13% loss in 1994. That means that by the end of 1994, many investors in the fund had either made no money or were even in the red.

That pattern of buying too late is a common one with sector-fund investors. So common, in fact, that if you don't buy any sector funds, you may already be investing more successfully than the typical sector-fund investor. It isn't that sector-fund investors are foolish, it's that they get caught up in the emotional side of investing. We all *know* that the ideal is to buy low and sell high but it's hard to buy a fund that's down (it could lose more money) and to sell one that's making money (it could keep going up!). As a result, we tend to buy funds that have already posted good gains—we have more confidence in them—and sell when they have been losing money for a while. At the extremes, we're buying when we should be cutting back and selling when we might do better to buy more.

The main reason sector funds can be pointless investments is that a portfolio of diversified funds should give you exposure to most major market sectors, and there's no need to double up. Our examination of sector funds also suggests that they can be more trouble than they're worth. Many are just plain bad ideas. One giveaway that sector funds are often more profitable for fund companies than for investors is that these funds tend to launch when a sector is red-hot. That's when they can pull in the most money by encouraging investors to jump in on a trend. It's also the worst time to buy a fund. Nearly two dozen technology funds debuted in 1999. Investors who bought in made some gains then, but they suffered huge losses in 2000 and after.

Sector funds also tend to be overpriced. Because they usually don't have much in the way of assets, they don't benefit from the economies of scale that can enable funds to keep annual expense ratios down. Further, fund companies seem to think they can justify higher expense ratios because these funds require more specialized research. (We don't really buy that, since the research also supports the family's diversified funds. Sector-fund investors are often effectively subsidizing a fund company's research efforts.) Sector funds generally will take a bigger bite out of your returns than will other funds and that can be a bum deal.

Given that costs are high, you certainly wouldn't want to build a portfolio composed entirely of sector funds. And in any case, not every single part of the market has sector funds. Owning a mix of diversified funds is a much better idea, both for covering the industries in which to invest and for keeping costs from undermining your investing success.

Using Sector Funds to Diversify

There is one sensible reason to own a sector fund, however, and that's to give your portfolio the diversification that it lacks. To determine whether a fund that focuses on a particular sector can add variety to your portfolio, you need to know your portfolio's sector weightings. We talked with an investor who had tens of thousands of dollars just in Microsoft stock. Although he owned other funds, he still had close to 20% of his portfolio in software stocks and he had little in steadier issues such as financials stocks. A sector fund dedicated to financials would have added variety to that portfolio.

Speculating with Sector Funds

It's so tempting: getting access to a part of the market that you think will soar based on some trend, an analyst's recommendation, or your gut instinct. Though it isn't a great idea, investing about 5% of your portfolio can't do too much harm. That said, it's not sensible to gamble on sector funds unless you have already built a diversified portfolio to provide a solid foundation for your portfolio.

How to Buy a Sector Fund

If you can't resist the temptation to bet on a sector, do one of two things. The first option is to play long-term trends (increasing demand for health care products and services on the part of an aging population is one such trend) and dollar-cost average into your sector fund. The discipline of dollar-cost averaging means that you can lower the overall cost of your shares, resulting in higher total returns. The strategy is even more effective with highly volatile investments, such as sector funds.

Alternatively, you might also make a bet on an out-of-favor sector, particularly one that most other fund investors are avoiding. Precisely because investors typically don't have such good timing, you can often outperform by buying what most investors are selling. The biggest sales likely will be in the sector categories that have posted the worst returns during the past 12 months. That doesn't mean you should buy the category with the biggest losses, though. Do some research, including reading Morningstar's analyses of the funds, to make sure you understand why the group is out of favor and to confirm that it has good potential.

When you have identified a sector in which you want to invest, use the criteria you learned in Chapters 1 through 5 to pick a solid fund within the sector category you are targeting. You will want to pay special attention to how the fund's risk and returns compare with its category and to expenses. Sector funds can be pretty pricey to begin with; you don't want to snap up one that's yet more expensive than its competitors.

In addition to the questions you would ask about performance, risk, portfolio holdings, management, and costs before buying any fund, ask two more questions that apply specifically to sector funds.

How Diversified Is It? Because some sector funds adopt an even narrower focus than their sectors, such as buying wireless communications stocks exclusively, it's important to know if the fund favors certain subsectors and totally disregards others. Examine the portfolio holdings and a shareholder report. Read the fund's prospectus to see if it is dedicated to just one subsector within a broader sector. (Internet funds are subsector funds. Biotechnology and wireless funds focus on subsectors of the health care and communications sectors, respectively.) Even if a fund doesn't claim to be a subsector fund, it might still be heavily focused on one industry. Amerindo Technology, for example, has tended to heavily emphasize Internet stocks and have little or nothing in computers and other technology hardware. Even if the fund doesn't focus on one subsector, check to see if it owns just a small number of stocks, which can also spell a high degree of volatility. Only a few holdings need to run into trouble to trash the fund's returns.

Does It Charge a Redemption Fee? Sector funds often charge redemption fees, or tolls you must pay if you sell the fund within a certain period of time from purchase. Redemption-fee information appears in the Fees and Expenses section of Morningstar.com's Quicktake Reports as well as in a fund's prospectus.

Funds with redemption fees are a great idea if you're a long-term investor. The fees penalize people who invest for less than a set period (often three months, but sometimes a year or more). Basically, they are penalties for early withdrawal that are paid back into the fund—to the benefit of remaining shareholders—instead of to the fund company. Funds use these fees to deter investors who rush into hot funds, then flee when returns turn cold. These shareholders can undermine a fund's performance with untimely buying and selling. A flood of money will dilute a fund's returns while heavy withdrawals can force managers to sell stocks that they would prefer to hang on to. The

Scudder Flag Communications	This fund's concentrated portfolio mean it's too bold for conservative types. However, the fund boasts a respectable long-term track record, and investors will have a hard time finding such qualified managers in this sector.
Gabelli Global Telecommunications	This global fund from value meister Mario Gabelli and son Marc should appeal to investors looking for a less aggressive way to play the communications sector. Management's prudent approach has resulted in superb long-term performance with below-average volatility compared with its peers.
T. Rowe Price Media and Telecommunications	Manager Robert Gensler has displayed some deft maneuvering within the tumultuous telecommunications sector. His management expertise, coupled with strong analytical support, makes this fund an attractive entrant in the group.

Figure 9.1 Our favorite communications funds.

result of that money rushing in and out is lower returns than the fund might have earned without such disruptions.

Figures 9.1 through 9.7 list our favorite sector funds. Not every fund will suit every investor. Be sure to carefully examine funds you are considering to determine which is best for you.

Using Real-Estate Funds in a Portfolio

Although we stand by our claim that no one really needs a sector fund, some funds are so useful that they merit further consideration. Real-estate funds can add a lot of variety to a portfolio. They're technically sector funds, but they play such a distinct role in a portfolio that they deserve to be treated separately.

The average real-estate fund has a strikingly low correlation with the S&P 500 index. That means that when the S&P 500 goes up or down, real-estate funds probably won't move in sync with the index. That makes real-estate funds appealing when large-cap stocks are down. The real-estate group is even less attuned to the bond market, with a negative correlation versus the Lehman Brothers Aggregate Bond index. (The negative number means that when the index goes up, the real-estate category is likely to move in the opposite direction.)

Davis Financial	This fund's nonfinancials picks have occasionally gotten it into trouble, but over time, its management team has executed its approach with distinction, producing some of the category's best returns.
Invesco Financial Services	This fund's management uses a sensible strategy, focusing on market leaders that are growing at a solid pace. In addition to one of the category's lowest expense ratios, this fund offers competitive longer-term returns.
T. Rowe Price Financial Services	This fund benefits from savvy stock selection across a broad range of financials subsectors. It has one of the best longer-term records of diversified financials funds. A well-below-average expense ratio gives the fund an edge.

Figure 9.2 Our favorite financial funds.

Eaton Vance Worldwide Health Sciences	This fund tends to own more foreign stocks than its peers, as well as a bigger serving of obscure domestic issues. The result of this quirky mix has been excellent long-term returns with surprisingly modest volatility.
Fidelity Select Health Care	This fund emphasizes large pharmaceutical companies, and while that focus can be a burden at times, its long-term returns remain competitive. This isn't a fund for those who value long manager tenure, though— like Fidelity's other sector funds, it's something of a manager training ground.
Vanguard Health Care	With $16.5 billion in assets, this is the biggest specialty fund in any category, and it's also among the best. Manager Ed Owens has consistently guided it to strong finishes, and a low expense ratio is a gift that keeps on giving.

Figure 9.3 Our favorite health funds.

In other words, real-estate funds do not behave much like large-cap U.S. stocks, which is what most investors have (or at least, ought to have) as the core of their portfolios. Nor do the funds behave much like bonds, which are the common choice to stabilize a stock portfolio. Adding a real-estate fund to a portfolio of stock and bond funds could add greater variety, resulting in steadier performance. A glance at this group's performance in 2001 and the first half of 2002 highlights this benefit: Most U.S. stock funds were underwater, but the typical real-estate fund gained nearly 25%. Most bond funds posted gains, but they were modest compared with real estate's success.

The real-estate category's solid showing is partly attributable to the high dividend yields of many real-estate securities. Most funds in the category invest predominantly in real estate investment trusts (REITs), which are required by law to pay out most of their income as dividends to shareholders. That consistent yield can bolster returns during rallies and offset losses in down years. Moreover, unlike other diversification mainstays such as gold and foreign funds, the yields of real-estate funds prevent them from being especially volatile. Real-estate funds are also more tax-efficient than other income offerings such as bond funds or funds with high-yielding stocks because part

Invesco Energy	Make no mistake about it—this is an aggressive fund that makes the most out of rallies in the energy sector. Investors should limit their exposure here, but it may be just the ticket for those looking to add some spice to their portfolios.
T. Rowe Price New Era	This fund has done nothing to sully its reputation as the slow-but-steady champ of the natural-resources sector. Charlie Ober is one of the category's more-experienced managers, and the fund is one of the few low-cost options in the group, too.
Vanguard Energy	Although longtime manager Ernst von Metsch will be stepped down at the end of 2002, this fund's sensibly diversified approach and rock-bottom expense ratio should help convince investors to give its new manager a chance to prove himself.

Figure 9.4 Our favorite natural resources funds.

of their dividend is considered a return of capital for accounting reasons. That means not all of the yield paid by a real-estate fund will be treated as income and taxed at that higher rate, whereas all of the yield from bond or other stock funds may be taxed as income.

That doesn't mean that real-estate funds are simply a fixed-income substitute. They're too volatile to provide that kind of sanctuary. When the economy

American Century Global Gold	This fund's manager focuses on gold to the near-exclusion of other precious metals, and that was a negative for much of the 1990s. But the fund has proven itself a powerful option for those looking for a fund that will rally when gold does.
Oppenheimer Gold & Special Minerals	This fund's manager stayed far ahead of his peers in the gold bear market of the late 1990s and also remained on top of his game in 2001, a strong year for gold stocks. Overall, he has produced a fine long-term record while generally keeping volatility in check.

Figure 9.5 Our favorite precious-metals funds.

Fidelity Select Technology	This fund has changed managers at a rapid-fire clip, but we're not overly concerned—Fidelity's considerable research muscle typically mutes the effect of such changes. It provides broad exposure to the tech sector, and its long-term results are sturdy.
Northern Technology	This fund's managers make sizable industry bets at times, but they've generally been on the mark. Thus, this fund's long-term returns are among the best in the category, and its costs are also reasonable for a sector fund.
PIMCO RCM Global Technology	This fund's managers have run money in this style together for more than a decade, and they've been very successful here since this fund's launch in late 1995. The pair spreads the fund's assets across emerging names, established blue chips, and value plays.

Figure 9.6   Our favorite technology funds.

buckles, the funds can suffer severely, as their average 14% loss in 1990 proved. Nevertheless, if you want to diversify a portfolio targeted to a long-term goal that is currently tilted heavily toward large-cap stocks, you'd be well-served by putting a small stake of your overall portfolio into a real-estate fund.

Figure 9.8 shows our favorite funds in the real-estate category.

AXP Utilities	Despite AXP's shaky overall record, this fund can't be ignored. Its returns have been consistently solid, and it has had the same manager since 1995.
MFS Utilities	This fund's growth bent has stung at times, but we like manager Maura Shaughnessy's broad-ranging approach. Plus, she has delivered superior returns in markets that have been more hospitable to her style
Vanguard Utilities Income	This fund won't wow you. Although it focuses on strong growers, it also emphasizes firms that pay dividends. The fund has one of the category's higher yields as a result. It also boasts an experienced manager and an ultra-low expense ratio.

Figure 9.7   Our favorite utilities funds.

Morgan Stanley Institutional U.S. Real Estate	The fund's comanagers have been on board since its 1995 inception and have amassed one of the finest risk/reward profiles in the category. Notably, the fund is the only real-estate option in Morningstar's 401(k) plan.
Security Capital U.S. Real Estate	Owing to its experience and deep research resources, management has had considerable success over time making big bets on its favorite stocks and property types. But because it's a concentrated portfolio, it's only for investors willing to live with some volatility.
Third Avenue Real Estate Value	Unlike the majority of his REIT-focused peers, manager Mike Winer loads up on real-estate operating companies (REOCs) are not required to pay a dividend. Investors seeking a nice income stream from their real estate fund should consider other alternatives, yet we think the fund's low dividend yield makes it uniquely suitable for taxable accounts.

Figure 9.8 Our favorite real-estate funds.

Using Foreign Funds in a Portfolio

French wine and Sophia Loren aren't the only imports dear to Americans. By mid-2002, U.S. investors had poured $420 billion into international funds that primarily buy stocks of foreign companies. What's the attraction? For starters, returns that are often alluring. In 1999, foreign-stock funds on average gained a phenomenal 44%, while the S&P 500 index rose only about half as much. Then, there's the diversification that foreign investing offers. Foreign markets are often influenced by different factors than the U.S. market, so adding foreign funds to your investment mix gives you a better chance of always owning something that's performing well.

To pick among these funds can be as difficult as for a novice to pick the right wine. Before you look at returns and even Morningstar ratings, it's essential to understand how your fund invests. You can then set reasonable expectations for the investment, uncover its hidden risks, and avoid surprises. The first thing to know is that foreign funds plug into the same style box and sectors as domestic-stock funds. That means you can use what you have learned about U.S. funds in scrutinizing foreign options. In this chapter, we look at issues such as country and currency exposure that are specific to foreign investing.

Start by asking the following four questions. (You can find most of the answers to these questions on a fund's Quicktake Report, on the fund family's Web site, or in the fund's shareholder report.)

Does the Fund Own Emerging-Markets Stocks?

In the late 1990s, a few international funds posted eye-popping returns of 50% or more. Their secret? Emerging-markets stocks of companies domiciled in less developed markets such as Indonesia, Chile, or Russia. Owning emerging-markets stocks has its benefits. In addition to occasionally top-notch returns, they add more diversification to a U.S. portfolio than stocks from developed international markets such as Germany and the United Kingdom.

There's a price for the exhilarating highs and the diversification that emerging-markets stocks can add: the threat of steep losses. Concerns about political and economic stability, which are usually less pronounced in developed markets, can cause investors to flee, driving down stock prices. In 2000, the MSCI Emerging Markets index was in a freefall: It shed more than 30% for the year. If such plummets make you sweat, limit your search to funds that are light on emerging-markets stocks.

If you want to avoid emerging-markets stocks altogether, you'll need to do more than just shun funds dedicated to emerging markets. You should also check the country exposure on mainstream diversified international funds, because many of these offerings also nibble at emerging-markets stocks. In 2001, the average foreign-stock fund held more than 8% of its assets in emerging-markets names. If you are concerned about the risks that emerging-markets investing can pose, check to make sure that your fund owns primarily European and Japanese stocks. If you see several companies from countries in Latin America, the Pacific Rim, or Eastern Europe, your fund is dabbling in emerging markets. Many excellent foreign funds invest in emerging markets, so some exposure isn't generally cause for concern. If you're a cautious investor and you see that 30% or more of the fund is in those markets, it may be a good idea to steer clear.

Does It Concentrate in a Specific Region?

While you are examining a fund's country exposure, get a feel for whether the fund prefers a few markets or a particular region (a handful of funds are even dedicated to single countries) or whether it casts a wider net. Morningstar places international funds that focus on a single region in one of these regional categories: Europe stock, Latin America stock, Japan stock, Pacific/Asia stock, and Pacific/Asia ex-Japan stock (that is, all Asia and Pacific Rim markets excluding Japan).

Even mainstream international funds are often heavily skewed toward a particular region. In 2002, Ivy International parked roughly 37% of its portfolio in Latin America stocks. Concentrating in a single region or country can deliver uneven results. It's comparable to a fund that focuses heavily on a single sector. To stay off the return trampoline, find funds that own stocks from a wide variety of markets.

What's Its Style?

A few years ago, style wasn't an issue for foreign-stock funds. Most funds bought reasonably priced stocks of the world's largest companies, taking what was essentially a growth-at-reasonable-price approach. International-investing pioneers such as the managers at EuroPacific Growth, the world's largest foreign-stock fund, had profited for years and even decades on such strategies. In the 1990s, though, Janus and American Century met with great success when they began applying the growth-focused strategies they used at home to investing abroad. Their styles were still novel among foreign-stock investors.

The question of investment style doesn't end with value versus growth. It also involves whether the fund focuses on stocks with large, mid, or small market capitalizations, or some mix of sizes. (To determine a foreign-stock fund's investment style, consult its Morningstar style box.)

The investment style you choose should depend on how much risk you can handle and the other funds in your portfolio. If your U.S. stock funds lean toward growth stocks, consider a foreign fund that's more inclined toward value. If you become queasy at ups and downs, steer clear of funds that emphasize small companies; they tend to be more volatile than funds that focus on large companies. Like volatile emerging-markets stocks, though, foreign small-cap stocks are generally better diversifiers than foreign large-cap stocks. That's because foreign blue chips tend to be big multinationals and often perform much like U.S.-based multinationals.

What Is Its Currency-Hedging Policy?

When fund managers buy foreign stocks, they're also effectively investing in the foreign currency in which the stock is denominated. Even if a British stock goes nowhere, a fund can still make a gain if the pound strengthens relative to the dollar. So a foreign stock's return is really a combination of two things: the performance of the stock itself and the performance of the country's currency versus the U.S. dollar.

Say you buy a Japanese stock, Sony. The stock itself rises 10%. But the yen (Japan's currency) falls 15% against the U.S. dollar. As a U.S. investor, you have lost money on that investment, because even though the stock price has risen, the currency's value has fallen. What if the yen rises 10% instead? Then your return is even bigger. You get the 10% rise in the stock's price *and* the 10% rise in the currency.

However, some managers take the currency component out of the equation altogether by hedging their foreign currencies. That is, they effectively trade their exposure to foreign currencies for U.S. dollars. In our preceding example, say you buy Sony, but hedge your currency exposure by buying a contract (known as a "future" because it's a commitment to conduct the transaction at some future time) to sell Japanese yen and buy U.S. dollars. Sony's stock rises 10% and the yen falls 10% against the dollar. What's your return? Because you hedged your currency exposure, it is 10%—the change in the yen doesn't affect your return.

Several academic studies indicate that currency hedging has only a minimal effect on returns over very long time periods. But over shorter spans, hedging can make quite a difference in a fund's performance. The managers of Putnam International Growth claim they added an extra two percentage points of return in 1997 by hedging the fund's exposure to falling currencies into the rising U.S. dollar.

Because we think it's important to invest for the long term, we don't believe it matters much whether a fund hedges its currency exposure. We focus instead on how consistent a fund is in its policy. To avoid the unexpected

American Funds EuroPacific Growth	Year after year, this giant fund has delivered solid returns with much less volatility than the norm. A very low expense ratio adds to this old favorite's charms.
Artisan International	Manager Mark Yockey has proven over a long career that he can adapt to just about any market conditions. Yockey uses an all-cap style that emphasizes companies with strong earnings growth, but he can't simply be labeled a growth manager because he goes where he thinks the best opportunities at the best prices can be found.
Harbor International	Manager Hakan Castegren has led this value-oriented fund to outstanding returns with relatively low volatility since its 1987 inception. It's worth noting that he is not a deep-value player—he's a bit more flexible than that— but this would certainly be a great choice for an investor looking for a foreign value fund.
Julius Baer International Equity	This is one of the most unusual funds in the category— and one of the most successful. Its managers, who have been at the helm since 1995, don't restrict themselves to a specific market-cap range or traditional value or growth strategies. They put much more emphasis on sector plays than most peers, and often let the fund's cash stake grow into double digits.
Liberty Acorn International	With a focus on fast-growing smaller companies, this fund is the polar opposite of Harbor International. This is the most aggressive choice on this list, owing both to its growth leanings and its smaller-cap tilt, but it provides more diversification for an S&P 500-focused portfolio than do foreign large-cap offerings.
Tweedy, Browne Global Value	This remarkable all-cap value-oriented fund hedges all of its foreign-currency exposure into the dollar. The fund can lag when growth strategies are in favor, but its managers have generally handled all kinds of market conditions well.

Figure 9.9 Our favorite foreign stock funds.

losses that can accompany badly timed currency plays, stick with funds that have consistent hedging policies, those that almost never hedge, or those that almost always do. That way, you are assured that your fund manager is focusing solely on picking stocks, not also trying to project currency movements. Foreign funds will usually indicate hedging policies in their prospectuses or shareholder reports. You can also call the fund company's customer service number to find out the fund's policy.

Figure 9.9 on page 123 shows our favorite foreign stock funds.

Using Small-Cap Funds in a Portfolio

In recent years, small has been beautiful. As of mid-2002, the best three-year returns among U.S. stock categories belonged to the small-value and small-blend groups, which had gained 15% and 12% per year, respectively. Apparently no one told these guys that a bear market was going on. It's a case study in why portfolio diversification is a good idea.

The Appeal Is Relative

The first thing to note is that small-cap stocks' success in the bear market turned the normal pattern on its head. Big-cap stocks tend to do better than small ones in bear markets. If they don't abandon stocks altogether, nervous investors tend to flee to the safe haven of familiar blue-chip names. The late 1990s ruled out that option, though. Big names led the market on the way up, and because their price multiples were sky-high, they were among the first to drop as investors turned cautious. For investors who still wanted stock exposure, smaller issues appeared to be a good deal.

Figures 9.10 through 9.12 list our favorite funds in each of the three small-cap stock fund categories.

How to Pick a Small-Cap Fund

Of course, going whole-hog into small-cap funds wasn't the answer to beating the bear, any more than staking everything on large-growth funds was the smartest way to run with the bulls. Investors who do that inevitably run into trouble when the bears stop prowling or the bulls stop running.

It makes sense to be especially circumspect with small stocks, because they can be a lot more volatile than large caps with the same investment style.

Ariel Fund	Manager John Rogers buys beaten-down value stocks and then holds on to them as they appreciate. Rogers runs a concentrated portfolio, so when his picks are out of favor, the fund's returns suffer. Still, the fund's long-term record stacks up well against its peer group.
FPA Capital	Manager Bob Rodriguez, a tried-and-true value investor who's twice been named Morningstar Manager of the Year, runs a highly concentrated portfolio that focuses on down-and-out stocks. Rodriguez bets big on individual names, which has led to bumpy returns. Those investors who have been willing to ride out the bumps, however, have been well rewarded for their loyalty.
Gabelli Small Cap Growth	Although it has "Growth" in its moniker, the fund certainly has a value bent. Manager Mario Gabelli buys stocks in tiny companies that are trading at a deep discount to his estimate of their private-market values. He's also willing to make substantial sector and industry bets, so this fund's returns have been rocky at times. Still, the fund's long-term record is solid.
Royce Total Return	Even when small-value stocks aren't in favor, this offering is likely to hold up well. It's one of the steady-eddies in the group, due mainly to manager Chuck Royce's preference for cheap firms that pay dividends and the limited size of individual positions.
Third Avenue Small-Cap Value	The fund's manager, Curtis Jensen, buys micro- and small-cap stocks that fit the fund's deep-value investing criteria, and this style has served investors well over the long term.

Figure 9.10   Our favorite small-value funds.

Small-value funds tend to have more dramatic ups and downs than their large-cap counterparts, small blend is more volatile than large blend, and so on. You don't want to have too much of your portfolio riding on their big ups and downs. In the late 1990s, small caps looked pretty sorry compared with their larger counterparts. In fact, the typical small-company fund lost money in 1998, even as the S&P 500 posted a 29% gain. Your best bet is to own a

Baron Growth	Manager Ron Baron's attention to valuations has meant that he has been largely inattentive to the technology sector since the fund's launch in late 1994. The fund's fairly conservative approach has made it one of the group's least-volatile members, so this a solid pick for more-moderate types.
Managers Special Equity	This offering's lineup of five subadvisors, whose specialties range from go-go growth to value, has produced a well-diversified portfolio that has performed well in varied market climates. That diversification means the fund doesn't knock the lights out in growth-driven years such as 1999, but it checks the fund's losses in tough markets for aggressive funds.
RS Diversified Growth	With its bold investment style, this offering is only suitable for aggressive investors. The fund can get crushed when growth stocks fall out of bed, but lead manager John Wallace has amassed an impressive long-term record.
William Blair Small Cap Growth	You won't always find a lot of sexy small-cap stocks here, but you will find a slug of micro-caps and some IPOs. This is a fairly aggressive choice, even by small-growth standards, although managers Michael Balkin and Karl Brewer don't tend to make huge bets on individual names or sectors.

Figure 9.11   Our favorite small-growth funds.

mix of large and small stocks. You will benefit when the market favors one type of stock without exposing yourself to serious losses when investors turn to the other. As we noted earlier, small-cap stocks should represent between 10% and 20% of the stock portion of most investors' portfolios.

When you're looking for the right small-cap fund for your portfolio, ask the same questions we discussed at the beginning of this book. Here are two more questions to consider.

How Big Is the Fund?   More so than with other mutual funds, asset size—the amount of money the manager has to invest—matters with small-cap fare.

FPA Paramount	This fund has improved markedly since its current co-managers, Eric Ende and Steven Geist, took over in mid-2000. Better still, the fund figures to be a great pick for taxable accounts, because the previous manager's snafus here make for a large tax-loss carryforward that can be used to balance future gains.
Royce Premier	Recommending a Royce fund for small-cap exposure is a pretty safe bet. The fund family and its venerable leader, Chuck Royce, are well-regarded for their expertise in this part of the market. Like most of its siblings, this one boasts a strong long-term record with only a modicum of risk.
T. Rowe Price Small-Cap Stock	Slow and steady is the name of the game here. With relatively low volatility, solid long-term returns, and below-average expenses, the fund deserves a place in Morningstar's 401(k) plan.

Figure 9.12   Our favorite small-blend funds.

Bigger funds are harder for managers to run and they're not likely to enjoy the same level of performance as smaller, more nimble funds because a small-cap manager needs to buy small companies. A manager with a lot of money to invest either has to find more "good ideas" (and idea 150 may not be as good as idea 35!) or has to invest more money in the same stocks. The problem with the latter approach is that many small-cap stocks don't have a lot of shares floating around to buy or sell, and there are practical and legal limits to how much of a company a fund can own. All told, it could be hard for the manager to find a home for all that money he or she wants to put to work. When a fund has too much in assets, the number of holdings will increase significantly or its market cap will go up as the manager has to buy bigger stocks or both. The result could be a fund that's very different from the one you picked out. In general, small-cap funds whose asset base starts to float above $1 billion can become unwieldy. For funds that focus on microcap stocks (the very smallest companies in the market), that threshold may be more like $500 million.

What Is Its Closing Policy? If you find an appropriate small-cap fund, the next logical question is: Will the fund company be willing to close the fund if it gets too big for the manager to run efficiently? Most fund companies haven't been very good about doing this. After all, it isn't easy to turn away money on which the fund company earns fees (through the expense ratio investors pay). That said, there were encouraging signs in 2001 and 2002—as small-cap funds suddenly became popular, fund companies such as Wasatch did close small-cap stock funds to prevent excessive cash from undermining their strategies.

When searching for a small-cap fund, check the prospectus for information on whether the fund might close. You can also call the fund's customer service line and ask about plans to close it. If you decide to go with a fund that *isn't* planning on closing, monitor it carefully to ensure that it doesn't wind up playing the wrong role in your portfolio by turning into a different kind of fund.

Investor's Checklist: Move Beyond the Core

▶ No one *needs* a sector fund, but one could be useful if there's a clear gap in your portfolio. If you own lots of growth investments, a financials fund could add diversification.

▶ Watch out for high costs. Because they tend to be small, sector funds are often pricey, which hurts returns.

▶ If you are speculating with a sector fund, limit that fund to 5% of your portfolio and stick with it for the long haul.

▶ Avoid excessively narrow sector funds such as Internet or biotechnology offerings.

▶ Redemption fees are good—they discourage market-timers who can undermine performance by jumping in and out of a fund.

▶ Real-estate sector funds can be great portfolio diversifiers because they don't behave like ordinary stock or bond funds.

▶ For straightforward foreign-stock exposure, pick a fund that focuses on big companies in developed markets and doesn't make big bets on emerging markets or single countries.

▶ Opt for funds that consistently hedge or don't hedge their foreign currency exposure.

▶ Small-cap funds add diversification and may boost returns. Watch out for the added risk, though.

▶ Beware of asset growth in small-cap funds. Some funds aren't hampered much by lots of money, but for many funds, assets greater than $1 billion can spell trouble.

10

Find the Right Bond
Fund for You

SAY YOU'RE AT a dinner party and someone starts bragging about his car. It's a safe bet that he's talking about a sports coupe or maybe an SUV. Could it be a minivan? Not likely. ("I swear, you can fit a couple dozen bags of groceries and still have room for a month's worth of dry cleaning! And there have to be at least half a dozen cup holders, not to mention . . .")

Bond funds are the minivans of the investing world. People talk about stock funds because those funds are often exciting. Bond funds mostly aren't exciting. Our bond analysts would heartily disagree with that assessment— they find bond funds utterly compelling. We concede that the ins and outs of how the funds invest can be interesting, but when it comes to dramatic performance, in gains or losses, they don't begin to compare with stock funds. In fact, that unstimulating performance is a big part of bond funds' appeal and what makes them such useful investments.

In this chapter, we explain what you need to know before choosing your first bond fund, maybe the only one you will need. We also discuss a few bond fund strategies, such as municipal bond investing and high-yield bond investing, to help you decide what type of bond fund is best for you.

To learn how to choose a bond fund, you first need to understand how bonds work. The essential difference between a bond and a stock is that when you buy a stock, you become part owner of the company. Buy a share of Ford and you own a fraction of Ford. It's a small fraction—there are 1.9 billion shares of Ford—but you do own a piece of the company. When you buy a bond, you are loaning money to the company (or, in the case of Treasury bonds, you're loaning money to the government). Your loan lasts a certain period of time—until the date when the bond reaches maturity—and you get a certain dividend payment every six months (commonly known as a coupon) as interest on the loan. Thus, the essential issues for bond investing are how long until the bond matures (that translates into interest-rate risk) and how confident you are that the business or government can repay the loan (known as credit quality).

Understanding Interest-Rate Risk

Two forces govern the performance of bonds and bond funds: interest-rate sensitivity (or duration) and credit quality. (The two are the dimensions of Morningstar's style box for bond funds, which we describe in detail in the Frequently Asked Questions section of this book.) Duration is a key consideration because bond prices move in the opposite direction of interest rates. When rates fall, bond prices rise. Bond prices go up because they pay higher coupons than new bonds issued with lower interest-rate payments. The opposite happens when interest rates rise: Bond prices fall because new bonds should have higher coupons. To determine how dramatic a fund's rises and falls might be, check out its duration. The longer the duration, the greater a fund's sensitivity to interest rate changes.

Duration boils down to the three risk factors of bonds: maturity, the cash flows from coupons and principal, and current interest rates. Think of a bond as a pro-basketball player's contract. In negotiating his first contract, a top draft pick wants a salary that will stay competitive with what's offered across the NBA. Looking at different contract proposals, he'll consider the length of a contract (its maturity), the salary (the coupon), and wages across the league (current interest rates). He will also take into account any clause that would permit his contract to be terminated early. In the bond world, those are terms that allow the bond issuer to "call" the bond, paying off bondholders before it matures. An issuer might call a high-interest bond, for example, because it can issue new bonds with a lower interest rate, thereby saving a lot of money.

Suppose the player is offered a five-year contract at $1 million a year. He likes the coupon, but he's nervous about the long-term commitment. If he signs the contract and the average NBA salary spikes up, his salary will be relatively worse than it was and may even be below average. Duration factors in these kinds of trade-offs produce a risk measure that investors can use for comparisons. Of two bonds, the one with the longer duration will be more vulnerable to a change in interest rates.

One of the less-than-intuitive aspects of duration is that it's expressed in years, just like maturity. The trouble is, duration isn't nearly as concrete a concept as maturity. Take a bond with a maturity of 11 years and a duration of 8.5 years. At the end of 11 years, we know that something happens: The bond is paid off. There are no more coupon payouts and bondholders get their premiums (the bond's face value) back. But what happens after 8.5 years? Nothing, really. Duration is a useful abstraction, the longer a bond's duration, the more it responds to changes in interest rates. So a bond fund with a duration of four years should be twice as sensitive to a change in interest rates as a bond fund with a duration of two years.

For most investors, bond funds with short- and intermediate-term durations—ranging up to about 6 years—are the way to go. They're less volatile than longer-duration funds and offer nearly as much return. Over the long haul, intermediate-term bond funds have delivered as much as 90% of the returns of long-term bond funds with 80% of the volatility. That's an appealing trade-off; opting for an intermediate-term bond fund means your returns drop about 10% but the volatility drops much more dramatically.

Understanding Credit-Quality Risk

In addition to interest-rate risk, bond funds also face credit risk. This is the risk that the issuers of the funds' bonds may not be able to repay their debts. Think of it this way. If your no-good brother-in-law who hasn't held a job in six years wanted to borrow $50 from you, you would probably wonder if you would ever see that $50 again. You would be far more comfortable loaning money to your super-responsible kid sister. The same dynamic occurs between companies and investors. Investors eagerly loan money to the government or to well-established companies that seem likely to repay their debts, but they think twice about loaning to firms without a solid track record or that have fallen on hard times. Because people have greater doubts about the ability of those businesses to repay their debts, the borrowers will have to promise higher interest rates to obtain money.

Judgments about a firm's ability to pay its debts are captured in a credit rating. Credit-rating firms, such as Moody's and Standard & Poor's, closely examine a firm's financial statements to get an idea of whether a company is closest to being a no-goodnik or a debt-paying good citizen. They then assign a letter grade to the company's debt. In Standard & Poor's system, AAA indicates the highest credit quality and D indicates the lowest. So if you hold a bond rated AAA, odds are excellent that you'll collect all your coupons, and then your principal when the bond reaches maturity. Bonds rated AAA, AA, A, and BBB are considered investment-grade, meaning that it's very likely the company that issued the bonds will repay its debts. Bonds rated BB, B, CCC, CC, and C are non-investment-grade, or high-yield (also known as junk), bonds. That means there is serious concern that the bond issuer will not uphold its obligations to pay interest to its bondholders. The lowest grade D, is reserved for bonds that are already in default.

If you're going to buy a bond with a low credit-quality rating (one that might not pay its promised coupons and return all your principal), you'll want an incentive. To encourage you, the bond will offer the higher yield mentioned earlier. All other things being equal, the lower a bond's credit quality, the higher its yield. That is why you can find high-yield bond funds with yields of 9% or more, while many investment-grade bond funds offer yields around 5%. Because investment-grade issuers are more likely to meet their obligations, investors give up higher income for that greater certainty.

Credit quality also affects a bond's performance. Lower-rated bonds tend to underperform—to drop in price—when the economy is in recession or when investors think the economy is likely to fall into a recession. Recessions usually mean lower corporate profits and thus less money to pay bondholders. If an issuer's ability to repay its debt looks a little shaky in a healthy economy, it will be even more suspect in a recession. High-yield bond funds usually take a hit when investors are worried about the economy. Because

most high-yield bonds are issued by businesses and are affected by the economy, a high-yield bond fund offers less diversification for a stock fund portfolio than do other bond funds.

Buying Core Bond Funds

When you're looking for a bond fund, follow the standard guidelines for
picking a fund from the beginning of this book. Pay special attention to these
three points, as well.

Look for Low Costs

A penny-pinching mentality is a must when evaluating bond funds. Because
bonds typically return less than stocks over the long haul, their costs become a
heavier burden. As if high expenses cutting into your returns weren't bad
enough, high-cost bond funds are also riskier than low-cost bond funds. Expenses get deducted from the yield the fund pays to its shareholders, so managers of high-cost funds often do hazardous things to keep yields competitive,
such as buying longer-duration or lower-quality bonds. In doing so, they increase the fund's risk. Managers with low expense hurdles, in contrast, can
offer the same yields and returns without taking on extra risk. Plenty of terrific bond funds carry expense ratios of 0.75% or less.

Focus on Total Return, Not Yield

Many bond fund investors are in the habit of focusing on yield. If you're
looking for income in retirement, it's natural to focus on yield—it tells you
something about the size of the checks you'll get when the fund makes its regular income distributions. But chasing yield can have its penalties. Some
funds use accounting tricks to prop up their yields at the expense of their
principal (also known as net asset value [NAV]). Managers will pay more
than face value for high-yielding bonds and distribute that entire yield as the
bonds depreciate to face value. Or they'll buy undervalued bonds and supplement their lower yields with capital gains. Although such moves can increase your income, the overall value of your account will decline in the
process. That's because part of what appears to be higher income is effectively
the fund paying you back your own money. That payout will be reflected in
a NAV, or share price, that shrinks over the years.

Instead of judging a bond fund by its yield, evaluate its total return: its yield plus any capital appreciation (capital appreciation comes from bonds increasing in value if interest rates change) plus compounding of those gains over time. Yield will be the lion's share of a bond fund's return; you just want to be sure that the fund isn't cutting into NAV to produce that yield. Funds with superior long-term returns will be your best bet.

Seek Some Variety

You wouldn't choose a fund that buys only health care stocks as your first equity fund, so why should your first (and perhaps only) bond fund be a narrowly focused Ginnie Mae fund? (Ginnie Mae funds focus on bonds backed by mortgages that the Government National Mortgage Association has guaranteed.) Yet many investors own bond funds that buy only government bonds, or Treasuries, or mortgages. For your bond fund, consider intermediate-term, broad-based, high-quality bond funds that hold both government and corporate bonds. You can get higher total returns plus the stability that diversification affords. (See Figures 10.1 through 10.3 for our favorites.)

Specialty Strategy 1: Municipal Bond Funds

If you're in one of the higher tax brackets, you might consider a municipal bond fund, whose income is exempt from federal income taxes. States, cities,

Fidelity Short-Term Bond	Manager Andrew Dudley succeeds through caution. He takes on limited interest-rate and credit risk and keeps the portfolio spread among hundreds of bonds, adding incremental gains through issue selection. The fund's modest expense ratio is a real plus.
Vanguard Short-Term Bond Index	This fund sticks to a mix of government bonds and investment-grade corporate issues. It carries the least credit risk of our short-term bond picks, and it also has ultra-low expenses, which helps make it difficult to beat.

Figure 10.1   Our favorite short-term bond funds.

Dodge & Cox Income	This fund gets a lift from low expenses, proving that you don't have to pay big bucks for good, active management. The fund's emphasis on government and high-quality corporate bonds has yielded consistently competitive results, and its low-turnover approach has minimized its volatility.
FPA New Income	This fund's management team, led by Bob Rodriguez, is one of the best in the business. It is more than willing to pile into unloved sectors of the bond market, often with impressive results, though its cautious interest-rate stance can hold it back when interest rates rally.
Fremont Bond	Bill Gross, Morningstar's Manager of the Year in 1998 and 2000, has made this fund a star. Although Gross shies away from most risky bets and sticks primarily to high-quality bonds, this fund has one of the best records in the intermediate-term bond category.
Metropolitan West Total Return Bond	This fund's management team boasts some of the best brains in the industry, as well as a solid, deep team of sector specialists. And though the fund isn't as cheap as Dodge & Cox Income or Vanguard Total Bond Market Index, its expense ratio is quite reasonable.
Vanguard Total Bond Market Index	This fund is not flashy, but it doesn't need to be. Its superlow expenses make it tough to beat over any extended period of time. Designed to track the Lehman Brothers Aggregate Bond index, this fund actually beats its benchmark by a small margin during most trailing periods, thanks to astute management.

Figure 10.2   Our favorite intermediate-term bond funds.

municipalities, and county governments issue municipal bonds, or muni bonds, to raise money. They use the proceeds to improve roads, refurbish schools, or even build sports complexes. The bonds are usually rated by a major rating agency, such as Standard & Poor's or Moody's, based on the quality of the issuer. Unlike income from bonds issued by corporations or the federal government, income from municipal bonds is exempt from federal and usually state income taxes (from the state issuing the bond). So when

Vanguard Long-Term Corporate Bond	The fund's biggest advantage is its low expenses, which are just a fraction of what its average peer charges. The fund also has benefited from its high-quality profile, which has helped it avoid many of the credit problems that have plagued its peers.

Figure 10.3   Our favorite long-term bond fund.

examining a municipal bond's yield, it's important to take the implicit tax advantage into account. Muni bonds usually pay lower rates specifically because of their tax benefits.

You don't need to be in a tax bracket that would allow you to drive a Jaguar or to shop routinely at Neiman Marcus for the tax-protected income from a muni fund to be a good deal for you. Say you're an investor in the 28% tax bracket. You want to know which investment offers you a better yield: a corporate-bond fund yielding 7% or a muni-bond fund yielding 6%. After taxes, the muni fund is the higher yielding investment: Take 28% in taxes off the corporate-bond fund's 7% yield, and you're left with an after-tax yield of a bit more than 5%.

Consider the following points when searching for a suitable muni fund. You can find this information in a fund's Morningstar.com Quicktake Report, in its shareholder report or prospectus, or on the fund family's Web site.

Look for Intermediate-Term Durations

Just as with taxable bond funds, if you're looking for an all-purpose muni fund, you probably will want an intermediate-term option. Like most bond funds, a municipal bond fund's value rises and falls depending on changes in interest rates. To determine a fund's interest-rate risk, check its duration. (A fund with a long duration will land in the right-hand column of Morningstar's bond style box.) A long duration usually means more potential for short-term gains and losses. Vanguard Long-Term Tax Exempt's duration was roughly twice that of Thornburg Limited-Term Municipal National at the start of 1999. No wonder the Vanguard fund lost twice as much as the Thornburg fund (0.4% vs. 0.2%) when interest rates rose in February of that year. But when rates fell in 2000, the Vanguard fund's longer-duration portfolio outpaced the Thornburg fund's and it gained 13.3% for the year while Thornburg gained 6.8%. Our suggestion: Choose the happy medium. During the past five years, intermediate-term municipal bond funds with durations between 4.5 and 7 years have returned about 90% as much as long-term offerings, but with only about 70% of their volatility.

Look for Solid Credit Quality

Just like funds that hold bonds issued by businesses, some municipal-bond funds are vulnerable to credit problems and bond defaults (i.e., the issuers of the bonds they own could fail to pay up on their obligations). Some aren't, though. Vanguard Insured Long-Term Tax Exempt, for example, only buys bonds that are insured against credit problems. Insured bonds earn AAA ratings (the highest) and are highly sensitive to interest-rate movements, but they generally yield less than lower-quality bonds. At the other end of the credit spectrum lies Franklin High Yield Tax-Free Income, which invests heavily in low-rated or nonrated, high-yielding municipal bonds.

For most of the 1990s, the strong economy masked the risks of high-yield municipal bonds. We have long been critical of funds that pumped up returns by owning bonds with dicey credit quality. With the economy strong, such funds had the wind at their backs; and Morningstar's analysts got into plenty of arguments with the fund companies' managers, who couldn't understand why we were warning investors when the funds were scoring great returns. The average high-yield muni fund returned about 3% more per year than the average high-quality offering during the decade ending December 31, 1999. Since the economy slowed and slipped into recession, though, more municipalities have threatened to default on their debts, which has hurt the performance of high-yield muni funds. Here too, we recommend a middle-of-the-road approach: Favor funds with average credit qualities of AA. They have enough high-quality bonds to skirt most credit scares but are still flexible enough to snap up higher-yielding, lower-rated issues. If you're inclined to be more cautious, a fund dedicated to AAA rated or insured bonds is generally safest.

Know Your State's Tax Rate

Some municipal bond funds can offer you shelter from both state and federal taxes. That's because while some municipal-bond funds invest all over the country, others focus on a single state. National muni funds offer geographic diversification and can seize opportunities from New York to New Mexico. Single-state funds, on the other hand, can provide residents of those states with income that's exempt from both federal and state taxes. (National muni funds only give you the federal tax break.) A Californian doesn't pay state income tax on the income from a California muni fund. Choose a single-state fund if you live in a high-tax state. Otherwise, go national for the diversification benefits.

Seek Low Costs

Costs are important for all bond funds, but especially for municipal-bond funds. In any given year, the difference between the highest- and lowest-returning muni funds can be minuscule. A small cost advantage therefore goes a long way. Invest in a muni fund with an expense ratio of less than 0.75%.

Avoid AMT, If Need Be

You can still owe taxes on the income of municipal-bond funds if you're exposed to the Alternative Minimum Tax (AMT) and the fund you own holds bonds subject to this tax. The AMT is designed to ensure that wealthy individuals pay at least some tax, but you could be subject to it even if you aren't in one of the higher tax brackets. For example, if you cash in a lot of employee stock options, you may be subject to AMT. (Read Internal Revenue Service Publication 525 "Tax and Nontax Income" and check Form 6251 "Alternative Minimum Tax—Individuals" or ask an accountant to determine if this could be a problem for you.)

Fund managers buy bonds subject to the AMT because those securities tend to yield more than non-AMT bonds. If you're concerned about the AMT, choose a muni fund that avoids bonds subject to the tax, such as T. Rowe Price Tax-Free Income. The prospectus will indicate if the fund has a mandate to avoid such bonds.

In Figures 10.4 through 10.6, there is a sampling of our favorite national municipal bond funds.

Specialty Strategy 2: High-Yield Bond Funds

If you are expanding your bond-fund horizons, high yield is one of the first areas to consider. High-yield bonds are often called lower quality bonds, or junk bonds. No matter what the name, these bonds offer much more income

Evergreen High Income Municipal Bond	This fund is not nearly as conservative as the Vanguard pick, but it has an excellent long-term record. Manager Clark Stamper is known for his ability to scour the market for underpriced bonds.
Strong Short-Term Municipal Bond	This fund takes on more credit risk than many rivals, but its moderate interest-rate sensitivity has kept a lid on volatility. The portfolio remains a good choice for those who don't mind taking on additional credit risk to capture more income.
T. Rowe Price Tax-Free Short-Intermediate	This fund is a solid all-around offering. It boasts a below-average expense ratio, sticks mainly with high-quality bonds, and delivers strong long-term returns. It has also consistently delivered a better-than-average income payout.
USAA Tax-Exempt Short-Term	This fund also takes advantage of its low expense ratio, which at just 0.38% is quite reasonable. Manager Clifford Gladson is keen on low- to mid-quality credits, but he usually limits the portfolio's interest-rate-related risk.
Vanguard Limited-Term Tax-Exempt	Ultralow expenses—that's the key here. This category's winners and losers are often separated by less than 1%, so the importance of this fund's expense advantage can not be emphasized enough. And because of that advantage, the fund doesn't need to take on lots of extra credit risk to keep up with the group's more-aggressive members.

Figure 10.4 Our favorite muni-short bond funds.

than Treasuries or other high-quality corporate bonds because they have more risk that their issuers may not be able to make the interest payments or pony up the principal they originally promised to return. (Hence the term *junk* bond.) If the economy slows down, or if the companies fall into trouble, they may not be able to keep their end of the bargain.

Given that credit risk, not interest-rate risk, is their Achilles' heel, a junk-bond fund could be a good complement to a high-quality bond fund, which will generally be more sensitive to interest-rate changes. Funds favoring

Fidelity Spartan Intermediate Municipal Income	Like most Fidelity bond funds, this fund avoids interest-rate bets and significant credit risk, instead preferring to add value with bond selection. That may be a tad conventional, but Fidelity knows how to do it right. The fund boasts a nice low expense ratio.
Scudder Medium-Term Tax-Free	Management focuses mostly on individual sector and bond selection. And as with similarly successful portfolios, interest-rate bets are only a small piece of this fund's puzzle.
USAA Tax-Exempt Intermediate-Term	What's particularly impressive about this fund is that despite assuming a greater-than-average level of credit risk, it has consistently been able to keep that risk in check. What really makes the story special is a very low expense ratio, something most investors don't expect from a fund that requires so much credit research.
Vanguard Intermediate-Term Tax-Exempt	Are you tired of this story yet? Vanguard equals cheap, giving the portfolio a huge head start on just about everyone else. Even a mistake here is almost never enough to derail it. Throw in a seasoned management staff, and you've got a juggernaut.

Figure 10.5 Our favorite muni national intermediate bond funds.

high-grade bonds with far-off maturities can be volatile when interest rates change. But because junk bonds offer so much more income and often have shorter maturities, they aren't as sensitive to interest-rate shifts as higher-quality, longer-duration bonds are. When interest rates shot up in 1999, the average long-term government bond fund lost more than 7%. The average junk bond fund, which is far less vulnerable to interest-rate movements, actually gained 4.2%. High-yield bond funds can therefore be a good supplement to a portfolio already well rounded with Treasuries, high-quality corporate bonds, and mortgages, all of which offer high credit quality. Junk-bond funds will behave more like stock funds, though, so keep them to no more than 15% of your bond exposure.

When shopping for a junk-bond fund, examine a fund's credit quality. (This information is available from the fund company and from the Morningstar.com Quicktake Reports.) Is the fund investing in the upper tiers of

Fidelity Spartan Municipal Income	The firm has come as close to perfecting the practice of muni-bond management as we've seen. With a terrifically modest price tag and analytics that match up against anyone's, it's a terrific choice.
Franklin Federal Tax-Free Income	This is the largest muni-national long-term fund, and for good reason. Manager Sheila Amoroso uses a buy-and-hold approach, looking for bonds offering competitive yields and trading at reasonable prices. This fund has earned an enviable record of solid returns and moderate volatility as a result.
Franklin High Yield Tax-Free Income	A good choice for those who are willing to take on a little more risk. The fund is run in a similar fashion to Franklin Federal Tax-Free Income, but it can buy lower-quality, higher-yielding bonds than that fund. The fund is well diversified, though, so its risks aren't likely to get completely out of hand.
Vanguard High-Yield Tax-Exempt	In some ways this fund has its cake and eats it too. Although it's considered a high-yield muni fund, its low costs mean it can deliver a decent yield without taking on as much credit risk as its rivals with the same mandate.
Vanguard Long-Term Tax-Exempt	This fund represents Vanguard's incredible cost advantage married to the muni world, where costs matter more than just about anywhere else. The fund makes occasional credit and interest-rate shifts, but they don't seem to affect the portfolio's long-term record—which is stellar—as much as its cheap profile.

Figure 10.6 Our favorite muni national long bond funds.

junk (say, bonds with credit qualities of BB and B), or is it dipping lower for added yield? Check, too, to see if the fund owns any convertible bonds (bonds that convert to stocks), or bonds from emerging markets. Some high-yield funds may even include stocks in their portfolios. These elements are likely to make the fund more volatile. Finally, examine how the fund performed during tough markets for junk-bond funds. That will give you a sense of how risky the fund could be in the future. Junk-bond investors experienced trying periods in 1990 and, more recently, in the third quarter of 1998, as well as in

2000 and 2002. In the 1990s, junk bonds performed quite well in the strong economy. But an economic slowdown can spell underperformance for these funds. Whereas all other categories of bond funds made money in the faltering economy of 2000, the average high-yield bond fund actually lost 7.6%.

Specialty Strategy 3: Prime-Rate Funds

There's almost no better place to pick up a lot of income with low day-to-day volatility than with a prime-rate fund. Prime-rate funds invest in leveraged bank loans. Banks typically make these loans to companies (most of which have poor credit profiles) and then sell the loans to institutional investors and mutual funds. The yields on the loans rise and fall along with short-term interest rates, so their prices can remain the same. That's how prime-rate funds keep their NAVs relatively stable.

Sound too good to be true? In some ways, it is. In fact, prime-rate funds come with plenty of caveats. For starters, most charge relatively high fees when compared with the average bond fund. Further, some use investment leverage, which boosts both gains and losses. Leverage is essentially borrowing to invest. That way a fund can get 25% more bond exposure, for example, than it would without borrowing. That can increase the fund's gains by 25%, but it also increases the losses by that much.

Another drawback to prime-rate funds is that most of them have a restrictive redemption policy. Because the market for corporate loans is so tiny, it's tough for prime-rate funds to sell these loans to meet shareholder redemptions. Therefore, most prime-rate funds will allow investors to sell their shares only on a quarterly basis. (You can buy at any time, though.) And if too many people want to cash out when you do, you may not be able to sell as many shares as you would like.

Finally, though prime-rate funds display little sensitivity to interest-rate shifts, that doesn't mean they'll never lose money. Most prime-rate funds were hurt by slight principal losses in 2000 and 2001, thanks in part to the telecom sector's meltdown.

Specialty Strategy 4: Inflation-Indexed Bond Funds

Inflation-indexed bonds are the holy grail of income investing: limited volatility and a guarantee that your returns won't be ravaged by high inflation. The principal value of an inflation-indexed bond rises with inflation, something that's almost as certain as death and taxes. Conversely, an inflation-indexed bond's maturity value can fall in a deflationary climate, but not below the bond's face or par value. Inflation-indexed bonds won't perform very well when inflation looks tame and conventional bonds are zooming up in price, but that diversification effect is part of the appeal.

Most funds focusing on inflation-indexed bonds stick with the highest quality bonds—those issued by the U.S. Treasury (commonly referred to as TIPS). A small number of other bonds issued by government agencies and corporations also try to keep pace with inflation. As of mid-2002, there were only a handful of dedicated inflation-indexed bond funds out there, including American Century Inflation-Adjusted Treasury, Fidelity Inflation-Protected Bond, and Vanguard Inflation-Protected Securities. If and when inflation heats up, though, fund companies will be clamoring to launch these types of funds.

Such funds can be a great idea for the bond portion of your portfolio because they address a key problem of all bond funds: Inflation cuts into any returns you make. Bonds do not deliver big gains, so the impact of inflation is more noticeable. Even a low inflation rate will gradually erode those returns, an important consideration if you are relying on your bond fund for income.

Putting It All Together

The key to bond-fund investing is understanding what your funds can and can't do. A basic high-quality fund can act as a good balance to a stock portfolio, but it shouldn't be expected to outperform stocks over a long period of time. (Because high-quality bonds promise much more certain returns than stocks, they do not have to offer such high returns to attract investors.) And because interest rates almost never stand still, a bond fund should not be expected to turn in positive returns every single year, either. That's where bonds with different structures, such as TIPS, or those with some credit sensitivity, such as junk bonds, can be a welcome elixir.

Investor's Checklist: Find the Right Bond for You

▸ Bonds with longer durations are more sensitive to changes in interest rates. Funds that own such bonds can rise significantly in value when rates drop or lose value when rates rise.

▸ Bonds with lower credit qualities pay higher yields to compensate investors for the risk of default on their obligations. Funds that own these bonds are particularly vulnerable to a weakening economy.

▸ Costs take a big bite out of bond fund returns. Look for low-expense funds.

▸ Focus on a fund's total return, which reflects income return plus capital return. Income can be appealing, but not if it comes at the expense of your principal.

▸ If you're going to own only one bond fund, make it an intermediate-term fund that owns both government and corporate bonds.

▸ If you need tax protection, buy a municipal bond fund that doesn't make big interest-rate or credit-quality bets. One dedicated to your state can shelter you from state and federal taxes.

▸ Prime-rate funds tend to be stable when interest rates are in flux, but there are often restrictions on when you can make withdrawals and they take on a fair amount of credit risk.

▸ Inflation-indexed bond funds are a great way to invest in bonds without having to worry about inflation eroding the value of your returns.

11

Finding the Right Fund Companies for You

As WE DISCUSSED in Chapter 4, knowing your fund family's capabilities is critical to picking strong-performing funds. This chapter provides descriptions of some of the best-known fund companies (as well as a few boutiques), along with pros and cons of each.

Kicking the Tires: No-Load Fund Families

American Century

Although American Century has been placing greater emphasis on its analyst resources of late, it's still a shop where the computers do much of the heavy lifting. On the growth-stock side, American Century practices a relatively risky strategy known as momentum investing. The aim is to find companies with accelerating growth rates in the hope that the market doesn't fully appreciate the degree of positive change at the firm. Computers can screen for a host of momentum factors such as profit growth, earnings growth, and earnings that exceed expectations. The catch is that companies with accelerating profits tend to trade for high prices, and that makes them vulnerable to jarring price drops when their earnings fall short of expectations. Although best known for its momentum funds, American Century has successfully expanded its lineup to include some fine value, foreign, and bond funds. The firm is partly owned by JP Morgan and partly owned by the founding Stowers family and other insiders at the firm.

Strengths: American Century is a classic B student. The funds are generally pretty good, but not many would make the top of our buy lists.

Weaknesses: The firm is improving its fundamental research capabilities, but it still has a ways to go before it can stand with the best on that front.

Fidelity

This privately held colossus offers the advantages and disadvantages that come with being the biggest fund firm. The positive aspect of its heft is that Fidelity has hundreds of very bright managers and analysts doing excellent fundamental analysis. In addition, Fidelity passes the economies of scale on to investors in the form of low expense ratios.

The bad side is that managing hundreds of billions of dollars limits the flexibility of Fidelity's domestic-stock fund managers. Just as asset bloat can hinder an individual fund, it can hinder a fund family, too.

The firm's huge number of portfolio managers also means that analysts spend a lot of time repeating themselves to all the managers interested in their stocks. (To make sure analysts' research has an impact, Fidelity compensates analysts based on how much their picks contribute to fund performance and how well analysts communicate with managers.) Finally, Fidelity has to constantly fend off poachers trying to hire away its smart young analysts and managers. In 2002, AXP Funds pulled off a coup when it lured three of Fidelity's rising stars and two analysts to head a new unit running large-cap AXP funds.

Size has made Fidelity's funds more mild-mannered than in the past. You won't get any unpleasant surprises from Fidelity funds, but you're not likely to see many funds crush their indexes, either. Expect Fidelity funds to quietly outperform over the long haul.

Strengths: Although its domestic-stock funds are enormous, the firm has plenty of room to grow in its bond and foreign-stock groups. The firm's government and high-quality corporate bond funds are wonderfully conservative portfolios where managers avoid making market bets and simply stick to researching companies and selecting bonds that appear undervalued. This strategy won't likely add more than 100 basis points (1 percentage point) to returns in a year. As for Fidelity's U.S. stock funds, they're not exciting, but the group's large-cap funds are well-run, dependable vehicles. The firm has also had success with its smaller-cap offerings, particularly the giant Fidelity Low-Priced Stock, but asset bloat is an ongoing worry.

Weaknesses: Fidelity runs a host of narrowly focused select funds, many of which we would recommend avoiding. Funds like Fidelity Select Air Transportation and Fidelity Select Defense & Aerospace are really only of use to speculators who want to make a bet on an industry. Unlike some firms, Fidelity's sector funds are not designed as places for managers to stay for the duration of their careers. Rather, a sector manager is supposed to learn about the sector and then move on after a year or two to learn about another sector. We've also been disappointed by Fidelity's high-yield bond funds.

Janus

Janus is good at growth-stock investing, but its funds are best used in moderation. Janus started as a small growth shop where everyone shared ideas, and that's still largely true today. Janus may have a lot more money under management now, but it still has that boutique atmosphere. That combination of focus (Janus funds have never shied away from big bets on stocks and sectors) and skill enabled Janus funds to put up amazing returns in the late 1990s, yet many of them also went down the tubes together when growth imploded in the following years. Some of Janus' portfolio managers have only a few years of experience running money. Although we believe they are good stock-pickers, they need a little more seasoning before we can be confident that they can manage portfolios well. In the past, many of the firm's funds had significant cross-holdings, but the firm has made strides to differentiate its portfolios so that they don't move in lockstep.

In 2002, Janus gained control of its parent company, thus resolving a long-simmering feud. The main result is that it gives investors greater confidence that Janus won't be struck by key managers defections. It also means a couple of good value funds from Berger will be re-christened as Janus funds.

Strengths: Led by Helen Young Hayes, Janus' international offerings are impressive. Though some got whacked in the 2000–2002 bear market, they've still got what it takes to deliver solid long-term returns. Hayes and company have made strong stock picks even as assets ballooned. Janus' many large-cap growth funds also have strong long-term performance records, though the funds are somewhat volatile. Janus also deserves kudos for its willingness to close funds; most of the firm's large funds are closed to new money.

Weaknesses: Janus' track record at small- and mid-cap funds such as Venture and Enterprise has been spotty. We'd also steer clear of Janus' domestic value-oriented funds because their analyst staff is largely focused on growth stocks.

TIAA-CREF

Known for managing teachers' pension funds, TIAA-CREF (Teachers Insurance and Annuity Association–College Retirement Equities Fund) has branched out into mutual funds. Because the firm is run solely for the profit of investors, its costs are among the lowest in the industry. In addition, the funds carry minimum initial purchase amounts of just $1,500, so they make a nice entry point for young investors. The funds are broadly diversified portfolios, some of which blend active with passive management. No niche products here.

Strengths: The main draws here are low costs and broad diversification, so TIAA-CREF is a fine place to shop when you're buying your first or second fund.

Weaknesses: The actively managed portions of some TIAA-CREF funds have been mediocre.

T. Rowe Price

T. Rowe Price offers mild-mannered style-specific funds. You'll find that T. Rowe Price's funds are among the more conservative options in just about any category because they all adhere to risk-reducing strategies. The funds avoid big stock or sector bets, and even T. Rowe Price's growth funds are wary about buying stocks with a lot of price risk. The firm has also done a great job of enticing managers to stick around. If strategy changes or manager exits have made a hash of your portfolio, give T. Rowe Price a call.

T. Rowe Price is a publicly traded company, but it has steered clear of the mergers that have spelled trouble for other publicly traded mutual fund outfits.

Strengths: T. Rowe Price has fine offerings across the board. If you want a specialized fund such as a regional or sector fund, an offering from T. Rowe makes a good choice because the firm tries to tone down the risk in volatile asset classes.

Weaknesses: T. Rowe's tech funds have been a disappointment during recent years, so we'd stay away.

Vanguard

More than any other firm, this one bears the imprint of its founder. Jack Bogle is a zealot when it comes to costs and shareholders' rights, and it shows throughout the organization. The firm is owned by fundholders, and it offers the lowest costs in the industry. Whereas most organizations create incentives based on market share, Vanguard pays out bonuses based on how low it's able to keep costs. Vanguard runs its index funds and bond funds in-house, but it farms out management responsibilities for its actively managed stock funds to other investment firms (subadvisors). The firm generally has proven adept at picking great subadvisors over the years.

Strengths: For index funds, bond funds, and tax-managed funds, Vanguard is tough to beat. The firm boasts some great actively managed funds, too, thanks to the firm's low costs and ability to choose solid managers. Among the actively managed Vanguard funds we like are Capital Opportunity, Wellington, and International Growth.

Weaknesses: Vanguard doesn't have a lot to offer in actively managed small-cap funds. In addition, due to quirks in their construction, the Value Index and Growth Index haven't behaved much like typical value and growth funds, respectively.

Kicking the Tires: Load Fund Families

American Funds

The watchword here is long-term. The privately-held American Funds get managers focused on the long haul and shelters them from any pressure to chase investment trends. As a result, the funds generally win out in the end even if they endure periods of looking extremely unfashionable. American does a great job of keeping managers and analysts at the firm for their entire careers. As a result, it boasts some of the longest-tenured managers in the industry. Adding to the firm's long-term success is the fact that fund expenses are the lowest of any advisor-sold firm. Also, the firm never chases a quick buck by launching trendy funds that bring in a ton of cash but may not be in shareholders' best interests. Remember how it seemed as if everyone had an Internet fund by early 2000? The American Funds group did not. And their funds largely avoided the overhyped stocks that would later crash to the earth when the bubble burst and accounting scandals scarred the market.

Unlike just about any other firm, American divvies up each fund's assets among a handful of independently acting managers. At most firms, a team-managed approach means that a group of managers swap ideas and come to a consensus, but American cobbles together managers with different styles and lets them loose. That gives American funds diversification among both strategies and stocks. American has never closed a fund to new investors because the firm believes it can always carve out another chunk and turn it over to another manager.

Strengths: American's fundamental research skills are second to none, and it shows across the board in its funds. Fundamental Investors and EuroPacific Growth, to name just a few, have produced outstanding performance without undue volatility. We also like American Funds' innovative take on emerging markets, the New World fund.

Weaknesses: The fund doesn't have much in the way of small-cap exposure: SmallCap World, its one small-cap option, is nothing to write home about. And if you're looking for a fairly aggressive fund, you'll have to look elsewhere because American doesn't go there.

AXP

Long the fund-world's doormat, AXP, the fund management arm of American Express, is finally showing signs of life. In 2002, the firm built an excellent new unit in Boston with the help of three ex-Fidelity managers. Those new managers have, in short order, built a 15-person staff with some impressive resumes. The Boston group runs AXP's domestic large-cap funds, and the firm has also picked some excellent subadvisors, including Mario Gabelli and Chris Davis (of Davis Selected Advisors), to take over some long-suffering funds. The funds that are still at the firm's Minneapolis branch don't inspire confidence, though, as they're run by the same crew that turned in dismal performance in the past.

Strengths: Large-cap funds such as AXP Growth and AXP Stock, which are being steered by the new Boston-based team, are worth a look, as are some of the AXP Partners funds, which are managed by superb subadvisors.

Weaknesses: Skip AXP's bond funds.

Franklin Templeton/Mutual Series

The Franklin Templeton umbrella covers five distinct groups under three names. Templeton is a value-oriented foreign-stock shop. Most of its funds are well managed but pricey. Under the Franklin name, you'll find some good municipal bond managers, a decent growth-stock group, and a separate small-value crew that runs Balance Sheet Investment and MicroCap Value.

Finally, the Mutual Series group runs outstanding low-risk deep-value funds out of New Jersey. The firm does rigorous balance sheet analysis and will not pay much for its companies. Over the years, the Mutual Series funds have produced excellent returns at very moderate risk levels. The one negative at these funds is that founder Michael Price and some other top managers have left in recent years.

Franklin is publicly traded.

Strengths: Thanks to combining the strengths of fund groups with different specialties, Franklin Templeton does a reasonable job of covering all the bases.

We like all the Mutual Series funds though our favorites are the ones with the longest-tenured managers. Mutual European is a nice choice. Franklin also runs some solid muni funds such as California Tax-Free Income and Federal Tax-Free Income. In addition, the huge Templeton Foreign, run by Jeff Everett, is an excellent choice if you're in the market for a foreign value fund.

Weaknesses: It's hard for investors to figure out what to do with Franklin Dyna-Tech. It is an oddball fund with a huge cash stake, some growth stocks, and some actual tech stocks. Meanwhile, the firm has let other funds, such as Franklin Small-Mid Growth, grow too large.

Oppenheimer

OppenheimerFunds isn't a bad choice for one-stop shopping. The firm offers a diverse lineup of funds that cover various asset classes and investment styles. Managers and analysts work in teams based on their investment disciplines, such as growth, value, and global. There is also a highly experienced quantitative team here that manages funds under the Main Street brand.

Oppenheimer's domestic-equity funds rarely shoot out the lights, but many of them offer a respectable risk/return profile. The fund's value lineup had been a weak area in the past, but the firm has taken steps to address the problem. It has brought in outside managers and analysts to build up the value team. The firm also brought in a new investment-grade bond team to take over a few middling fixed-income offerings. That team, which came from the former MAS division of Morgan Stanley, follows a disciplined process that places great emphasis on risk control. Finally, the firm's Rochester municipal-bond division has recently assumed responsibility for the firm's national and state tax-exempt funds.

Oppenheimer is owned by MassMutual.

Strengths: Under the guidance of Bill Wilby, Oppenheimer's global lineup is the firm's crown jewel. A unique theme-based approach to uncovering hidden gems across the globe has generally delivered superb results. The firm's large-cap options, such as Oppenheimer Capital Appreciation and Oppenheimer Main Street Growth & Income, are also worth a look.

Weaknesses: Besides relative newcomer Oppenheimer Main Street Small Cap, the firm's small-cap lineup fails to impress. Oppenheimer Emerging Technologies is also a fund to avoid. Many of the fund's municipal-bond funds have been lackluster performers, so we'd steer clear.

PIMCO

Most of PIMCO's assets are in institutional accounts, not load funds for retail investors, but this is a firm worth getting to know. PIMCO's prowess in fixed-income management is second to none. PIMCO Total Return is by far the biggest bond fund around and it's also one of the best. PIMCO's size has enabled it to build a great staff of analysts, managers, and traders. In addition, its size has given its institutional share classes low expenses. We named PIMCO's bond guru, Bill Gross, our Fixed Income Manager of the Year twice because of his uncanny ability to regularly turn in great results. PIMCO also runs some very respectable stock funds, some of which are subadvised by other firms.

Allianz bought PIMCO in a deal that moved Bill Gross from rich to superrich. PIMCO hasn't suffered any key defections since the deal went through.

Strengths: If you invest through a 401(k) or a planner with a large practice, you might be able to buy into the low-cost institutional share class of PIMCO Total Return. If not, PIMCO subadvises some low-cost virtual clones of that offering that are available to no-load investors: Harbor Bond and Fremont Bond.

Weaknesses: Stock funds PIMCO Innovation and PIMCO Opportunity are two funds that haven't impressed us. Returns have been poor for the amount of volatility shareholders have had to endure.

Putnam

How many Putnam employees does it take to screw in a light bulb? Five to examine whether it's the right light bulb for that particular socket, four to make sure the light bulb is positioned correctly relative to other light bulbs, three to make sure the task isn't too risky, and four to screw it in. Putnam is all about teams and process. Each fund is run by a team of managers who receive inputs from fundamental analysts, quantitative analysts, risk and strategy analysts, and product-positioning analysts.

Despite that uniform process, performance has been decidedly mixed. The fund's value and foreign funds have done just fine, and the bond funds have acquitted themselves respectably, but Putnam's growth offerings drove off a cliff in 2000. Although every growth fund lost money in the bear market of 2000–2002, Putnam's growth funds lost much more because they remained aggressively positioned and their stock-picking was weak. Putnam's error was in confusing style monitoring with risk control. For example, Putnam OTC Emerging Growth, a high-octane mid-growth fund, followed the game plan set out for it and invested in high-growth, high-valuation stocks. Although style controls confirmed that the fund was doing what it was supposed to be doing, Putnam didn't apply the risk controls that would have questioned why a fund should be positioned in such dangerous territory to begin with.

Chastened by its lapses, Putnam has begun to take risk control more seriously. Most of its funds are now aimed squarely at the middle of the Morningstar style box—no extremes, thank you very much. The firm has also built its risk-control group into a more formidable operation and has made some other shareholder-friendly changes, such as closing funds before asset growth spoils performance.

Putnam is owned by Marsh & McLennan.

Strengths: Putnam's value and blend funds are solid options. We're also fans of the firm's foreign funds. Putnam Equity-Income is one of the firm's solid value offerings, and Putnam International Growth exemplifies the latter.

Weaknesses: Putnam appears to have its growth funds aimed in the right direction, but we wouldn't jump in just yet. Putnam has shown some of its growth managers the door in recent years leaving it a little thin on the management side. The firm has filled the void by giving its quantitative analysts greater say in the management of growth funds. That seems reasonable, but we'd like to see some good results before we hop on funds such as Putnam OTC Emerging Growth.

Kicking the Tires: Boutiques

For investors who like to cherry-pick among offerings across a number of firms, here are some of the best boutiques.

Davis/Selected

This family of funds is built on a fundamentals-driven, buy-and-hold strategy. Although mainly associated with value investing, and financials stocks in particular, the firm will invest in any sector. Management is loath to sell a stock and will allow appreciating stocks to move into the growth side of the style box without selling. Our favorites in this lineup are the large-cap Selected American and Davis New York Venture. We would avoid the expensive Davis Government Bond and the unproven Davis International Total Return.

The firm is owned by the Davis family.

Harbor

This isn't quite a boutique, but Harbor Funds are too good to leave off the list. Think of this firm as Vanguard Jr. Harbor doesn't offer index funds, but it does offer moderate-cost actively managed funds run by outstanding sub-advisors. Three highlights: Harbor Bond is run by fixed-income superstar Bill Gross, Harbor International is run by value stalwart Hakan Castegren, and Harbor Capital Appreciation is run by Sig Segalas' outstanding team.

Harbor Capital Advisors, the advisor to the Harbor group of funds, is owned by Robeco, an asset manager based in the Netherlands.

Longleaf Partners

Founded by Mason Hawkins and Staley Cates, this Memphis firm is a stickler for value. A stock has to be trading at least 40% below management's estimate of intrinsic value before the firm will buy. If management does like a stock, it won't be shy about buying. Longleaf typically runs focused portfolios of just 20 or 30 names. This can make performance erratic, but over the long haul the firm has put up strong returns. The best option here is Longleaf Partners Fund, which invests in cheap stocks of all sizes. Longleaf Partners Small Cap is closed to new investment, and Longleaf Partners International, while a promising performer, has a steep expense ratio that dims its appeal.

Longleaf Partners is employee-owned.

Marsico

Founder Tom Marsico runs some of the better large-growth funds around. Marsico put up great returns at Janus Twenty before setting out on his own. He has continued to produce strong relative performance since then. Marsico blends stock selection with top-down analysis (playing on macroeconomic trends) to make a pleasing mix. More recently, the firm has launched funds run by former Marsico analysts. Marsico is the proven quantity here, however, so we favor his Marsico Focus and Marsico Growth funds. If you invest with a broker, you can find similar funds under the Nations Marsico label. The firm is owned by BankAmerica.

Oakmark

In some ways, Oakmark is the anti-Janus. When growth is in favor, they're goats; and when value is in favor, they're heroes. We like Oakmark's domestic- and foreign-stock funds. The crown jewels here are Oakmark Fund and Oakmark Select, which are run by 2001 Morningstar Domestic Stock Manager of the Year Bill Nygren. We wouldn't recommend building a portfolio exclusively of Oakmark funds, however, because that would leave you without growth stocks or fixed income. The firm is owned by the French company CDC, which has generally taken a hands-off approach to Oakmark's investment operation.

Royce

This firm offers a seemingly vast spectrum of small-value funds. Not that you need more than one, but if you did, you could find about 20 here. When they're feeling bold, they might venture off into small-blend, but that's about it. More importantly, founder Chuck Royce and the firm's other managers and analysts are skilled in this patch of the market. We like Royce Total Return for its blend of respectable returns and relatively low risk. Legg Mason owns the firm.

Tweedy, Browne

These value stalwarts are throwbacks to the Graham and Dodd investing style, in which Warren Buffett was also schooled. They look for cheap, well-run businesses. The biggest difference between Tweedy, Browne's funds and

Longleaf's is that this team avoids big stock bets. Thus, you get a much smoother ride here. The firm offers two appealing choices: Global Value (a foreign-stock fund) and American Value, a mid-value offering.

Tweedy, Browne is majority-owned by Affiliated Managers Group (AMG).

Wasatch

These small-cap specialists are that rare boutique that can actually manage both growth and value funds well. Led by Sam Stewart, the firm has produced outstanding results. We also like Wasatch's willingness to close funds while assets are still small. The downside to the firm's closing policy is that expenses are high for some of the firm's funds.

The firm is closely held.

Investor's Checklist: Finding the Right Fund Companies for You

▶ The company behind your fund can be almost as important as its manager. Make sure you understand the company's research capabilities, management philosophy, and ownership.

▶ Every fund company has both strengths and weaknesses. We've summarized our views on all the big ones in this chapter, so be sure to check out our opinions before signing on with a particular fund company.

▶ Some of the key things to focus on when checking out a fund company are the expense structure, asset size, management depth, and track record with different asset classes (such a stocks, bonds, and international securities).

PART FOUR

Monitoring Your Portfolio

12

Schedule Regular Checkups

WE'VE TALKED ABOUT some of the biggest mistakes investors can make—chasing hot funds, paying too much, and not having a diversified portfolio. You could avoid all those mistakes, but if you fail to monitor and periodically adjust your portfolio, you might still have only limited success as an investor.

You have determined just the right mix of assets and have chosen solid funds to fill those roles. But they won't just stay in one place. You will need to rearrange your portfolio precisely because it's a mix of different kinds of investments, which will perform differently over time. Take one of the fundamental portfolio splits, stocks versus bonds. Stock returns usually outpace those of bonds over long stretches, so over time the proportion of stocks in your portfolio will grow.

So what? That means your stocks are prospering. It may seem foolish to cut back on a winner. But the more you let winners run, the greater the risk in your portfolio. Imagine that in early 1995 your ideal portfolio was a 50/50 mix of stocks and bonds. To simplify things, you put $10,000 in Vanguard Total Stock Market Index and $10,000 in Vanguard Total Bond Market Index. If you then let them ride for five years, you would have had 69% in stocks and 31% in bonds.

You would have made a lot of money, but an additional 19% of your portfolio would be vulnerable to a downturn in stocks. If you had held as the stock market dropped in 2000 and through 2001, your portfolio would have lost a cumulative 10.5%. If you went into the market downturn with your portfolio split equally between the two funds, you would have lost just 2.7% for the period.

The asset mix you came up with originally was the best one for meeting your goals. If that gets out of whack, then you don't have the right portfolio for you anymore—it makes sense to restore the mix.

Still, rebalancing can be challenging psychologically. It requires you to take money from your best-performing funds and divert it to the ones that are lagging and may even be losing money. If you shift money from your strong-performing stock funds to bond funds, though, you aren't selling off everything; you're protecting the gains that you made by effectively taking some of them off the table. Alternatively, if your stock funds are in the red and you shift money from your bond funds, you're getting more shares on the cheap, which can enhance your returns.

Knowing When to Rebalance

The common rule is to rebalance your portfolio once a year. Just choose a date such as January 1 (or maybe a different date, depending on how you like to usher in the new year) and review and rebalance your portfolio then. You could rebalance your portfolio more often, but our research indicates that more frequent rebalancing, such as every three or six months, doesn't do much to limit volatility. And if you're rebalancing funds in a taxable account, frequent selling could be bad for your tax bill because you're typically taking profits on your winners.

When rebalancing a taxable portfolio, pay attention to when your funds make their annual distributions. Most funds make them sometime between October and December. (You can contact your fund company in the fall to find out the scheduled distribution date.) If you sell after a distribution, you'll be paying taxes on shares that you later got rid of. Better to sell before-hand. When you're buying shares, do so after distributions have been made. Otherwise you could wind up getting a taxable distribution on shares that you have owned for just a matter of days.

Your Annual Portfolio Review

Before rebalancing you need to determine what is out of balance. That's why you should start with an annual portfolio review. You will want to check the percentage of your portfolio that is devoted to the following areas:

- ▶ Cash, stocks, and bonds.
- ▶ Various investment styles, such as "large value" or "small growth."
- ▶ Key sectors.
- ▶ Specific individual securities.
- ▶ Foreign exposure.

Asset Mix: You'll probably find that your mixture of cash, stocks, and bonds shifts the most dramatically over time. Stocks typically post better returns than bonds or cash, and therefore continue to grow in importance in your portfolio if left untouched. When the market is in the doldrums, the opposite may be the problem: Your stock portfolio loses money, leaving your equity allocation smaller than you'd like. Either way, it's important to pay close attention to the balance of stocks, bonds, and cash, and to be ready to readjust as necessary to meet your approaching goals.

If your stock funds are taking up more than their allotted share of your portfolio, trim them back and shift the money to bonds. If you are investing in a taxable account, cutting back on stocks could mean incurring a taxable gain. Instead of selling stocks, you may want to invest new money in your bond funds to restore the balance.

The simple step of restoring your stock and bond mix is hands-down the most important thing you can do to keep your portfolio's volatility in check and to protect the gains you have made. Excessive stock exposure will make your portfolio much more vulnerable to stock market slumps. At the other extreme, parking too much in bonds will hinder you from getting the long-term returns you need to meet your goals.

Investment Style: Just as your stock/bond mix can change, your portfolio's investment style can also shift over time. In a given year, different kinds of stock funds can perform very differently from each other—that's the reason you want to hold a variety of stock funds in your portfolio. In the late 1990s, large-growth funds posted the best returns of any style category. As a result, such funds grew to be considerably larger portions of investors' portfolios. Investors who neglected to rebalance suffered tremendously in 2000 and 2001, when large growth turned into the worst performing style category.

Your portfolio mix can shift for other reasons, too. Your managers may have decided to emphasize growth stocks, even if they don't run growth funds, because that part of the market is too compelling to overlook. Industry trends could also cause stocks that are typically growth investments to gravitate toward value, or vice versa. When many health stocks took a big hit in the early 1990s, health-care investors ended up holding a basket of beaten-down value stocks. At the same time, many value-fund managers picked up on those stocks. If you owned both a health-care fund and a value fund, you might have been overexposed to that area.

As explained in Chapter 7, a good mix of both growth and value can protect you from dramatic downturns in any given style. In the late 1990s, value investors were disappointed year after year, as growth stocks climbed ever higher, and value fare stagnated in comparison. Many investing commentators were claiming that value investing was dead and growth stocks and funds were the way to go. Investors seemed to believe them. Of the 10 funds that got the most new money in 1999, seven were growth offerings: Alliance Premier Growth, Fidelity Aggressive Growth, Janus Mercury, Janus Twenty, Janus Worldwide, MFS Massachusetts Investors Growth, and Vanguard Growth Index.

Despite the words of commentators and the actions of investors, growth was not the only way to go, nor was value a waste of time. On average, those seven growth funds that got huge amounts of new money in 1999 took a 21% loss in 2000, an even more painful 27% in 2001, and were down 33% for the first nine months of 2002. While growth was plummeting, value rebounded and provided diversified investors with some respite from growth stocks' tumultuous returns. Those who had bothered to throw some new money into once-unloved value funds were amply rewarded.

Sector Exposure: It's also important to be mindful of your exposure to specific sectors and to rebalance to avoid getting burned by a single area. After technology stocks came into vogue in 1998, investors who were previously well diversified among a handful of mutual funds discovered that a large chunk of their assets were actually directed toward just two sectors: computer hardware and software. A portfolio made up of the seven preceding popular funds would have had more than 40% of its assets in the information supersector, with especially heavy stakes in the computer hardware and software sectors. Focusing on one or two areas of the market might pump up your returns temporarily, but it will also leave you dangerously exposed to downturns in those areas, as the experience of those seven funds illustrates. Conduct a regular checkup of your sector exposure, and consider scaling back on those funds that are skewing your portfolio heavily toward a certain sector.

Concentration in Individual Securities: Letting your portfolio concentrate heavily in a few stocks can also ruin your plans. While Microsoft, General Electric, or (for many investors) your employer's stock may play an important role in your portfolio, you'll want to know exactly how much you're devoting to such holdings. Checking on "stock overlap," as it's called, will help to ensure that you don't inadvertently go into one year with 15% or more of your assets dedicated to the best-performing stock of the previous year, which could be ready for a downturn. Consider all the Enron employees who lost their shirts because they had so much of their portfolios tied up in company stock.

To accurately assess the largest stock positions in your portfolio, you'll need to add together any individual stocks you own and any exposure from the top holdings of your mutual funds. It's not unusual to discover that many of the most popular mutual funds are investing in the same securities. As the bull market was nearing its March 2000 peak, it was hard to find a large-cap growth fund that didn't own Cisco Systems, Nokia, or Amazon, if not all three. If you own overlapping funds, you could end up paying for that duplication of effort with greater portfolio volatility. Use the Stock Intersection tool in Morningstar.com's Portfolio Manager to see the largest stock positions in your portfolio based on your individual stock holdings and the top holdings of your funds. If you have more than 5% of your portfolio in a single security, consider scaling back on the fund that's heavy on that holding.

Foreign Exposure: Finally, review the percentage of your portfolio devoted to specific countries or regions of the world. Your foreign-stock funds may change weightings frequently, and you will want to keep tabs on how each fund's weighting works with other holdings that you own. Even some domestic-equity funds are allowed to invest outside the United States, so don't rely solely on the word "foreign" or "global" to spot a fund's international ambitions.

When examining your foreign exposure, watch out for single country or emerging-markets exposure that takes up more than 30% of your overall foreign stake. Check your exposure to the often-risky Japanese market as well as to developing regions such as Latin America and the Pacific Rim. If you have more than one foreign fund, you might be able to reduce that focus by shifting assets between them. If you own just one foreign fund, you might want to add another one that puts greater emphasis on other parts of the world.

Tweaking Your Portfolio: Getting More Conservative or Aggressive

Maybe your investment portfolio could use a little conservatism. Perhaps you overdosed on technology stocks during their 1990s bash and suffered a miserable hangover in the wake of the crash that began in 2000. Or you thought that the stock market could only go up. Or maybe your portfolio doesn't need to be very aggressive for you to meet your goals. Here are some tips on adjusting your portfolio's volatility.

Alter Your Asset Mix: The most effective way to influence your portfolio's long-term returns and volatility level is through your mix of stocks, bonds, and cash. Although other factors, such as what investment styles you follow, what sectors you have exposure to, and what individual securities you choose, also have an impact, your asset allocation has an enormous influence. The more of your portfolio you have in stocks and the less you have in bonds and cash, the more volatile your portfolio's performance will be.

Alter Your Bond Mix: In addition to altering your asset mix, you can curtail or increase volatility within specific asset groups. Many portfolios include intermediate-term bonds at their core. Such funds are fairly tame to begin with, but to dampen the volatility of an intermediate-term-bond portfolio, consider adding a short-term bond fund to your mix. Because of their shorter durations (meaning less sensitivity to interest rate changes), short-term bonds tend to be less volatile than intermediate-term bonds; they gain less when interest rates fall, but lose less when rates rise. They often yield less as well.

Conversely, if you're looking to become more aggressive, invest in longer-term bond funds or high-yield bonds, which offer more capital appreciation potential than shorter-term offerings (along with higher volatility, of course).

Alter Your Stock Mix: Your portfolio's overall volatility is closely connected to the size and type of your stock investments. To decrease volatility, investigate funds that focus on very large companies. As discussed in Chapter 3, small-cap funds simply tend to be more volatile than their large-cap counterparts. If curtailing volatility is your goal, focus the U.S. stock portion of your portfolio on funds that buy the very largest companies. They may not have the same growth potential as smaller companies, but they don't have the same volatility, either. You might consider adding a fund that focuses on dividend-paying stocks, such as an equity-income fund.

Dividend-paying stocks are often called "buffers" because their dividends provide a cushion in difficult markets. Although a company's stock price may fall, it will usually pay its dividend. And that dividend props up total return. For example, say Acme Cement Company's stock price falls from $100 per share to $95 per share in one year. That's a 5% loss. However, the company pays a $7 per-share dividend each year. At the end of the year, shareholders have a $95 share price and a $7 dividend. So they haven't really endured a 5% loss. Even with the drop in the stock's price, they have still made a gain of $2 per share. Funds that land in Morningstar's large-value category are the most apt to pay ample dividends.

Reasonably priced stocks can also buffer your portfolio's volatility level. Funds that buy companies whose stocks trade at high prices relative to their earnings, their sales, or their cash flows, harbor what's called price risk. Investors have high expectations about the futures of these companies and are therefore willing to pay a premium for the stocks. If the earnings, sales, or cash flows of these companies don't live up to expectations, however, their stock prices can plummet. Our studies show that the price/earnings ratio is a pretty good indicator of such risk. If you're comparing two funds, the one with the higher P/E ratio is likely to post bigger losses in an unfriendly market. High prices are what did in many technology stocks in 2000 and on into 2001 and 2002. To avoid such price dives, stick with valuation-conscious funds in one of the value or blend categories.

Alter Your Foreign Mix: If you have been on the daring side with your foreign mix, you have most likely been drawn to mid- and small-cap foreign
stocks, or to emerging-markets stocks. Though these groups hold out the
promise of big returns, they are also very volatile. To curtail volatility in your
foreign position, focus on large international companies that are domiciled in
developed markets (mostly Europe, Japan, and Canada). They may not have
the same growth potential as smaller companies or emerging-markets stocks,
but they don't have the same volatility, either.

Conducting a Quarterly Review

If you review your portfolio every year, paying specific attention to the preceding factors, you'll be well on your way to meeting your financial goals.
One more tip, though, can make your life even easier between annual re-
views: Invest just 15 minutes every three months in a "minireview" to look for
major portfolio developments. Not only will this make your annual review
less time-consuming, but it will also tip you off to any burgeoning trouble
spots that might require action during your annual portfolio checkup.

The goal of the quarterly minireview is to check for major changes or
trends within your holdings and portfolio overall. It's not meant to be a substitute for the more thorough review; nor is it meant to trigger major buy or
sell decisions. To keep your quarterly review short and to the point, you'll
need to review only a few items within three key areas of your portfolio:

Quarterly Review Checkpoints

1. Performance-Related Data:
   ▶ Overall portfolio return for past three months and year-to-date.
   ▶ Biggest gainer and loser for past three months and year-to-date.
   ▶ Best and worst performers relative to an appropriate benchmark, such
     as the correct mutual fund category.

The first question you'll probably want answered when you conduct your
quarterly review is: "How much money did I make?" (Or, sadly but possibly,
"How much money did I lose?") The key here is not to put too much emphasis on the gains or losses of a single quarter. More important than knowing

your overall return in a short, three-month time period is determining which holdings contributed the most, and the least, to that return. These are the holdings that you'll probably need to adjust (either buying more or selling) during your year-end checkup.

Also, keep in mind that it's not just absolute returns that matter. Your worst performing holding, in absolute terms, may actually be doing better than any of its peers. If that holding is playing an important diversification role in your portfolio, you may end up keeping it even though its style is out of sync with the broad market. That's why it's important to note each holding's performance ranking relative to the appropriate category or industry peer group.

2. Portfolio Allocations:
    ▶ Asset allocation.
    ▶ Investment style allocation.
    ▶ Stock sector percentage.

In each quarterly review, you'll want to check in on your asset allocation to see if, and how, the big picture of your portfolio has changed. Striking alterations over a three-month timespan don't indicate that it's time to rebalance. But by keeping tabs on major portfolio-related changes as they develop, you'll make your year-end review easier and will be tipped off to trends before your overall portfolio changes too dramatically.

3. Fundamental Changes and News:
    ▶ Manager changes.
    ▶ Fund company news (mergers or acquisitions).

This is probably the most important part of the quarterly review. Unlike the other two areas that we've checked (your portfolio's performance and changes in its composition), this area that actually might trigger a midyear sale or purchase. If, for example, you find that your mutual fund has undergone a manager change, you'll want to do some research on the new manager. You'll want to learn about his or her background and what changes, if any, he or she intends to make to the portfolio. A management change in and of itself isn't a "sell" signal, but it does entail further investigation.

Investor's Checklist: Schedule Regular Checkups

► Rebalance your portfolio annually to restore the mix that you determined was right for your goals.

► Rebalance by first reviewing your portfolio's mix of cash, bonds, and stocks; its mix of investment styles and sectors and country exposure; and its concentration in individual stocks.

► If you want to keep portfolio volatility in check, restoring the balance of cash, bonds, and stocks is most important.

► The easiest way to make your portfolio more conservative or aggressive is by adjusting the amount in stocks versus bonds. Devoting more to stocks will increase your portfolio's long-term return potential but will also increase short-term volatility. For steadier performance, put more in bonds.

► Make your bond mix more conservative by shifting toward short-term bond funds and higher credit quality. The trade-off for greater stability will be lower long-term returns though. Get more aggressive by shifting toward the longer term and/or lower credit quality.

► Make your stock portfolio more conservative by increasing its focus on the biggest companies, on dividend-paying stocks, and on stocks with reasonable valuations. Shift foreign investments toward blue-chip stocks in developed markets.

► Do a quick portfolio review each quarter to help anticipate any changes you'll need to make at year-end.

13

Know When to Sell

SMART INVESTORS ALWAYS take a fresh look at their holdings. They do not fall in love or get angry—they simply reassess their investments' potential. Mutual funds change and you have to be ready to sell when those changes indicate a problem.

Here are some important warning signs. These aren't sell signals per se; we talk about specific reasons for selling a fund later in this chapter. Think of these as signals that a change for the worse may be on the way.

Keeping an Eye on Asset Growth

As funds attract new investors and grow larger, their returns often become sluggish, weighed down by too many assets. They lose their potency, and their returns revert to the average for their group. Some funds stop accepting money from new investors when their assets grow too large. Ideally, a fund will do that well before it is bloated, but most don't. Excessive size often explains why so many once-hot funds become mediocre.

There are worse things than being average. But you may still want to keep an eye on your funds as they grow, especially funds that focus on smaller companies and whose strategies involve a lot of trading. American Century Ultra is one fund that was utterly transformed by mushrooming assets. The fund put up terrific numbers in the early 1990s by buying fast-growing small-company stocks and quickly selling them when their earnings growth slowed. The fund's performance drew lots of attention from investors, and its asset base swelled. Returns slowed because the managers couldn't execute their fast-trading, supergrowth strategy with so many assets in tow. Performance suffered as a result. So what did the managers do? They changed their strategy. They now buy large companies and trade far less often. The fund became competitive in its new style, but it no longer plays the same role in a portfolio.

Morningstar has studied where asset growth can be the biggest problem, and we have found that you must pay the most attention to funds that focus on smaller-cap or growth-oriented stocks (see Figure 13.1). Funds that land in the small-growth category are the most vulnerable to asset bloat. Booming assets can also burden other small-cap or growth funds, but the negative effects may not be as great.

Along with weaker performance, American Century Ultra displayed another significant consequence of asset growth: Its managers had to alter their strategies to put large amounts of money to work. In some cases, a fund will simply buy more stocks. Others will buy larger companies or trade less frequently.

Concerns about how much of a single company a fund can reasonably own will force the manager of a growing fund to invest in more stocks, or bigger companies, or both. A fund with a burgeoning asset base will often

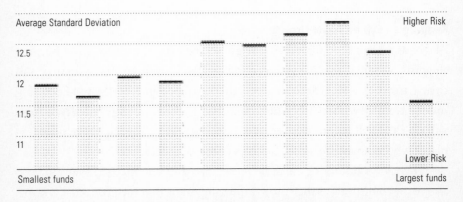

Figure 13.1   Asset size related to risk. As assets increase, many funds tend to take on more risk.

trade less frequently because its activities can affect a stock's price. Because the manager has a lot of money to throw at a single stock, that buying can drive up the stock price by upsetting the balance between supply and demand—more money will be chasing shares of that stock. It is virtually impossible for a manager to buy all the shares wanted at one time, so the last share purchased could cost significantly more than the first. Because of this effect, a growing fund can create its own headwind, hurting performance by trading too frequently.

No matter whether the fund buys more stocks, bigger ones, trades them more slowly, or all the above, the manager has to make some kind of change. And as a shareholder, you need to be aware of the change, and consider whether this altered fund fits into your portfolio. American Century Ultra shareholders no longer own a small-growth fund; they own a large-growth fund.

Knowing What to Make of Manager Changes

As we discussed in Chapter 4, mutual funds are only as good as the people behind them: the fund managers. Because the fund manager is the person who is most responsible for a fund's performance, many investors wonder if they should sell a fund when their manager leaves. The short answer is, it depends; that's why this is a yellow flag, not a red one. It's possible that the new manager will do just as well as—and maybe even better than—the old. And some types of funds are less affected by manager changes than others. For example, managers of index funds are not actively choosing stocks; they're simply mimicking a benchmark. Thus, manager changes at index funds are less important than manager changes at actively managed funds.

Whenever your fund undergoes a change, it's worthwhile to check the Morningstar Analyst Report on the fund. A fund company will often claim that a manager change is just incidental and that everything is business as usual. That may be the case, but our analysts are always skeptical. They assess the likely impact of the change by looking at factors such as whether the departing manager was the only person at the helm or worked as part of a team, and what kind of analyst support the incoming manager can draw on. Our analysts also take a hard look at the incoming manager's experience, including his or her record running other mutual funds.

Monitoring Fund-Family Growth, Mergers, or Acquisitions

Maybe the family behind your fund is adding some new funds to its lineup. Or maybe a bigger company is going to buy it. Why should you care? After all, your manager will still be there calling the shots. Such changes can matter a surprising amount, because they can distract managers from doing their job—running investors' funds.

Once-great funds such as PBHG Growth stalled as their families expanded. Fund managers can lose their focus when their families launch new funds, and working on those new funds means that the managers are spread very thin.

Changes in fund company ownership also can lead to a slowdown in performance. Robertson Stephens (now called RS Funds) spent a large part of 1998 trying to cut its ties with owner Bank of America. The group finally succeeded, but its funds suffered. Nearly all its offerings had subpar returns in 1998, and the managers admitted that the company's business issues were distracting.

Spotting Yellow Flags

How can you find out if your funds are on the verge of change? For starters, keep tabs on your fund families. Regularly visit their Web sites looking for news of growth plans and new fund launches. You can also gain access to information on funds in the pipeline at the Securities and Exchange Commission's Web site (www.sec.gov); before launching new offerings, fund families must register them with the SEC. And scan whatever fund company marketing materials jam your mailbox. Pay attention to what independent sources, including Morningstar, have to say about your funds and your fund families. Scan our news and see what other investors in your funds are saying on Morningstar.com's Conversation boards. Our Analyst Takes are also helpful. The Morningstar analysts who follow the funds will cover any significant changes that the fund has undergone.

Finally, check up on your funds periodically to make sure the status quo hasn't changed. What do their assets look like? Are their managers still in place? Is anything notable going on with the fund family? Some investors prefer to check on their funds monthly. Lots of us quickly look over our funds every day, but that's much more often than necessary. Looking over your funds each quarter should be often enough for you to keep on top of any significant changes.

If you find that changes may be afoot, ask questions. If your fund family is launching a new fund that sounds a lot like the fund you already own, call the family's customer support number and ask how the funds will differ and if this will mean more work for your fund manager. Or if you're worried about asset size, find out if the family plans to close the fund anytime soon.

Using the Star Rating to Flag Changes

As explained in Chapter 3, Morningstar's star rating isn't designed to be a buy or sell signal. It puts the fund's returns and volatility in context, but you need to dig a bit deeper to assess the fund. That said, a change in your fund's star rating is worth investigating. If your fund sheds a star, it might not mean the fund is in trouble. Because we calculate the star ratings every month, the drop could be reflecting a short-term performance shift. Maybe your growth fund emphasizes health-care stocks, but technology stocks have been doing better lately. Also, a fund that is 4 years 11 months old is rated just for the past three years. If that fund got off to a terrible start, it might lose a star when it's old enough for us to rate its five-year record. Yet the fund was better in recent years, which should be encouraging to shareholders.

When the rating changes, you should find out what has been going on, then base your decision to hang on or sell on that information. The easiest way to get the scoop on significant changes in the fund is to read the Morningstar Analyst Report. Our reports always discuss what has been driving both the fund's long- and short-term returns. We often highlight stock or sector bets that have done notably well or badly, and you can also check the fund's top holdings for names that have been in trouble lately. Good shareholder reports will also address what has been hindering performance as well as what has been working. Most funds post the reports on their Web sites, and some post basic shareholder letters every month or quarter.

Also use significant drops in the star rating as your indicator to dig into the issues mentioned here. See if you may have missed any yellow flags then consider the factors in the following section to determine whether it makes sense for you to sell or to hang on.

Spotting Red Flags

Be on the lookout for other signs of a strategy change. A big surge in assets might force a manager to alter his or her strategy by investing in larger companies, holding more cash, or trading less. If the fund is no longer doing what brought it past success, it's time to leave.

Shrinking assets can be a different kind of warning sign. If a firm loses a lot of assets, they might have to cut back on staff. It's worth checking to see if the fund has the same amount of support that it had in years past.

Finally, beware of funds that are constantly tweaking their strategies. This usually happens because a fund is adjusting to what's working in the markets at that time. The problem is you'll always be a day late and a dollar short when you chase trends. To beat the market, you need a fund that can stand by its strategy even when that leaves it temporarily out of fashion.

Knowing When to Sell

The first step in deciding whether to sell is identifying *why* you own the fund. What was your rationale for buying it? Did you admire the portfolio manager's track record? Then you'll need to keep an eye open for manager changes. Did you love the industries the fund invested in? Then you need to look for changes to the portfolio's sector weightings. Did you buy the fund to fill the large-cap value slot in your portfolio? Then you should pay particular attention to its style.

The tricky part is figuring out when to sell. Most of us can agree on what to look for when buying a fund—good risk-adjusted returns, long manager tenure, and so on—but we part ways on when to sell. Just check out some of the long and lively debates raging on Morningstar.com's Conversation boards. None of us wants to undermine our returns by buying and selling at the wrong times. Yet some situations almost demand that we hit the sell button.

Seven Good Reasons to Sell

You Need to Rebalance: As we discussed in the previous chapter, even if your investment goals have remained the same and you have not tinkered with your asset allocation, you'll probably need to get your portfolio mix back to its original state. If your stock funds didn't fare well in a given year, rebalancing probably will require putting more money in those laggards.

The Fundamentals Have Changed: Presumably, you buy a small-value fund because you want exposure to small-value stocks. If the manager starts buying large-value stocks, you may have a problem. You may now have multiple large-value funds in your portfolio and no small-value fund. You may need to sell one of your large-value funds and pick another small-value one to restore your original balance of styles.

Be careful how you define a change in style. Sometimes a manager's stocks will change, but his or her strategy won't. Baron Asset is a case in point. The fund didn't migrate from the small-growth to the mid-cap growth category because manager Ron Baron began buying larger stocks. He still buys small-cap issues; he just holds on to them as they move into mid-cap or large-cap range. Similarly, Longleaf Partners occasionally wanders from mid-value into mid-blend. Like Baron Asset, Longleaf Partners keeps turnover low—as its holdings prosper, they may shift into a different box, but the strategy hasn't changed. If you are concerned about strictly maintaining your asset allocation, you may want to avoid such funds.

We mentioned that a manager change should be a yellow flag. To decide whether you should sell, you need to assess how good the replacement manager is. If the replacement already has a long-term record at a similar fund, then it should be easy to figure out if he or she is a worthy successor. If it's a manager from the same firm who doesn't have much of a record, take a look at the record of other funds in the same asset class. Some families have deep benches and can replace departing managers without missing a beat. In other cases you'll find that the firms do a lousy job at most of their funds in an asset class and you were holding the only good one. If that's the case, it's time to bail out.

You Misunderstood the Fundamentals: Closely related to changing fundamentals are misunderstood fundamentals. If you buy a compact disc that's cracked or a shirt that doesn't fit, you return it. Sometimes investments need to be returned, too.

Let's say, for example, that back in 1999, you picked up a fund like Invesco Blue Chip Growth expecting a steady, diversified investment style. The fund wasn't as tame as the name implied, however. (In fact, its name changed to Invesco Growth in 2001.) It took big risks that sometimes paid off and sometimes failed. It lost 24% in 2000 and 49% in 2001 due to a stake in tech stocks that reached as much as 71% of the portfolio. Shareholders who thought they were buying a boring blue-chip fund had every reason to sell. They had made a mistake. Rather than hang on to a mistake in the hope that it works out, it makes sense to switch the money to a more compelling investment that you feel comfortable with. After reading Chapter 5, you may also have realized that you have been overlooking one of the most basic issues—the effect of high costs. If your fund is overpriced, you could save a lot of money and improve your returns by picking a cheaper option.

The Fund Isn't Living up to Your Expectations: Although one year of underperformance may be nothing to worry about, two or three years of falling behind can get frustrating, to say the least. Before cutting the fund loose, though, be sure that you're comparing your underperformer to an appropriate benchmark, such as its Morningstar category or a suitable index.

Taxes are particularly important in making your decision. If you have owned your fund for a long time, you may have built up significant gains, resulting in a tax hit when you sell. Your new pick would have to make many percentage points per year more to make up for the tax damage. (Morningstar.com has a tool called Trade Analyzer to help you figure out the tax aspects of a swap.) That means that if your star fund has faded to average, selling may not be a good idea. If you think you can do better but want to avoid the taxes, put new money to work in a new fund. (Yes, we're suggesting you break the rule against fund overlap—there's no sense in shifting everything to the superior fund when you will face a hefty tax bill as a result.) On the other hand, if your fund is down enough, you can give yourself a tax break by selling. It could be a win-win deal.

Surprisingly, you may also need to sell if your fund is *gaining* more than it should. If your intermediate-term bond fund is returning more than 10% per year, it's probably taking on more risk to achieve that return than you would expect to come from the "boring" part of your portfolio. You should at least check the fund's Morningstar Quicktake and Analyst Report to see where those outsized returns are coming from and to determine if that could spell trouble.

Your Investment Goals Have Changed: You don't invest to win some imaginary race, but to meet your financial goals. As your objectives change, your investments should change as well. Suppose you start investing in a balanced fund with the goal of buying a house within the next five years. If you get married and your spouse already owns a house, you may decide to use that money for retirement instead. In that case, you might sell the balanced fund and buy a portfolio of stock funds. Your goal and the time until you draw on your investment have changed. The investment should, too. For the same reason, bonds should become increasingly prominent in your portfolio as you near your goal.

You Can Get a Tax Break: If your fund account is in the red, it might make sense for you to sell and take a loss that you can use to offset future taxable gains. The IRS allows you to use $3,000 of capital losses to offset ordinary income—which is taxed at much higher rates than capital gains. And capital losses that exceed the $3,000 threshold may be carried forward indefinitely. (Be sure to take into account any deferred loads or redemption fees when determining whether to recognize a tax loss. And keep in mind that if you work with a broker, you will also be paying a commission to invest the money.) Selling sooner instead of later is a particularly good idea if the fund looks poor for any of the preceding reasons. You can even sell a good fund if you really need the tax break; just keep in mind that you can't buy it back for at least 30 days or the IRS won't let you take the tax writeoff.

You Just Can't Take It Anymore: Even meeting your goals isn't worth it if you develop ulcers or wind up sleep-deprived along the way. Maybe your fund is so volatile that not even the vision of your brand-new house calms you down—every time the fund takes a dip, you see yourself losing another room off your dream house. Sell, by all means (so long as you never buy the fund or a fund like it again). The moral: Know your funds, know yourself, and never make the same mistake twice. To avoid getting in that situation again, pay particular attention to how your prospective fund invests and do the gut check. Examine the fund's worst annual and quarterly losses and ask yourself if you would be able to stick out those periods, not knowing if things might get worse, without undue stress.

Investor's Checklist: Know When to Sell

► Watch out for excessive asset growth. Funds that focus on smaller companies or growth stocks and trade frequently are especially vulnerable to problems from asset bloat.

► If there's a manager change, answer these four questions:

–Is the manager solo or part of a team?

–What past experience does the new manager have?

–How successful has the fund company been at handling past changes?

–Does the fund company have a strong roster of managers and analysts?

► Treat big changes to the fund family as yellow flags. Watch out for the family launching lots of new funds or merging with or acquiring other fund companies.

► A change in a fund's star rating alone isn't reason to sell, but it is an indication that you should dig deeper to find out what's going on.

► In deciding whether you should sell a fund, review the seven good reasons for selling:

–You need to do basic portfolio rebalancing.

–Fundamentals such as the fund's investment style have changed.

–You misunderstood the fundamentals.

–The fund hasn't met your expectations.

–Your investment goals have changed.

–You can use a tax writeoff.

–A fund has been too volatile for your taste.

14

Keep a Cool Head in Turbulent Markets

SUPPOSE THAT YOU'RE planning on buying a car. You want to see great financing deals and sales, right? Automakers would prefer otherwise, but if you're buying, the cheaper the better.

Yet most people don't see things that way when stocks are down. If you're going to be buying stocks and holding them for at least five years, a bear market should see you cheerfully pursuing bargains or contributing more to your mutual funds so the managers can pick up deals on your behalf. Instead, investors tend to retreat, taking their money out of stock funds. When the market starts going up, then they buy. It's like waiting until prices and loan rates start going up to buy a car.

That example is courtesy of the great Warren Buffett. He's right, as he often is—how you think about a bear market, just like how you think about car prices, depends on whether you're a buyer or a seller. If you're building up your nest egg, low stock prices are good. For retirees and others making withdrawals from their funds, declining stock prices are bad news.

The market's travails since early 2000 have driven this point home emphatically, but one key to investing success is understanding how volatile stocks can be. Many investors simply don't appreciate how variable the stock market's returns have been. Take the oft-quoted statistic that over the long haul, stocks have delivered double-digit annual gains. It is true that since the mid-1920s, stocks have risen by an average of over 10% per year, but in any given year, their returns frequently deviate from the norm.

In fact, although market commentators often refer to a 10% gain as a normal return, stocks hardly ever deliver that sort of increase in a single year. Between 1975 and 2001, there was only one calendar year—1993—in which the S&P 500 index achieved a return that was within 2 percentage points of normal (i.e., between 8% and 12%). During that time, the index's yearly returns ranged from a high of 37.53% to a loss of 11.9%. Instead, over the past three decades, the S&P 500 has posted an annual loss about one fourth of the time.

That statistic highlights the importance of having an investment plan that works in both rising and falling equity markets. By keeping a cool head and sticking to sensible investing principles, investors can limit the bear-market damage to their portfolios and be positioned to benefit when stocks rebound.

Investing in Bear Markets

First off, it's important to know what *not* to do when stocks start falling: Don't try to time the market. Although plenty of so-called market commentators and investment advice-givers claim to be able to foresee the market's near-term direction, few, if any, manage to do so on a consistent basis. The events that move the market in the short term—currency crises, a terrorist attack, a series of surprisingly good (or bad) economic reports—are difficult to anticipate.

Elaine Garzarelli, the onetime star fund manager who correctly advised clients to sell stocks before the October 1987 equity-market crash, understandably reaped a whirlwind of favorable publicity after her 1987 market call, but her subsequent money-management efforts were less successful. Her record during the 1990s was spotty at best, and she ultimately stopped trying to incorporate market-timing into her fund-management strategy.

Garzarelli isn't alone. Another prominent fund manager who implements market-timing strategies, Paul Merriman, has built an abysmal long-term record at Merriman Growth and Income and other funds. In fact, his funds' records are among the worst in their respective Morningstar categories, even after the recent bear market, in which a market-timer ought to have shone. We don't know of any fund manager who has consistently added value with a market-timing strategy. Given that fund managers have more resources at their disposal than a typical investor would have, their inability to execute market-timing strategies profitably should give average investors pause.

A mountain of evidence also suggests that in the aggregate, mutual-fund investors are lousy market-timers. Time and again, they have pulled money out of equity funds after the market has already fallen and therefore haven't fully participated in the subsequent rebound. For example, equity funds suffered their greatest outflows ever, as a percentage of assets, in October 1987. Spooked by the dramatic 25% one-day drop in the market, investors sold in droves. Many fund investors therefore missed the S&P 500's 17.4% gain between December 1987 and February 1988.

Dollar-Cost Averaging

Because it's impossible to foretell the near-term direction of the market, the disciplined approach afforded by dollar-cost averaging is often the best course for investors trying to build wealth for their long-term goals. Take, for example, the different paths chosen by two hypothetical investors in 1987. One invested $1,200 in Vanguard 500 Index on July 1, 1987, then made no further contributions. Another instead invested $100 in the fund on July 1, 1987, then contributed a similar amount for the next 11 months, for a total investment of $1,200. Because the latter investor kept buying shares even after the market's October 1987 free fall, he profitably picked up shares going for bargain prices. By June 2002, the dollar-cost-averaging investor would have had $6,071, while the account of the former, who stopped his contributions, would have been worth $500 less.

Of course, the dollar-cost averager benefited from having less at stake when the market dropped. In that sense, this is a rigged example. But that investor was also at a disadvantage for the first few months; he was paying higher prices as the market went up. The point is simply that by continuing to invest regularly (i.e., in your retirement plan) you can turn even difficult markets to your advantage.

We've discussed the benefits of dollar-cost averaging elsewhere, but it's worth noting that the strategy works especially well during market downturns.

By continuing to invest in bear markets, you acquire more shares at cheaper prices than you would by purchasing only when the market is near its peak. In effect, you're letting the market's volatility work to your advantage.

Diversify, Diversify, Diversify!

In addition to maintaining a disciplined contribution schedule, it is also critical to properly diversify your portfolio both by asset classes and by investment styles. (For more on diversification, see Chapters 8 and 9.) This is especially true for retirees and others who are taking distributions from their accounts and who need to avoid precipitous losses.

Although many investors had their portfolios heavily concentrated in the large-growth funds that suffered especially steep losses, there were plenty of places to hide from the bear. Small-value funds, which tend to own a lot of banks, industrials, and other Old Economy firms, therefore rose 39% between April 2000 and June 2002. Funds that invest in real estate investment trusts (REITs) also prospered, in relative terms.

Does that mean small-value stocks and REITs will perform well in every market meltdown? No. It is difficult to predict, in advance, which segments of the equity market will hold up well during downturns. But we know that certain asset classes, ranging from REITs to small-value and natural-resources stocks, often zig when the market zags. By spreading money across several of these largely uncorrelated segments of the market, investors can avoid suffering disproportionate losses in bear markets.

Add Bonds for Ballast

It is even more important to remember that bonds are a necessary part of any well-diversified portfolio. It was easy to forget that between 1995 and 1999, when the S&P 500 delivered gains exceeding 20% in each year, and bonds put up comparatively paltry return numbers. But in addition to providing the income needed by retirees and others, bonds can help stabilize a portfolio, as high-quality debt tends not to move in sync with equities. During times of stock-market turmoil, bonds often rally, as investors seek refuge from riskier assets. From May through July 2002, the S&P 500 suffered a punishing loss of more than 20%. Most bond funds posted slight gains during that period. Because interest rates fell, pushing up bond prices, most long-term government offerings gained at least a few percentage points (some gained several percent) for the three months.

A comparison of Vanguard Total Stock Market Index and Vanguard Balanced Index vividly illustrates bonds' steady-Eddie natures. The former fund tracks the Wilshire 5000 index of all regularly traded U.S. companies. The latter tracks that same index within the 60% of the fund that's devoted to equities, but it also stashes 40% of its assets in bonds. The bond slice of the portfolio tracks the Lehman Brothers Aggregate index of investment-grade debt issues. The pure-stock fund, Total Stock Market Index, delivered a 32% loss between April 1, 2000, and June 30, 2002. In contrast, the Balanced Index held up much better, losing just 13.5% during that period, thanks to its bond allocation.

Consider Foreign Stocks

Bonds can provide ballast to a portfolio heavy on U.S. equities, but the same is true for foreign equities and foreign bonds. Although the markets of the United States and other developed nations sometimes move in lockstep, that's not always the case, and international investing can add important diversification to a portfolio that will help in a bear market.

We don't expect the U.S. economy or its currency to crumble, but investing a portion of one's assets overseas buys insurance against just that. Could such an economic calamity afflict a major industrial country? Just ask Japanese investors. During the 1980s, the Japanese equity market posted gains that handily exceeded those in the United States. Articles about the superiority of the Japanese economic system, as well as its progressive labor/management relationships, filled the popular press in the United States. Japanese companies were thought to be more farsighted, and there was a consensus (not to mention a slew of best-selling "how-to" books) suggesting that the United States businesses would do well to emulate Japan.

Pity the poor Japanese investor who thought there was no need to invest overseas. From its peak in 1989 to June 30, 2002, the Nikkei index of Japan's major companies shed nearly three fourths of its value. Income-hungry Japanese bond investors haven't done much better. With persistent deflation racking the Japanese economy, the nation's bond-issuers haven't had to offer much in the way of a payout. Indeed, the yields of many high-quality

Japanese issues have been near zero for years. Ask those long-suffering Japanese investors whether it makes sense to diversify and invest a portion of their assets overseas. We are willing to wager that most of them will say "Yes!"

During the 1970s, U.S. investors also benefited greatly from investing overseas. The Watergate political scandal, the bursting of the Nifty Fifty bubble in 1973 and 1974, and economic woes—including rising inflation and interest rates, as well as a weakening dollar—gave U.S. investors several body blows throughout the decade. The main index of foreign shares, MSCI EAFE, handily outpaced the S&P 500 during the period. Compared with those who stuck to investing in the United States, investors who diversified by purchasing foreign stocks and bonds achieved much better returns during that turbulent decade.

The recent bear market also has reminded U.S. investors of the importance of diversifying their investments across borders. For the first half of 2002, the typical foreign-stock fund was down 1.2%, less than one tenth the loss experienced by the S&P 500 index. And foreign funds were down an annualized 3.8% for the trailing three years. The index's loss for the period was roughly two and a half times as much.

What to Do When Your Fund Owns a "Scandal Stock"

One of the things that makes it particularly hard to hold on to your fund in a bear market is that you might find that it owns some companies that went bankrupt or played fast and loose with accounting rules. Unfortunately, even the best managers make mistakes and will get burned by some of their investments. In the 2000–2002 bear market, great managers like Marty Whitman, Wally Weitz, Bill Nygren, Chuck Freeman, and Bill Miller got burned by deceptive accounting. When this happens to one of your funds, you should ask a few questions to figure out if it's an isolated problem or a sign that the manager just isn't doing his homework.

1. Did the Investment Fit with the Fund's Stated Strategy?

Third Avenue Value manager Marty Whitman lost some money on World-Com debt, but that was just what you'd expect from a vulture investor. Whitman makes his living by buying stocks or bonds of companies that the market hates. He knows the ins and outs of bankruptcy laws so he can make sure he's first in line to get paid when a company goes bankrupt. He creates worst-case scenarios and will generally buy only if he thinks he won't lose money in a close-to-worst-case scenario. He bought WorldCom debt rather than stock because he figured bankruptcy was a real possibility. While Third Avenue's WorldCom investment passes this test, others don't. For example, some funds that are supposed to pay attention to valuations bought Enron near its peak when it was trading at extreme valuations. That should have been a red flag, and fraudulent accounting just made matters worse.

2. Was This an Isolated Incident or Was the Portfolio Chock-Full of Mistakes?

Every investor makes mistakes, and it's very difficult to spot all of the accounting games that have been played lately. However, if you find a fund full of companies that were more focused on hype than building a business, you'd have to have some questions.

3. How Badly Did It Hurt the Fund?

We don't get daily portfolios on funds, but returns don't lie. If performance is dreadful, the manager may have doubled down on his bet the way Alliance Premier Growth did with Enron. If you think a manager was window-dressing, take a look at the day a stock blew up and compare the fund's daily return for that day with the return of an appropriate index. If the fund did much worse than the index, the fund probably held the stock that day.

After you've looked at the details of a fund's mistakes, step back and get some perspective. Most funds own a good number of stocks, and a bad investment that loses 1% of assets is hardly a disaster. Take a look at the fund's long-term record to see if the good investments outweigh the bad ones.

4. How Thoroughly Did the Fund Managers Research the Company?

Admittedly, the managers have to help you out on this by publicly commenting on the subject. Sometimes they are surprisingly candid. About 10 years ago, a momentum shop admitted to *Barron's* that is was hoodwinked by a fraudulent company when it said that *Barron's* clearly had researched the company more than the fund shop had. Ugh! More recently, one manager who owned Enron asked, "Who reads footnotes?" Yikes. Conversely, some thoughtful managers go over their reasons in great detail; it's clear they did their homework even when they were wrong.

Plan for Taxes

Although we normally encourage investors to hold tight and continue contributing during market downturns, sometimes you can do yourself a favor by selling. We covered some reasons to sell a fund in Chapter 13, but a big market downturn presents some selling opportunities that investors should not miss.

For one thing, if you're sitting on sizable unrealized losses in taxable accounts, you may wish to recognize some of those losses and give yourself a tax break. To be sure, selling a fund at a loss is no fun, but it is often sensible. What are the advantages of booking these losses? You may use capital losses on your fund or stock sales to offset gains elsewhere in your portfolio.

Selling funds at a loss may make sense even if you are comfortable with your current holdings. By recognizing losses now and gaining the tax benefit, you will have more dollars to invest at the depressed prices available in a bear market. You may be able to take the proceeds of the sale and direct them to better, lower-cost funds.

From a tax perspective, a bear market can also be a great time for investors to rebalance their portfolios. Maybe you realized that your portfolio tilted far too much toward growth funds, and now you want to spread this money across all types of equity offerings, including value funds. Because your growth funds are underwater, you can earn a tax benefit by selling them and shifting assets into value funds. In this situation, you're getting paid to rebalance.

Rebalance

As illustrated in Chapter 12, it's always important to rebalance. But it can be particularly critical during times of great market turmoil, when various asset classes and investment styles may deliver markedly different returns.

An investor who had a well-diversified portfolio split 50/50 between stocks and bonds in March 2000 would have had a very different allocation by the middle of 2002. Because bonds have outperformed equities so handily, that portfolio would probably be closer to 64% bonds and 36% stocks. When the market rebounds, the portfolio probably won't perform as well as it would if the investor had restored the 50/50 split. Furthermore, stocks have tended to deliver higher returns than bonds over long periods of time. A portfolio that has such a hefty bond weighting might be too conservative to deliver the long-term gains the investor needs.

Investing in Bull Markets

Okay, that's enough of the depressing stuff. Most of us invest because we want to make money, not because we want to win relative victories in bear markets. So what is the smart way to make money when the stock market is on the rise? As it turns out, a lot of the precepts that lead to successful investing in bear markets are also important when the bulls are charging.

Diversify

At the risk of sounding like a broken record, diversification is no less important in a bull market than in a bear one. Ignore the market commentators and self-styled prognosticators who say they have identified the slice of the market that has outperformed and will continue to beat the market in the future. What they are really advocating is a strategy of buying when prices are already high, which is never a smart investment approach.

For example, pity the poor (and getting poorer) shareholders in Bob Markman's funds. Markman frequently ridiculed the importance of diversification, and in the late 1990s preached that large-growth stocks, especially those in technology, were the only place to invest. Shareholders at his funds, including Markman Aggressive Allocation, have gotten pummeled during the bear market, and his funds' long-term returns are now among the worst in their respective Morningstar categories.

Rebalance

Even if you don't willfully hike your exposure to hot-performing asset classes during a bull market, a failure to rebalance can produce much the same results. If an investor had built a well-diversified portfolio in the mid-1990s—split between value and growth funds, stocks and bonds, domestic and international—without rebalancing, it would have become dangerously focused by 2000. Growth handily outperformed value, stocks beat bonds, and domestic stocks and bonds outperformed international investments. An investor would have had a lot of exposure to all the asset classes and investment styles that got pummeled during the bear market.

Unfortunately, there is often a cost to rebalancing in a bull market. If one asset class or investment style handily tops another, you may have to sell some appreciated holdings to rebalance, thereby incurring some taxable capital gains. Still, if you talk with investors who had large-growth-heavy portfolios as the bear market began, they will probably tell you they wish they had focused less on their tax bills and more on diversification.

The good news is that there are some tax-friendly ways to rebalance during a bull market. One is to use new contributions to rebalance your portfolio. In this scenario, an investor who needed to up an allocation to value funds in the late 1990s could have done so, at least in part, by directing new contributions to those offerings, instead of selling growth-fund shares at a gain.

You can also use taxable and tax-sheltered accounts in tandem to minimize the tax impact of rebalancing. An investor with a too-heavy stock allocation in the late 1990s might have sold off some equity funds in an IRA or 401(k) and redeployed that money into bonds. During a bull market, it makes sense to use a tax-protected account for rebalancing.

If rebalancing forces you to sell shares out of a taxable account, you may be able to use a technique called "specific identification" to cut your tax bill. That refers to some fund companies' policies of allowing investors to select specific shares of a fund to sell. For example, if your fund currently has an NAV (net asset value, or price per share) of $20 and you own shares that you bought at $12.50 and $17 per share, sell the $17 shares. Your gain will be less and so will your tax bill. If your fund company allows this (and a large number of shops ranging from Stein Roe to Vanguard do so), you may identify and sell shares with the highest cost basis, which will effectively limit your gains and cut your tax bill.

As a general rule, you should keep a close eye on the tax consequences of trading of any kind during a bull market. Whereas it is often sensible to trade out of a fund and recognize a tax loss during a bear market, the opposite is sometimes true in a bull market. Investors who sold value funds in taxable accounts during the late 1990s (often to chase performance and buy growth offerings) frequently faced significant tax bills as a result. As mentioned, rebalancing is important, but swapping wholesale out of a fund because you're trying to trade up isn't the same thing. If you have to pay a big tax bill because you sold a fund, the fund you replace it with has to be much better than the one you sold. You have to have a fund that not only is better than the one you sold, but also is good enough to earn back the extra taxes you paid. After paying the tax bill to sell, you'll be investing less money than you otherwise would have, and that can hurt in a bull market.

Aside from taxes, another cost that deserves attention in bull markets is a fund's expense ratio. Investors tend to pay more attention to fund costs when returns are modest and expenses would eat up a higher percentage of their returns. But in actual dollars, a higher expense ratio costs more in vigorous bull markets than in times of more moderate returns because of the effects of compounding.

Use Common Sense

It's also important to use common sense during a bull market. Investors who ignored technology stocks when the Nasdaq Composite index stood at 1,500 were rushing to buy in when the Nasdaq reached 5,000. Sure, technology stocks were growing rapidly, but did it make sense to be more interested in tech shares after they had become three times more expensive? Investors sometimes forget that when they buy stocks, they are actually acquiring small stakes in businesses. If you had an eye on purchasing a local restaurant for $2 million and the owner raised its price to $6 million, would you be more interested in buying it? Of course not. Yet, investors frequently make that very mistake when they are buying stocks.

That is particularly unfortunate because in the late 1990s, companies in many less sexy industries like banking and manufacturing had continued to post earnings gains, even though their stock prices had faltered. Therefore, relative to the earnings power of those businesses, their share prices were getting increasingly cheaper. Yet investors were selling these so-called Old Economy stocks in droves to shift money into what were, in hindsight, very overpriced technology shares. Using our hypothetical example, if the restaurant's price went from $2 million to $1 million even as its operating fundamentals improved, buying it would make even more sense than before. But many investors sized up the stocks of these dowdy, slow-growth firms and made the opposite decision.

Keep It Simple

As illustrated, certain investment precepts are sensible in both bull and bear markets. Keep a strong focus on the things you as an investor can control. Buying low-cost funds gives you an edge. Sticking to an investment plan and continuing to buy shares, even in a big market downturn, makes sense. Maintaining a well-diversified portfolio lowers risk, and in many cases, it enhances returns. Finally, you can't control the short-term movements of the market, but you can exercise considerable discretion over how much you invest. Many poor investment decisions result because investors feel as if they haven't saved enough and therefore need to take extra-large chances to acquire an adequate nest egg. Slow and steady usually wins the race, in both bull and bear markets.

Investor's Checklist: Keep a Cool Head in Turbulent Markets

► Market-timing doesn't work. Whether you are in a bear or bull market, stick to your long-term plan and rebalance accordingly.

► Dollar-cost averaging can be a particularly powerful way to invest in a down market because you are automatically buying as prices decline.

► Be sure to maintain a properly diversified portfolio, whatever the market. For most investors that means investing in a variety of stock types—large and small, growth and value, U.S. and foreign—and owning bonds for stability.

► Don't overdo bond exposure in a bear market. Because bonds will be outpacing stocks, they could become too big a portion of your portfolio, meaning that you won't benefit as much from a stock's rebound as you otherwise might.

► Do sell to give yourself a tax break. Watch out for the wash-sale rule: You don't get to write off your loss if you buy the fund back within 30 days.

► To limit taxes in a bull market, rebalance by investing new money and making the biggest shifts in tax-protected accounts.

► Limit bull-market taxes by selling higher-cost shares first to minimize the size of your taxable gain.

► Be wary of trying to trade up in a bull market. If you incur a taxable gain, your new fund will have to be dramatically better to make up for the tax hit.

► Don't neglect expenses—they cost you whether the market is up or down.

PART FIVE

Bringing It All Together: Morningstar Portfolios

15

Look Inside Morningstar's Portfolios

PICKING GREAT FUNDS is the fun part of the investment process. After all, what fund junkie isn't thrilled to know that Oakmark's Bill Nygren or the folks at Tweedy, Browne are managing part of his or her portfolio? On the other hand, building diversified portfolios is, to put it nicely, less fun.

Yet, putting great funds together into a cohesive portfolio is a critical and underappreciated part of the investment process. No one fund can do it all for you, prospering when different kinds of stocks are thriving and holding up when stocks are in the doghouse. Thus, it's important to hold a mix of investments appropriate for your specific goal.

You have acquired a lot of knowledge from this book that you can use to build your own portfolio from scratch. But you don't have to start from zero. Taking our Morningstar portfolios, culled from our fund newsletter, *Morningstar FundInvestor,* and adjusting them to fit your needs is an easier way to target your goals.

We have created three portfolios—diversified mixes of some of our favorite funds for investors with short-, medium-, and long-term time horizons.

Our Aggressive Wealth Maker Portfolio is geared toward investors with 10- to 20-year time horizons and features an aggressive 85% equity/15% bond allocation. Moderate investors with time horizons of five to 10 years are the target audience for our Wealth Maker Portfolio, which features a 65% equity/35% bond allocation. Finally, our Wealth Keeper is designed to do just what its name suggests. Because it's geared toward investors who place a premium on capital preservation, it holds 65% of its assets in fixed income funds and 35% in stock funds.

With all the portfolios, our goal is to let fund selection shine through. As a result, we generally avoid bets on a given style or sector; we aren't gambling on the short-term direction of the market. Instead, the idea is to maintain a mix of funds that you can stick with in varied markets.

Using the Portfolios

You can adopt one of the portfolios wholesale. But because we're hesitant to make one-size-fits-all recommendations, we urge investors to adjust the asset allocations of any of the portfolios to suit their goals and risk tolerance. For example, if you're an aggressive investor who's attracted to indexing, you might stick with the same basic fund lineup that appears in our Wealth Maker Portfolio, but ratchet up its equity weighting and take smaller positions in bond funds. We recommend rebalancing once a year to restore your target asset-allocation mix.

To help investors who want to replicate the portfolios, we have avoided those funds whose minimums are too high to fit within the framework of a total investment of $100,000. Instead, investors can purchase all the funds in our portfolios in smaller increments, either by buying directly from the specific fund company or by going through a fund supermarket. Finally, we avoid closed funds.

Our Fund-Selection Process

In selecting the funds for the portfolios, we look at all the usual factors: strong past performance, moderate costs, manageable asset bases, and bright managers with good analysts behind them. Essentially, we look at the same factors we highlighted in earlier chapters of this book.

Putting the Pieces Together

In bringing funds together in our portfolios, we sought out offerings that complement one another. As a result, we have excluded a number of funds that are every bit as good as the ones in our portfolios. That's because we didn't want our aggregate stock portfolio to take big bets—either in sector weightings or market capitalization—versus the broad market as represented by the Wilshire 5000 total stock market index.

If one of our value funds owns a lot of financials, for example, another of our value funds might be underweight in the sector to neutralize our overall portfolio's weighting there. In a similar vein, we strive to remain neutral to the market capitalization breakdown of the Wilshire 5000. That way, we avoid making bets on small companies, for example.

In determining how a fund fits with the others, we have also tried to account for where a fund is headed. For example, we expected Oakmark Fund to gradually increase its weighting in large caps as more investors took note of manager Bill Nygren's talents, so the portfolios in which that fund appears were set up to accommodate more large-cap exposure.

Here are descriptions of each of our three portfolios, along with discussions of their component funds and what investors should be looking out for.

Aggressive Wealth Maker Portfolio

Because this portfolio (outlined in Figure 15.1) is geared to investors whose goals are far off and who are willing to take on more risk, we aren't hemming our managers in. Most of the funds we've picked will make aggressive bets at times. The portfolio features an 85% equity, 15% bond asset allocation.

Harbor Capital Appreciation (Large Growth)

This fund is by no means small, but Sig Segalas and his team at Jennison Associates deserve a lot of credit. Few growth-oriented funds have managed to be as consistent as this one; with the exception of its slight underperformance in 2000, it has landed in the top half of the large-cap growth category year-in and year-out. We chalk that up to the deep research team at Jennison, which has driven superior stock-picking, as well as Segalas' attention to diversification. We also like that this fund's expenses are low relative to other actively managed large-growth funds. Within the context of our Aggressive

Fund Name	Category	% of Assets
Harbor Capital Appreciation	Large-Cap Growth	20.00
Artisan International	Foreign Stock	15.00
Dodge & Cox Income	Intermediate-Term Bond	15.00
Turner Midcap Growth	Mid-Cap Growth	10.00
Oakmark I	Mid-Cap Value	10.00
Selected American	Large-Cap Value	10.00
ICAP Select Equity	Large-Cap Value	10.00
Third Avenue Small-Cap Value	Small Value	5.00
Managers Special Equity	Small Growth	5.00
Portfolio Total	—	*100.00*

Aggressive Wealth Maker Portfolio Analysis

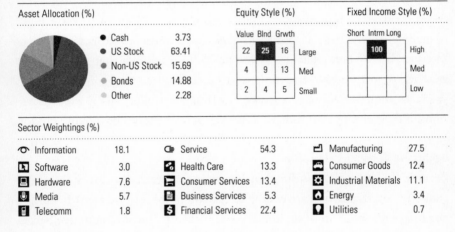

Asset Allocation (%)

● Cash	3.73
● US Stock	63.41
● Non-US Stock	15.69
● Bonds	14.88
● Other	2.28

Equity Style (%)

Value	Blnd	Grwth	
22	25	16	Large
4	9	13	Med
2	4	5	Small

Fixed Income Style (%)

Short	Intrm	Long	
100			High
			Med
			Low

Sector Weightings (%)

● Information	18.1		● Service	54.3		● Manufacturing	27.5
● Software	3.0		● Health Care	13.3		● Consumer Goods	12.4
● Hardware	7.6		● Consumer Services	13.4		● Industrial Materials	11.1
● Media	5.7		● Business Services	5.3		● Energy	3.4
● Telecomm	1.8		● Financial Services	22.4		● Utilities	0.7

Figure 15.1 Morningstar's Aggressive Wealth Maker Portfolio. Fund holdings are current as of 9-30-02 and subject to change. Updated portfolios can be found in *Morningstar® FundInvestor*™.

Wealth Maker Portfolio, this fund gives exposure to mega-cap, high-quality growth companies. (Selected American is also a mega-cap portfolio, but its picks lean toward the value side of the spectrum.)

Turner Midcap Growth (Mid-Cap Growth)

Although this offering's bear-market returns have been terrible, it's worthwhile looking past its weak defensive prowess because of the fund's potential to thrive when growth stocks rule the roost. Manager Chris McHugh and the team at Turner are disciplined investors who focus on companies that are delivering accelerating growth, solid fundamentals, and price momentum, and they don't shy away from stocks with high price tags. That unwavering focus on growth has helped this offering deliver topflight returns in growth-led markets. Although the fund's steep losses over the past few years should scare off hot money for the time being, keep an eye on this fund's asset size when growth investing takes off. Our research has shown that momentum-driven styles can be particularly vulnerable to asset bloat.

Dodge & Cox Income (Intermediate-Term Bond)

Although the Aggressive Wealth Maker Portfolio is designed to take on a fair amount of risk in exchange for strong long-term returns, we wanted our sole bond holding, at 15% of assets, to be a model of stability. This venerable offering fits the bill. Like all Dodge & Cox offerings, it uses a management team approach, with 11 manager-analysts contributing bond research. The presence of such a deep bench lessens the risk that any one individual's departure will undermine this offering's nearly unbroken string of successful years. Management spreads the portfolio across all major areas of the fixed-income market, but has historically emphasized corporate bonds over government issues—a tactic that has enabled the firm's credit research to shine through. Low expenses—a critical consideration for bond funds—seal its appeal.

Artisan International (Foreign Stock)

Although some foreign-stock managers have a doctrinaire focus on growth or value, this fund has managed to survive—and thrive—in varied market conditions. For example, this was a rare foreign fund that stayed in the game in 1999's go-go market but also held its own when technology and telecommunications stocks took a powder in the ensuing years. That all-weather quality is what made it a natural choice for the sole international option in our Aggressive Wealth Maker Portfolio. Manager Mark Yockey's phenomenal success has attracted a lot of cash, though, so keep an eye on whether growing assets are crimping his investment style.

Oakmark Fund (Large Value)

This fund's fortunes took a turn for the better the day Bill Nygren took the helm in early 2000. Nygren's record on the closed Oakmark Select, as well as his contributions as Oakmark's director of research, lead us to believe that he's one of the most talented managers of his generation. We picked this fund for the Aggressive Wealth Maker Portfolio with the expectation that it would increasingly focus on large-cap stocks. Although its charter allows Nygren to invest in both mid- and large-cap stocks, the fund has been getting a lot of new assets in the door, prompting him to gravitate toward larger-cap names.

ICAP Select Equity (Large Value)

Manager Rob Lyon isn't as well known as Bill Miller (Legg Mason Value) or Bill Nygren (Oakmark Fund, Oakmark Select), but we think his fine value funds deserve to be on investors' radars. Although this offering's track record is fairly short, Lyon and his team have built a dazzling record at sibling ICAP Equity, and this concentrated offering should be just as good, if not better. Along with Oakmark Fund, this fund gives the Aggressive Wealth Maker Portfolio exposure to some deep-value stocks, including a healthy dose of financials and cyclicals. But this is a fairly young fund and a concentrated one to boot. Keep an eye on outsized sector or stock bets, and consider making a change if a bet becomes too extreme.

Selected American (Large Blend)

This offering is coming off a rough stretch, but it would be hard to overlook it when assembling a basket of our favorite funds. Simply put, Chris Davis and Ken Feinberg are among the most talented managers working today. Their record on both this offering and sibling and near-clone Davis New York Venture has been superb. Davis and Feinberg focus on buying great companies on the cheap. They have recently boosted the firm's research efforts in tech and health care, and will likely devote more assets to these areas than in the past. For managers like these, who hate to sell, investing in rapidly changing sectors may present a new challenge. Another issue is asset growth. Davis Advisors has recently added to its analyst staff, so that could help the firm's funds grow gracefully.

Managers Special Equity (Small Growth)

This fund is different from others we're highlighting—it draws on the talents of managers from several different firms who each run a portion of the assets.

The subadvisors' specialties run from go-go growth to value investing. The overall mix is growth leaning, but less daring than many other small-growth offerings. The result has been greater consistency than its competition. The fund rarely posts a subpar year, regardless of the market environment. That has spelled great long-term returns and a smoother ride than most competitors offer. Because the portfolio is spread among managers with different styles, this fund can handle more money than most, but asset growth could prove a liability.

Third Avenue Small-Cap Value (Small Value)

For the small-cap value role in the portfolio, we turned to a shop that knows this area as well as any other: Third Avenue Funds. Although this offering is run by Curtis Jensen, instead of value-investing legend (and Third Avenue Value manager) Marty Whitman, we liked its explicit focus on smaller companies. The key issue to watch out for with this fund is simple: Is Jensen as good as Whitman? With Whitman's guidance, Jensen has done just fine, but Whitman is more than 70 years old and plans to gradually turn over more responsibility to Jensen. Keep tabs on how Jensen fares.

Wealth Maker Portfolio

This portfolio (see Figure 15.2) is suitable for investors who have shorter time horizons or aren't comfortable enough with volatility to follow our aggressive portfolio. This mix devotes more to bonds (35% of the portfolio versus 15%) and focuses on funds that don't make big style bets, such as index funds.

At Morningstar, we have always argued that index and actively managed funds can coexist peacefully in a portfolio. We have both in our company 401(k) plan, and we brought them together in the Wealth Maker Portfolio, too. Around the Vanguard stock and bond index funds that form the core of this portfolio, we've included actively managed funds whose managers have done a good job of adding value in their market segments. We chose active managers in the small-cap and international realms, for example, where we have found the benefits of indexing to be less clear-cut. Thus, an investor who already has significant index exposure might consider supplementing it with one of these fine actively managed funds.

Fund Name	Category	% of Assets
Vanguard Total Bond Market Index	Intermediate-Term Bond	25.00
Vanguard 500 Index	Large-Cap Blend	20.00
Oakmark I	Mid-Cap Value	15.00
Janus Mercury	Large-Cap Growth	15.00
Tweedy Browne Global Value	Foreign Stock	10.00
Western Asset Core	Intermediate-Term Bond	10.00
T. Rowe Price Small-Cap Stock	Small-Cap Blend	5.00
Portfolio Total	—	*100.00*

Wealth Maker Portfolio Analysis

Asset Allocation (%)

Cash	4.57
US Stock	51.99
Non-US Stock	9.46
Bonds	31.64
Other	2.33

Equity Style (%)

Value	Blnd	Grwth	
21	28	20	Large
6	7	8	Med
5	3	2	Small

Fixed Income Style (%)

Short	Intrm	Long	
	100		High
			Med
			Low

Sector Weightings (%)

Information	21.8	Service	50.8	Manufacturing	27.3
Software	2.6	Health Care	15.3	Consumer Goods	10.7
Hardware	7.4	Consumer Services	10.1	Industrial Materials	10.2
Media	9.7	Business Services	6.2	Energy	4.6
Telecomm	2.1	Financial Services	19.3	Utilities	2.0

Figure 15.2 Morningstar's Wealth Maker Portfolio. Fund holdings are current as of 9-30-02 and subject to change. Updated portfolios can be found in *Morningstar® FundInvestor™*.

Vanguard Total Bond Market Index (Intermediate-Term Bond)

In the bond world, staying cheap is the best way to improve your chances of success. To underscore that point, we made Vanguard's ultracheap bond index fund one of the centerpieces of our Wealth Maker Portfolio. Going for low expenses hasn't meant settling for less, either: This offering's returns have been extremely competitive with those of other intermediate-term bond funds.

Vanguard 500 Index (Large Blend)

We also like this fund's sibling, Vanguard Total Stock Market Index, for investors who like the simplicity of indexing, but we opted for this offering instead because it gives the portfolio more exposure to the market's biggest stocks. Further, the committee that assembles the S&P 500 index often eschews the most speculative stocks, many of which have flamed out in spectacular fashion over the past two years. And, of course, rock-bottom costs help cut the drag that expenses can put on returns.

Oakmark Fund (Large Value)

This fund lands in the Wealth Maker Portfolio for many of the same reasons we picked it for the Aggressive Wealth Maker Portfolio. Again, Bill Nygren is simply one of the most talented managers in the business. In this portfolio, the fund provides the bulk of our value exposure and complements the growth-oriented Janus Mercury quite well.

Janus Mercury (Large Growth)

Since the bull market collapsed in March 2000, everyone seems to hate Janus. We believe that many of the firm's funds are still solid choices in a well-diversified portfolio. And there can be little doubt that Warren Lammert—one of the firm's most senior managers—knows how to get the most out of a growth-stock rally. Thus, when growth rebounds, we expect to see this fund perform extremely well. If it doesn't deliver the goods, that will be cause for concern. Finally, watch for that biggest of scourges at Janus: asset growth. Even with the outflows they've suffered, the funds are big, and a strong rally could bring in many new investors.

Tweedy, Browne Global Value (Foreign Stock)

This value-leaning foreign-stock fund does not participate much when growth stocks rally, but that's okay with us. For the Wealth Maker Portfolio, which is generally more conservative than the Aggressive Wealth Maker Portfolio, we wanted a foreign-stock fund that was fairly conservative, too. The folks at Tweedy, Browne stick mainly with developed markets, focus on stocks without much price risk, and maintain an extremely diversified portfolio, all of which have kept a lid on volatility. To boot, management has lots of experience, smarts, and motivation to perform well. The fund could underperform should the U.S. dollar lose strength—management hedges all of its foreign-currency exposure back into the dollar—but that's a risk we're willing to take. And studies show that, over the long term, the impact of hedging or not on a fund's returns is pretty much a wash.

Western Asset Core (Intermediate-Term Bond)

Western Asset Management, this fund's advisor, isn't as familiar to retail bond investors as PIMCO, but it's a heavyweight in the world of institutional bond-fund management. Management uses all the tools at its disposal—duration bets, yield-curve and sector plays, and issue selection—to add value versus its competitors. Although some of these maneuvers have led to short-term setbacks, management's bond picks have typically been spot-on.

T. Rowe Price Small Cap Stock (Small Blend)

We chose this fund because manager Greg McCrickard delivers steady performance with a mix of value and growth stocks. Under his guidance, this fund has tended to edge ahead of the pack, with a knack for finishing most years in the small-blend group's top half. The result has been well-above-average, long-term returns without too much volatility. The one thing to watch out for here is growing assets interfering with performance.

Wealth Keeper Portfolio

This portfolio (see Figure 15.3) is designed for investors who don't want to completely miss out on the returns that stocks can deliver but whose primary focus is on preserving their principal. Thus, the portfolio is conservative not just in its 35% equity, 65% bond asset allocation, but also in the types of funds we chose for it. We steered clear of funds that make big bets, instead favoring offerings with disciplined strategies, stable management teams, and a history of consistent returns within their respective categories.

At the Wealth Keeper Portfolio's core is a fund that epitomizes all those qualities: the superb Dodge & Cox Income, an intermediate-term bond fund. We've supplemented that with another core bond position in Vanguard Total Bond Market Index and smaller, "kicker" positions in three more specialized bond funds that add variety and could boost returns. For the core equity positions, we've paired a growth fund, ABN AMRO/Montag & Caldwell Growth, with a traditional value fund, T. Rowe Price Equity-Income. We've taken smaller positions in the small- and mid-cap-focused

Fund Name	Category	% of Assets
Dodge & Cox Income	Intermediate-Term Bond	25.00
Vanguard Total Bond Market Index	Intermediate-Term Bond	17.50
T. Rowe Price Equity-Income	Large-Cap Value	13.00
ABN AMRO/Montag & Caldwell Growth N	Large-Cap Growth	13.00
Fidelity Short-Term Bond	Short-Term Bond	10.00
Northeast Investors	High-Yield Bond	7.50
Vanguard Inflation-Protected Securities	Short-Term Gov't Bond	5.00
Selected Special	Mid-Cap Blend	5.00
Julius Baer International Equity A	Foreign Stock	4.00
Portfolio Total	—	*100.00*

Wealth Keeper Portfolio Analysis

Asset Allocation (%)

- Cash — 4.13
- US Stock — 29.52
- Non-US Stock — 3.95
- Bonds — 61.15
- Other — 1.24

Equity Style (%)

Value	Blnd	Grwth	
19	38	17	Large
7	13	4	Med
	2		Small

Fixed Income Style (%)

Short	Intrm	Long	
8	66		High
16			Med
		10	Low

Sector Weightings (%)

Information	15.1	Service	41.8	Manufacturing	40.8
Software	1.8	Health Care	12.6	Consumer Goods	19.4
Hardware	4.2	Consumer Services	7.0	Industrial Materials	12.1
Media	4.9	Business Services	7.1	Energy	7.3
Telecomm	4.3	Financial Services	14.9	Utilities	2.0

Figure 15.3 Morningstar's Wealth Keeper Portfolio. Fund holdings are current as of 9-30-02 and subject to change. Updated portfolios can be found in *Morningstar® FundInvestor™*.

Selected Special and in Julius Baer International Equity, a versatile though little-known foreign-stock fund.

Dodge & Cox Income (Intermediate-Term Bond)
This fund is stability defined. Its management team is experienced and skilled, and its results have landed near the front of the intermediate-term bond pack year-in and year-out. Management generally shies away from big bets and instead has let research-based security selection drive results here.

The portfolio has long emphasized corporate over government bonds because management's strong credit research enables the fund to get a few extra basis points of yield without taking on a lot of additional risk. We're so comfortable with that approach, in fact, that we gave this offering greater prominence in our portfolio than Vanguard Total Bond Market Index. Low expenses seal this fund's appeal as a terrific core bond holding.

Vanguard Total Bond Market Index (Intermediate-Term Bond)

Vanguard's ultracheap bond index fund is one of the centerpieces of this portfolio. The fund's broad diversification, solid management, and low expenses make it tough to beat.

ABN AMRO/Montag & Caldwell Growth (Large Growth)

Growth funds have been a dicey proposition since early 2000, but this offering has managed to hold up much better than the rest. Manager Ron Canakaris didn't follow many of his growth-fund peers into speculative stocks in the late 1990s, sticking instead with his usual emphasis on high-quality mega-cap companies. The merits of that approach are evident in this offering's fine long-term returns. This fund might lag higher-octane growth offerings when technology stocks rule the roost, but that's a price we're willing to pay in exchange for its relatively smooth ride.

T. Rowe Price Equity-Income (Large Value)

Even as many of his rivals were throwing in the towel on dividend-focused strategies in the late 1990s, manager Brian Rogers stuck with his stodgy approach, and shareholders in this offering have been the better for it. The dividend-paying stocks Rogers favors are usually selling at very cheap price multiples relative to the market, which has enabled the fund to hold up quite well when pricier fare takes a dive. Rogers' emphasis on deep-value stocks means this offering is bound to look a bit slow in big growth rallies, but we think it's a terrific core stock fund for conservative investors.

Fidelity Short-Term Bond (Short-Term Bond)

Short-term bond funds are supposed to be conservative. Investors can park money in them without worrying too much about losing money. This fund fits the requirement exactly. Any short-term fund could have a losing year, but this one hasn't since Andrew Dudley took the helm in 1997. Dudley succeeds through caution. He takes on only small amounts of interest-rate and credit risk and keeps the portfolio spread across hundreds of bonds. He focuses on adding incremental gains through issue selection. The fund's modest expense ratio is real plus.

Northeast Investors (High-Yield Bond)

No doubt about it: High-yield bond funds have struggled in recent years. This fund has avoided the worst of the downturn, however, thanks to management's decision to downplay the hard-hit telecommunications sector. Chalk that wise move up to experience: Comanagers Bruce and Ernest Monrad are among the most seasoned hands in the category. The fund focuses on lower-rated bonds than many of its peers, but we're confident that management will continue to steer clear of the sector's diciest areas.

Selected Special (Mid-Cap Blend)

This fund recently underwent a management change, but we're excited about its prospects under the team of Chris Davis and Ken Feinberg. Unlike their large-cap charges, Selected American and Davis New York Venture, this one focuses on faster-growing companies in the mid-cap realm. The fund's latitude to range across small- and mid-cap names, both growth- and value-oriented, made it an appealing choice as the sole small- to mid-cap option in the Wealth Keeper Portfolio.

Vanguard Inflation-Protected Securities (Intermediate Government Bond)

This fund focuses on a relatively new asset class, Treasury Inflation-Protected Securities (TIPS), which are great diversifiers for a bond portfolio. The beauty of TIPS (and funds that focus on them) is that they stand to fare well at the very time conventional bonds are suffering—when inflation fears are on the rise and interest rates are heading up—because they're set up to allow the bond's principal to adjust to keep up with inflation. Although many investors obtain Treasury exposure by buying individual bonds, buying a TIPS fund instead is a smart strategy because the TIPS market is still fairly new and inefficient, giving skilled managers a decided advantage.

Julius Baer International Equity (Foreign Stock)

This little-known fund deserves to be on investors' radars, so we featured it as the sole foreign-stock option in the Wealth Keeper Portfolio. We like management's versatile, free-ranging strategy; this is a rare fund that stayed in the game in the growth-led market of 1999, for example, but didn't flame out in the ensuing sell-off. In fact, the current team here has delivered top-third results in every calendar year since they came aboard in 1995. Management's penchant for bold positions could get it into trouble—it currently holds a big stake in Eastern Europe, for example—but we've liked what we've seen here thus far.

PART SIX

More on Mutual Funds: Frequently Asked Questions

1. How Does the Morningstar Rating for Mutual Funds Work?

SUCCESSFUL INVESTING BEGINS with building a good plan. The Morningstar Rating (often known as the "star rating") helps investors assemble a multiple-fund, well-diversified portfolio and guides them to funds that have provided shareholders with superior risk-adjusted returns. Though investors should not buy or sell funds on the basis of the star rating alone, it is a quick and easy way to identify funds worthy of further research.

The Morningstar Rating for funds is a measure of a fund's risk-adjusted past performance, relative to similar funds, as classified within each of Morningstar's 50 categories. Funds are rated from 1 to 5 stars, with the best performers receiving 5 stars and the worst performers receiving a single star. We grade on a curve so that there are as many 5-star funds as 1-star funds in each category.

Although our star rating was designed by finance PhDs, you don't need to go back to school to use it as a guide for selecting superior mutual funds. The star rating helps investors determine which funds have best compensated shareholders for the risks the managers have taken. It is calculated by subtracting a risk penalty from each fund's total return, after accounting for all loads, sales charges, and redemption fees. The risk penalty is determined by the variation in the fund's monthly return, with emphasis on downward variation. The greater the variation, the larger the penalty. This rewards consistent performance and reduces the possibility of strong short-term performance masking the inherent risk of a fund.

Once we calculate the risk-adjusted return for all funds in a category, we rank them according to the results. Funds with scores in the top 10% earn 5 stars; the next 22.5%, 4 stars; the middle 35%, 3 stars; the next 22.5%, 2 stars; and the bottom 10%, 1 star.

Only funds that have a 3-year record receive a star rating. Funds are rated for up to three periods, the trailing 3-, 5-, and 10-year periods, and ratings are recalculated each month. For funds that remain in the same Morningstar category for the entire evaluation period, the following weights are used to calculate an overall rating:

Age of Fund	Overall Rating
At least 3 years, but less than 5	100% 3-year rating
At least 5 years, but less than 10	60% 5-year rating
	40% 3-year rating
At least 10 years	50% 10-year rating
	30% 5-year rating
	20% 3-year rating

If a fund changes Morningstar categories, its long-term historical performance is given less weight, based on the magnitude of the change. (For example, a change from a mid-cap category to large-cap category is considered less significant than a change from small-cap to large-cap.) Doing so ensures the fairest comparisons and discourages fund companies from changing a fund's style and shifting to another Morningstar category in an attempt to receive a better rating.

Important Things to Remember When Using the Rating

▶ The star rating is a strictly quantitative measure—a high rating doesn't imply the approval or endorsement of a fund by a Morningstar analyst.

▶ The rating is based on the fund's historical performance. Not only does the boilerplate warning about past performance not guaranteeing future returns apply here, but a highly rated fund may no longer have the same portfolio manager or employ the same strategy responsible for that performance.

▶ Because funds are rated within their respective categories, not all 5-star funds are equal. A star sector fund, for example, might have the best risk-adjusted return within its specific category, but it's probably far more risky than a highly rated diversified fund.

▶ The star rating is time sensitive and can change as new fund and category data evolve. (See the response to Question 2 for more information on this subject.)

Instead of selecting funds based solely on their ratings, investors should use them as an initial screen to help develop an overall portfolio strategy and to identify funds worthy of further research.

2. What Should I Do When My Fund Loses a Star?

SIT DOWN AND take a deep breath. Above all, don't panic and immediately sell your shares in the fund.

Though the star rating system has helped build Morningstar's name, we recognize its limitations. It's not intended to provide investors with strict buy/sell recommendations for funds. It is merely a quantitative tool helpful in analyzing a fund's past performance. Therefore, a fund's star rating should only be used as the first step in a wider analysis of a fund.

When a fund's star rating slips, it implies that the fund's risk-adjusted returns relative to its category peers have declined. However, that may not actually be the case. And even if the fund's relative performance has declined, that may not warrant a decision to exit the fund.

A fund's star rating can fluctuate for a couple of reasons. A star rating is based on trailing risk-adjusted returns for a fund and its category that are re-calculated each month. (See the answer to Question 1 for more information.) As an exceptionally strong or weak month of performance for a fund enters into the calculation or is excluded from it, risk-adjusted trailing returns can vary greatly. If the other funds in the category did not experience as much change due to the new time period, the fund's rank within the category could change and so, too, could its star rating. Since we adhere to strict cutoffs for a fund's relative ranking the fund's star rating can change even if its relative ranking has only changed slightly. For example, if a fund's ranking fell from the top 9% to the top 12% of its category, the fund's star rating would decline from five to four stars. A change such as this probably doesn't merit raising a red flag.

Similarly, a fund with a 4-year 11-month record will establish a 5-year record the following month and the calculation for its star rating will change from one based on its 3-year record to one based on its 5-year record. This change could potentially have even more dramatic consequences for the fund's star rating than the simple changes attributable to monthly recalculations described previously. If the fund had a terrible record during its first two years, that legacy suddenly appears in the calculation of its star rating. In such a case, the fund's star rating may very well decline, but it may not reflect the strength of more recent performance.

Clearly, a decline in a fund's star rating should not be read as an automatic sell signal. It is a warning sign that merits further research. Even if that analysis reveals that the fund's performance relative to its peers has slipped considerably, you must still think carefully about whether to sell it. You have to consider the possible alternatives, which is where the real fun begins. Sure, there are higher rated funds, but are you comfortable with the strategies the managers of the outperforming funds have used to garner these superior results? And speaking of managers, are the track records for the managers of the outperforming funds strong enough to earn your trust that they can continue to outpace the field? Also analyze the fund shops of the higher-rated funds. Do they have stronger or weaker reputations than the fund family whose fund you are considering selling? Are their track records longer or shorter? Finally, don't forget to consider the tax consequences of selling your fund.

When a fund loses a star, you should probably start to monitor the fund more closely than you did in the past. Since the change may only be transitory, you certainly don't want to act rashly. You should try to determine the cause for the change and what it means for your portfolio. Though this means some additional work, it's your money that's at stake and your time will be well spent.

3. How Does Morningstar's Style Box Work?

THE STYLE BOX is a tool that represents the characteristics of a security in a graphical format. For stocks and stock funds, two pieces of data determine where the security falls within the style box. One is market capitalization: how large or small a company is. Large companies show up in the top row of the style box, middle-size companies show up in the middle row, and small companies show up in the bottom row.

The other factor that determines a security's placement in the style box is its investment style. Investment style is based on a growth score and a value score. Half of a stock's growth score is based on its long-term projected earnings growth relative to other stocks in its market-cap range. The remainder of the growth score is based on a combination of historical earnings growth, sales growth, cash flow growth, and book value growth relative to the stocks in its market-cap range. The resulting score will range from 0 to 100. Half of a stock's value score is based on its price-to-projected earnings relative to other stocks in its market-cap range. The remainder of the value score is based on a combination of price-to-book, price-to-sales, price-to-cash flow, and dividend yield relative to the stocks in its market-cap range. This score will also range from 0 to 100.

Morningstar arrives at a stock's investment style by subtracting its value score from its growth score. A stock with a strongly negative score is assigned to value and one with a strongly positive score is assigned to growth. Those in between land in the core column of the style box (for funds, this is known as the blend column). The breakpoints can vary over time but, on average, each style will account for one third of the stocks in each market-cap range.

A stock mutual fund's style-box position is based on all the stocks in its portfolio. The portfolio's market cap is based on the geometric mean of the portfolio. That calculation takes the market cap of each stock and its weighting in the portfolio into account to come up with a number that best represents how the fund is positioned. The portfolio's overall stock style is based on the weighted average of the style scores for all its stocks (the weighting is based on the percentage of the portfolio each stock takes up). Funds with averages on the low side land in the value column, those on the high side land in growth, and those in between are blend.

The Fixed-Income Style Box

The fixed-income style box is a nine-square box that pulls together credit quality and duration. The style box allows investors to quickly gauge the risk exposure of their bond fund. The horizontal axis of the fixed-income style box displays a fund's interest-rate sensitivity, as measured by the average duration of all the bonds in its portfolio. Morningstar breaks interest-rate sensitivity into three groups: short, intermediate, and long. Short-term bond funds are the least affected by interest-rate movements and thus the least volatile. Long-term funds are the most volatile. Taxable-bond funds (as opposed to municipal-bond funds, which are protected from taxes) with average durations of less than 3.5 years fall in the short-term column; those with average durations longer than 6 years fall in the long-term column. Everything else is intermediate. (The cutoffs for municipal-bond funds are slightly different, but not appreciably so.)

The vertical axis of the style box indicates credit quality. It is also broken into three groups: high, medium, and low. A fund's placement is determined by the average credit quality of all the bonds in its portfolio. Funds with high credit quality tend to own either U.S. Treasury bonds or corporate bonds whose credit quality is just slightly below that of Treasuries. On the other hand, funds with low credit quality own a lot of high-yield, or junk, bonds. Funds that have an average credit rating of AAA or AA are categorized as high quality, and those with an average credit rating lower than BBB are classified as low quality. Medium-quality funds fall between the two extremes.

The style box can make it far easier for investors to find appropriate funds. Say you need a fund that offers slightly more yield than a money market fund and you don't want it to be much riskier, either. Just look for funds that fall within the short-term, high-quality square of the style box. Or perhaps you want a rich income stream but you aren't comfortable buying junk bonds. A fund that falls within the long-term, medium-quality square might be the answer.

4. How Do I Buy My First Fund?

As a GO-IT-ALONE investor, you can buy funds directly from fund companies such as Fidelity, Vanguard, and T. Rowe Price. Many fund companies offer both load and no-load versions of the same fund, so be sure to specify that you are interested in the no-load version. The first step in the purchase process is to request a prospectus and an application from the fund group by calling its 800-number or visiting its Web site. (You can find this contact information on Morningstar.com's Quicktake Reports.)

If you are thinking of buying more than one fund—and most fund investors do own multiple funds—you might want to work with one of these larger fund families. These fund families run many funds. They offer stock and bond funds, U.S. and international funds, and large- and small-company funds. You can build a well-diversified portfolio of funds without venturing outside the family. By investing with one of the major fund families, you can easily transfer assets from one fund to another. You'll also consolidate paperwork, getting one statement for all of your funds instead of a separate one for each fund you own.

Another way to diversify is to invest with a series of fund-family boutiques that do one thing particularly well. You could buy a large-cap growth fund from Janus, a small-company value fund from Royce Funds, a bond

224 MORE ON MUTUAL FUNDS

fund from Metropolitan West, a foreign-stock fund from Tweedy, Browne, and so on.

Making the Purchase

If you're doing it yourself, you need to contact the fund family or supermarket you have chosen. That means calling to request a prospectus and an application, going to the Web site to request that they be mailed to you, or downloading them from the site. Once you have filled out the application, you'll mail it back with a check or money order to open your account. Many funds and supermarkets also allow you to open an account online without having to go through the process of mailing back the application.

When you fill out the application, don't worry about how many shares you're buying. Focus on the dollar amount you want to invest. Unlike stock shares, you can own partial amounts of fund shares. If you invest $1,500 in a fund with a share price, or NAV, of $122.50, you'll get 12.245 shares of the fund.

In the application, you will see a number of options for buying the specific fund you want. The key ones are whether to reinvest dividends and other distributions and whether to invest a lump sum or a smaller amount each month.

Unless you're planning to use the fund for income, be sure to reinvest distributions. Instead of getting a check in the mail whenever the fund makes an income or capital gains distribution, you'll get more shares of the fund. Reinvesting makes a big difference for your long-term returns—studies have shown that 20% or more of the money shareholders make from a fund comes from such reinvestment. Keep in mind that the total-return numbers you see for a fund assume that you do reinvest distributions. You can't pocket the distributions and expect to get comparably good returns.

Lump Sum or Automatic Investing

The choice of whether to invest a lump sum all at once or set up what is known as an automatic investment plan is less clear-cut. The automatic investment plan automatically deducts a set amount from your checking account every month. It's easy and you can invest small amounts at a time, allowing you to invest without having to lay out a large sum of money all at once. This may sound familiar—if you participate in a retirement plan at work, you're in an automatic investment plan. The process is also known as dollar-cost averaging, because your purchase prices average out over time.

If you're buying a load fund, however, the more you can invest at once, the better. Load funds usually have breakpoints above which the front-end sales charge drops. If you invest at least $25,000 in one of the American Funds offerings, for example, the sales charge will be 5.00% instead of 5.75%. The charge declines further for larger investments.

Tracking Your Purchases

Whether you invest a lump sum or dollar-cost average or use some combination of the two, be sure to keep copies of the fund statements recording your share purchases. These are vital for keeping track of the fund shares you own. If you own the fund in a taxable account, knowing exactly when you bought shares and how much you paid for them can be a big help. When you redeem, or cash in, shares, you can minimize your taxable gains by paying attention to share price and how long you held the shares.

Gains in shares that you have owned for at least 12 months are taxed at a lower rate than those you have held for less than a year, which are taxed at your income tax rate. And by selling shares priced close to the current price, you'll minimize gains. If the current share price is $20 per share and you sell the shares you bought 15 months ago at $17 per share, your taxable gain will be much less than if you had sold the shares you bought 20 months ago for $13. When selling, be sure to tell the fund company that you want to sell designated shares and which shares you want to sell.

Great First Funds

Unless you're pretty flush, you'll want to find a fund that doesn't charge a high initial investment. Unfortunately, one of the best "first fund" choices, Vanguard's Total Stock Market Index, requires at least $3,000 up front. (We like total stock market funds as first funds because they ideally fit the requirements outlined previously. They own a mix of value and growth and in-between stocks, they give investors exposure to many stocks in a variety of sectors, and they hold mostly large-cap stocks while offering diversification into mid and small caps.)

You can often get around such a large investment minimum by setting up an automatic investment plan as discussed earlier in the book. If you commit to have your investment automatically taken out of your checking account every month, you can often buy into a fund for just $50 or $100. Vanguard still wants $3,000 up front, even if you set up an automatic investment plan, but families such as T. Rowe Price, Fidelity, and TIAA-CREF offer total stock market index funds that allow you set up automatic investment plans with considerably less money.

If you don't want to set up an automatic investment plan, there are two other options for getting into funds with minimum initial investments that are out of your reach. One is to set up an individual retirement account. Even funds with a steep minimum will often cut it to as little as $1,000 for an IRA. You can't draw on an IRA until retirement, however, so that isn't a good option if you're hoping to use the money before then. Fund supermarkets usually also allow you to invest for less. If you wanted to buy Weitz Value directly from the fund company, you would have to put in at least $25,000 in a lump sum. But most supermarkets allow you to buy the fund for just $2,500.

First Funds to Consider	Minimum Initial Purchase
Conservative Funds	
Dodge & Cox Balanced	$2,500
T. Rowe Price Capital Appreciation	$2,500
Vanguard STAR	$1,000
Vanguard/Wellington	$3,000
Moderate Funds	
TIAA-CREF Growth & Income	$1,500
Vanguard Total Stock Market Index	$3,000
Selected American	$1,000
Aggressive Funds	
Baron Asset	$2,000
Marsico Growth & Income	$2,500
T. Rowe Price Mid-Cap Growth	$2,500

FAQ Figure 4.1   Here are a few funds to get you started, grouped by risk level.

Specific Ideas for That First Fund

Figure FAQ 4.1 lists some of our analysts' best ideas for that first fund. We have arranged our list into three groups—conservative offerings, moderately risky funds, and aggressive funds. The four funds in the conservative group are all hybrid offerings that invest in both stocks and bonds. They should provide a smoother ride, but their long-term returns will probably be lower than those of the other funds on the list. The last four funds have the promise for the greatest long-term returns, but they are also more likely to suffer losses.

5. *What Should I Do When My Fund Manager Leaves?*

AN EXCELLENT QUESTION. Fortunately, we have an excellent answer:
Wait and see.

Bold, no? But we're serious. Investors shouldn't rashly sell a fund when the jury is still out about the new manager. There's no set period for passing judgment, either. But there are four questions to ask when your fund manager quits.

Is This Fund in a Taxable or Nontaxable Account?

If your fund is in a taxable account, you don't want to hightail it without good reason, especially if you've owned the fund awhile. Selling could mean a sizable realized gain, which in turn would mean writing a sizable check to the IRS. However, if you own the fund in a tax-deferred account, such as an IRA or a 401(k), selling won't have the same tax ramifications.

Will the Strategy Change?

If the new manager brings a new strategy, the fund may no longer play a role in your portfolio, and that's a valid reason to sell. For example, a small-company fund that has turned into a large-cap offering clearly won't fill the same slot for you. Even if the new manager vows to the stay the course, though, check in on the fund more regularly than you did before, just to make sure. New managers usually say things will stay the same, but most do at least *some* tinkering once they arrive.

As soon as you hear about a manager change, keep a close eye on its portfolio and performance. You can use Morningstar.com's Quicktake reports to get a summary of all the essential facts on the fund. Make sure to print out the report to make it easier to track changes. Revisit the Quicktake page on the site every few months, and compare it with your printed version. Confirm that the essential strategy is still in place.

How can you tell? First, make sure the fund's style-box position remains the same. Also monitor turnover. Because turnover represents how frequently a fund's holdings change, a surge could indicate that the manager is ditching his predecessor's stocks in favor of a new strategy.

Who Is the New Manager?

Fund companies don't want to gamble with funds that have solid track records. In these cases, new managers are often known factors: Either they've been hired away from competing funds, they run other funds in the family, or they're high-profile analysts.

Use the Quicktake Reports to check out the performance records for any funds the new manager has previously been in charge of. Read what the Morningstar analyst has to say about the new manager's skill, too.

How Is the Rest of the Family?

If your fund is the only one in the family, a manager change definitely deserves close watch: There isn't the same type of backup staff to pick up the slack. Big fund families, such as Fidelity or Janus, have deep research and management resources and can therefore absorb manager changes better than one-fund shops.

Even a good-size fund family might have just one illustrious offspring. That's currently the case with Legg Mason funds to name one example. Bill Miller's Legg Mason Value Fund is the family's only standout. Once Miller retires, investors here should certainly watch the fund more closely, monitoring the fund's returns relative to its peers every quarter to see whether the new manager measures up.

6. Should I Buy a Rookie Fund?

TO FIGURE THIS out, ask yourself the following five questions.

What Is the Manager's Record?

Just because the fund is a rookie doesn't mean the manager is. See how successful the manager has been at other funds. Check the new fund's prospectus or the fund company's Web site to find out what other funds the manager has run and when; then look up the Morningstar.com Quicktake Report for each of the manager's former charges. When Morningstar analysts cover rookie funds, they'll tell you how the manager has done in the past.

What Is the Fund Family's Record?

If the manager is a rookie, too, then you should have confidence in the family. Consider whether the rookie's parent company has several good funds. If the family is full of mediocre funds, or worse, what makes you think this one is going to be any different?

Pay attention to the fund family even when you're considering an index fund. Indexing can take more skill than you might think.

What Does the Fund Do?

Knowing the fund's strategy gives you an idea of what the fund is likely to own. That tells you the level of returns and risk you can expect from the fund. Say the fund will focus on fast-growing small companies. That indicates that you could score high long-term returns, but you're likely to endure a rough ride along the way.

What Will It Cost?

The annual expense ratio is the one predictable thing about any fund, rookie or veteran. You don't know how much money your funds will make next year, but you do know what percentage of your investment they're going to charge you.

Rookie funds tend not to be particularly cheap—low expenses result from the economies of scale that come with big, well-established funds. A rookie may not be big enough to pass savings along to shareholders. So investigate the family's other funds. Do they have modest expenses compared with their category peers?

Check with the fund company to find out whether the new fund's expenses have been temporarily capped. Many rookie funds will charge a set expense ratio for a year or so but might charge significantly more after that.

Does the Fund Offer Any Extras?

Favor rookie funds that vow to close to new investors before assets can hinder their performance. Small-company and focused funds are particularly likely to suffer if they bloat.

If you're going to hold the fund in a taxable account, determine whether the fund is committed to minimizing taxes. Even if the fund holds out the prospect of great returns, that means little if you have to surrender large sums to the Internal Revenue Service.

7. Should I Buy a Fund That's Closing?

GROUCHO MARX ONCE remarked, "I could never join a club that would have me as a member." That joke reflects something of the peculiar allure of closed funds. If they aren't letting people in, there must be something pretty cool going on in there, right?

Sometimes there is, often there isn't. Closing is a sign of success, but it usually comes after the real glory days have passed.

Why Funds Close

There's only one reason to close a mutual fund: to preserve the manager's strategy. For example, if fund managers rapidly trade a small number of small-company stocks and are successful, investors will likely take notice and throw money at those funds. Faced with a growing asset base, these managers may have to increase their number of holdings, slow their trading pace, invest in larger companies, or take all of these steps. That creates a tension between the manager who takes pride in crushing the competition and the fund company, which makes more money when assets increase. (Fund companies often get managers to share their interests by compensating them according to the amount of money they manage, not just by how well they perform.)

It's no wonder, then, that funds often close when the damage is already done. It isn't so much a matter of trying to cover something up as of trying to prevent the situation from worsening. Morningstar conducted a study on just this issue and discovered that closed funds on average went from performing in the top 20% of their categories in the three years before closing to just average performance for the three years following closing.

Moreover, for every fund that saw its relative performance improve after closing, three more suffered a decline in the three years after they closed. On average, closed funds' returns relative to their peer groups fell from the top quintile to slightly below average and the median performance was a dismal 62nd percentile.

Does that mean closing a fund actually does damage? No. In fact, the performance slump probably has little to do with closing. The explanation is simply that hot funds usually cool off. While a fund may get steady inflows over most of its life, it usually closes at the point when inflows become a torrent. And that almost always happens when a fund's strategy or asset class is generating abnormally high returns. Pick any strategy that's producing big returns for a stretch and it's a good bet that performance will slide back to average or worse over the following period. Take T. Rowe Price New Horizons. It produced an awesome 120% return over the three years prior to its closing. However, it closed just as small- and mid-cap growth stocks were peaking and only returned 17% over the next three years.

The general performance dropoff for closed funds stands more as further evidence against chasing short-term performance than as an argument against closing. Still, it's sobering to know that a fund's best days are probably behind it by the time it closes.

Another reason closed funds produce sluggish performance is that fund companies wait too long, failing to close until performance hits the skids or assets are gargantuan. By then, it's too late. If performance is already slumping, it may be a sign that it should have closed billions of dollars ago. Closing off new investment won't slim a fund down to its playing weight from its glory days.

Performance isn't the only thing eroding returns of closed funds. Their tax efficiency slumps, too. Unlike the drop in performance, however, this one is attributable to being closed. While inflows can have negative effects on trading costs, they have a positive effect on tax efficiency. They reduce the tax burden on all shareholders because the fund distributes capital gains to more people. Morningstar found that tax efficiency fell five percentage points after the closing date.

When Closing Works

There is some good news in all this. Closing can work, if it's planned in advance. That's because the fund company gives some thought to how much money the fund can handle, then commits to closing it at that point. Most of the funds in our study, meanwhile, closed only after the company finally woke up to size problems.

If you're shopping for a fund, especially one with a concentrated portfolio, a fast-trading strategy, or a small-cap focus, consider the promise to close a plus. It's the kind of promise Morningstar analysts like, so they'll probably mention it in their fund analyzes. But don't let this proclamation bias your decision too much. Make sure that you've chosen a fund worth buying and that meets your needs. Otherwise you might find yourself a member of a club that you really wish hadn't admitted you.

8. Should I Buy a Fund That's Doing Really Well?

MOST INVESTORS CAN'T help but notice funds that are up 30%, 40%, or 50% in a six-month period. Who wouldn't? But many do more than just look. They give in to temptation and buy these funds, chasing their attractive returns. Temptation like that can be hard to resist.

Resist, virtuous investors!

Buying hot funds is a bad idea. Since styles, market caps, sectors, and industries tend to move in and out of favor in the marketplace, some funds are bound to soar for short periods if the manager's style happens on the sweet spot. In the late 1990s, technology and large-cap growth funds skyrocketed, drawing the attention of many investors whose portfolios were tepid compared with these sizzling funds. Health care followed in 2000. For the past two years, small value funds and long dormant gold funds have been "the place to be." So is now the time to increase your portfolio's allocation of small-value funds or pick up a gold fund?

Not if your motivation is simply because they're hot. Here's why:

A fund that blazes in one market environment usually is as cold as ice in others. Furthermore, what's hot now has to cool off at some point. And investors have the uncanny ability to notice what's hot right before it's ready to cool down.

Take the case of PBHG Growth. From 1992 through 1995, the fund quietly built a superb record, though it wasn't attracting a lot of attention (in the form of cash) from new investors. In early 1996, when the fund's annualized three-year gain of more than 30% placed it on many a leader's list, the money started rolling in. Nearly $2.5 billion poured in during the first six months of 1996, just in time for the fund's 10% slide in July. New money slowed. Then, in early 1997, after the fund had suffered several months of losses, shareholders started bailing out, missing a strong second-quarter rebound.

The history of PBHG Growth illustrates a typical pattern. Investors treat strong near-term returns as evidence that a fund is good. "Where there's smoke, there's fire," they reason. But by the time investors see enough smoke, the fire's fuel is often almost spent.

Need more proof? Morningstar studies have found that investors across all fund types—both stocks and bonds—have paid a price for buying hot funds. The damage is greater on the stock side, especially with aggressive funds, where volatility and temptation are highest. It's not surprising that in the small-growth category one Morningstar study found that investors had surrendered 1.8 percentage points of return annually over one five-year period by chasing performance instead of simply investing a little each month (dollar-cost averaging). The small- and mid-cap growth categories are land-mine territory.

Look for Consistency

It's easy to get caught up in the excitement of exceptional returns. Try not to. What should you do instead? Emphasize consistent performers in your portfolio. Such funds rarely shoot out the lights, and they don't get nearly as much attention as their more volatile counterparts. What they do offer, however, is reliability and comfort. They make it easier for you to stay committed, and that often translates into good long-term returns.

A consistent fund lands in the top half to top third of its Morningstar category from one year to the next. Few funds will do that all the time, of course. But when a normally top-half fund lags, it usually isn't by very much—unlike a fund that is top of the heap one year and buried under the pile the next.

With a consistent fund, you can feel confident that no matter how its category does for a given period, your fund will be competitive. And because you'll be more comfortable with the fund, you'll be more likely to stick with it for the long haul. Investors who get caught up in chasing hot funds dump them when they turn cold. Too many PBHG Growth shareholders dumped the fund when it was down and missed the rebound. Those who bought it near the peak locked in losses by selling.

In 1998, Morningstar did a study comparing a very consistent fund, William Blair Growth, with Delaware Trend, a more volatile but also higher returning fund. Delaware Trend had higher 10-year returns, but when we adjusted for cash flows to reflect the typical investor's experience, William Blair Growth was superior. That's because investors found it hard to stick with Delaware Trend during the down periods; it lost as much as 43% in just three months, whereas William Blair Growth fell 25%. By missing the early stages of Delaware Trend's rebounds, investors cost themselves about three percentage points per year in returns. If you had invested $10,000, those three percentage points would have translated into $3,400 less in your pocket after 10 years.

Investors who chase hot funds usually get burned. They buy after a fund has generated big gains and sell when the fund loses steam. If you aren't the sort of investor who is thrown by a fund's gyrations, you're a rarity. Go for reliable consistency and you're likely to be more successful.

9. Should I Buy a Fund That's in the Dumps?

ASTUTE READERS MAY have noticed that this is a trick question. The answer to this question depends on whether it is directed at *absolute* or *relative* performance. Though our response to the question about hot funds tackled the question from the perspective of absolute performance only, here we will provide a more nuanced answer.

It depends. (How's that for nuance?)

Funds that are in the dumps in absolute terms may very well be good investments. We know that's counterintuitive, but playing *against* the crowd may let you catch a future trend today. Fund investors, as a group, have lousy timing. Most investors buy high and sell low, instead of the other way around. Opportunists can therefore make a bundle by buying what everyone else is selling.

This contrarian approach is best suited to buying a fund whose style is out of favor in the marketplace; hence many of the funds in its category are in the dumps as well. Therefore, if you are thinking about purchasing a fund because its category in general is in the dumps, looking for funds that are doing relatively well within that category is a good place to start your search.

That said, even funds that are doing worse than their peers when the group is down shouldn't be excluded from your search entirely. Though it's a harder call to justify purchasing such a fund, assess whether the fund does better than its peers when its style is in favor. For example, Scudder Dreman High Return Equity was trounced by its large-value peers in 1999, when large-value funds in general were being trounced by large-growth funds. However, manager David Dreman had a proven record of besting his rivals when value investing was strong, and the fund's long-term relative record was superior. Though it would have been a tough call to make at the time, investors who bought the fund when it was in the dumps (say in the middle of 1999) would have been handsomely compensated for signing on, since it has crushed its peers and the broader large-cap market since then. Similarly, now that growth and tech funds have taken a beating, it's a useful exercise not only to search for funds that have done relatively well during this downturn, but also to look for those that have done well both prior to the downturn and during brief periods when these areas have shined.

It makes most sense to buy a fund that's in the dumps when its style is not represented in your portfolio. When a fund's style, sector, or asset class is out of favor, it may provide you an opportunity to diversify your portfolio. Since certain types of investments will do well at certain times while others won't, a diverse portfolio helps smooth your ride and generate better long-term returns.

However, never buy a fund just because it's in the dumps and you don't hold a similar fund in your portfolio. Not everyone needs to own a bond fund, an international fund, a small-cap fund, a real-estate fund, and so on. Nor must everyone have exposure to value and growth styles. You should nonetheless consider the ways that such investments might add diversity to your portfolio—and looking while they're down is a good time.

10. How Can I Pay Less in Taxes?

WE HAVE GOOD NEWS and bad news.

Let's start with the bad news. Even if you don't sell any shares of a fund you own during a given year, you can still end up owing Uncle Sam come April 15. By law, the fund has to distribute income and realized capital gains (gains are realized when your fund manager sells a stock at a profit) to its shareholders. Otherwise, the fund itself has to pay the taxes, and you know that isn't going to happen. (Even if it did, the money would come out of the fund's assets, so you'd still be hit.)

"But," you counter, "I elected to reinvest all my distributions. It isn't like the fund cuts me a check whenever it makes a distribution."

That just doesn't matter. If you reinvest, you're getting more shares of the fund just as if the fund sent you a check and you used the money to buy those additional shares.

Don't hang your head, though. Here's the good news: There are ways to minimize the tax bite. For starters, avoid funds that pay out a lot of income. Income is taxed at the highest rate. If you're investing in bonds, opt for a municipal-bond fund; municipal-bond income is free from federal taxes, and if the bond is issued in the state where you pay taxes, it's likely free from state taxes as well. If you're investing in stocks, find funds that don't pay out income.

Whether the fund pays out capital gains is another matter. Some funds have consistently minimized taxable gains, allowing investors to keep most of their pretax returns. But even funds that historically have limited taxes don't always stick with that strategy. Longleaf Partners and Legg Mason Value both have good records of avoiding the tax man, but in 1999, both funds wound up selling stocks after strong runups, leading to taxable events for shareholders.

The most reliable way to identify taxpayer-friendly funds is to look for ones with the tax-managed moniker. Managers of tax-managed funds avoid income and capital-gains distributions. A lot of fund companies have introduced such funds in recent years, as investors realized that a 30% gain isn't so great if tax bills leave you with just two thirds of it in hand. Vanguard offers a variety of tax-managed choices covering different investment styles. Fidelity, American Century, and T. Rowe Price are just a few of the other fund families with tax-managed offerings.

Investors can face a lot of other tax situations. The following tips don't cover them all, but they should help you become a more tax-efficient investor.

Sell Specific Shares

When you sell shares in a fund, your taxable gain is determined by the sale price minus your cost basis in the fund. Say you dollar-cost averaged into a fund, thereby picking up shares at different prices. What's your cost basis when you sell? For most fund companies, the default cost basis is the average of the cost basis on your individual shares.

Many investors can save on taxes by identifying specific shares to be sold. Suppose that your average cost basis in a fund is $10, but you recently purchased individual shares with a cost basis of $16. If your fund now sells for $20 per share, you'd have a much lower taxable gain by selling the shares with the $16 cost basis, than by using the default $10 cost basis.

The specific-shares method involves a lot more record-keeping and hassle than the default average-cost method, but the tax savings may be worth it. You can apply this rule only to funds on which you've never sold shares using the average-cost method because once you use that method on a fund, the IRS requires that you continue to use it.

Sell Purposefully

Suppose you own a fund that's been a longtime loser. In fact, it has under-performed to the extent that you have a loss on your investment. Think about using that loss to your advantage. Sometimes we hang on to funds that we don't particularly like and that aren't performing well because we want to break even on our investment. Instead, use the loss on that fund to offset gains elsewhere in your taxable portfolio.

Shelter like Crazy

Take full advantage of all the tax-deferral options available to you, whether they are 401(k)s, 403(b)s, or IRAs. Once you've contributed the maximum amount to those accounts, consider the following suggestions.

Buy Tax-Managed Funds for Nonsheltered Accounts

A well-run tax-managed fund will keep taxable distributions to a bare minimum. Vanguard and T. Rowe Price both offer diverse lineups of tax-managed funds.

Go the Direct Route

The most tax-efficient investment may not be a fund at all, but a stock. When you put together a stock portfolio, you have complete control over when to sell a holding, except in cases when the company you own is taken over by another.

Steer Clear of Funds That Have Been Horribly Tax Inefficient for Taxable Accounts

A fund's tax efficiency may not always repeat, but it's probably best to steer clear of funds with poor tax efficiency versus their peers. You can find information about a fund's tax efficiency on its Morningstar.com Quicktake Report. Simply click on Trailing Returns, and scroll down to Tax Analysis.

Following these guidelines won't guarantee that you'll never pay a penny in taxes, but the rules will allow you to sensibly maximize your aftertax return. Hooray to that.

11. How Can I Determine Whether a Fund Is Best for a Taxable Account or a Tax-Sheltered Account?

WE HAVEN'T EXHAUSTED the exhilarating topic of taxes. Now that you've learned how to identify tax-efficient funds, you need to determine what to do with investments that are less tax-efficient but are worthy holdings nonetheless.

If you're beginning to yawn, here's something to jolt you awake. Between 1999 and 2001, the typical investor with a mutual fund in a taxable account kept only $77.50 of every $100 he or she earned in returns: The rest went to taxes. And that figure is based just on the income and capital gains distributions made; it doesn't factor in any additional damage investors might have done by realizing gains themselves.

Though paying attention to the tax efficiency of funds is important, it is equally important to maximize the benefits of tax-sheltered accounts.

Let's start with a basic principle—put the funds that generate a lot of income or distributions in tax-sheltered accounts.

Of course, you say, but should I protect the income from my taxable bond funds or try to protect myself from the capital gains I might be assessed from my high-turnover (yet superior) growth fund?

Some tax advisors say bond funds should go into tax-protected accounts, because income is taxed at a higher rate than capital gains. Others say that if a stock fund pays out a lot of capital gains, it should be in a tax-sheltered account.

Tax experts at T. Rowe Price studied this question. They looked at three varieties of funds: growth, growth and income, and taxable bond. They assumed $10,000 investments in each fund, with holding periods of 10, 15, and 20 years. They also assumed that the accounts were cashed in at the end of the period. The tax specialists ran the numbers for all income-tax rates. The study showed that your holding period, your expected tax rate when you cash in the account, and whether the account is tax deferred (i.e., a traditional IRA) or allows tax-free withdrawals (i.e., the Roth IRA) are the key determinants of where tax sheltering will work best for you.

Guidelines
The conclusions from T. Rowe Price's study can be boiled down to three essential rules for the kinds of investments that should have tax protection.

1. The closer you are to retirement and the higher your tax rate will be in retirement, the better off you'll be putting your bond funds in tax-protected accounts and your stock funds in taxable accounts. There are two subsections to this rule:

    ▶ If you have 15 years or more until retirement and expect to be in a lower tax bracket then, protect your stock funds from taxes and keep your bond funds in taxable accounts.

    ▶ If your retirement is fewer than 15 years off and you expect to be in a higher tax bracket in retirement than you are now, seek tax protection for your bond funds and store the stock funds in taxable accounts.

2. Because the Roth IRA permits tax-free withdrawals, put your stock funds in a Roth account, no matter what your time horizon and expected tax bracket are. Stock funds should make significantly higher

long-term gains than bond funds, and a Roth ensures that you won't be taxed on those big gains.

3. If you are investing in a tax-deferred account such as a traditional IRA instead of a Roth, tax-managed and other tax-efficient stock funds should go into taxable accounts. Such funds avoid capital-gains distributions. If you hold them in a traditional IRA, your withdrawals will be taxed at your income-tax level, which will always be higher than the capital-gains rate you would pay when cashing in a taxable stock fund.

12. How Can I Find the Best Fund Supermarket?

"CLEAN UP IN aisle six, clean up in aisle six—someone spilled Janus Olympus all over the place!"

Sorry, we can't help ourselves. Fund supermarkets are, in fact, a lot like regular supermarkets. In your parents' or grandparents' day, they had to visit the butcher, the baker, the greengrocer, and maybe even the druggist and the bootlegger to get everything they needed. Now we can get all those things—and a lot more—in a supermarket.

Fund supermarkets share one of the best features of real supermarkets—they offer all kinds of stuff in one place.

What a Supermarket Is

A fund supermarket offers investors a one-stop shop for buying funds—typically thousands of them. Fidelity, Vanguard, numerous other fund companies, and most major brokers offer a version of the supermarket. Charles Schwab was one of the first brokers to offer the supermarket service, and others operate in much the same way. Typically, you'll find two kinds of funds: those for which there is no load and no transaction fee (NTF is the fund industry's shorthand) and those for which there is a load or transaction fee, or both. The first thing you should know is that NTF funds aren't really free. To be included in the supermarket, they pay a fee. (More on that later.) The other group of funds may charge a load or be unwilling to participate in the NTF side of the supermarket.

The Big Catch

The real drawback to any fund supermarket is that funds have to pay for shelf space. That adds to a fund's annual expenses, and those expenses come out of the returns on your money. You might think of that fee as the price you pay for convenience. After all, instead of contacting five different fund families and setting up accounts with each of them, you can set up one account with the supermarket and buy all the funds there.

What's really annoying, though, is that investors pay for the convenience no matter how they buy the fund. If a fund is among Schwab's NTF funds, for example, you pay the fee even if you buy the fund directly from the fund company. Now that's irritating.

Also, some observers, including Vanguard founder John Bogle, have suggested that fund supermarkets encourage rapid trading among funds. Most supermarkets offer online trading, and with so many funds from so many families that invest in so many different things, the temptation is great. But trading too much can hurt your portfolio's overall performance.

The Advantages of Supermarkets

The main appeal of the fund supermarket is its convenience. Setting up a no-load mutual-fund account isn't very difficult to do, but if you buy your funds from several different fund companies, you have to go through the same steps multiple times. If you use a supermarket, you only have to set up one account.

Not only does a supermarket allow you to buy your funds in one location, but you also get consolidated reports on them. That's a huge plus, especially at tax time. Totaling up short-term and long-term gains from six different funds is a hassle. All fund companies have to report the same information on their 1099 forms, yet no two forms are laid out in the same way. You have to scrutinize them carefully to make sure you enter the right information on your tax forms.

Even if you don't care much about convenience, you might still find that a supermarket has something for you. Say you're interested in a particular fund but can't begin to meet the minimum investment requirement. Rydex Electronics, a technology fund, has a minimum initial investment of $25,000. Many of us would stumble at that hurdle. But if you look up the fund's Quicktake report on Morningstar.com and go to the bottom of the column at the left of your screen for Purchase Information (under Nuts and Bolts), you'll see that it's available through a slew of brokerages. Most of them can get you into the fund for less than $25,000. If you go through Schwab, for example, the minimum is $2,500.

So Where Should I Shop?

There are a number of fund supermarkets today, including versions from Jack White and Fidelity. More and more fund families are getting into the act, too: T. Rowe Price, Vanguard, and USAA have supermarkets that include funds from outside their families.

Generally speaking, bigger is better. Beyond the convenience of consolidated statements and one-stop shopping, savvy investors want choices, particularly among NTF offerings. There's no sense signing up for an account with a fund supermarket that doesn't offer that Vanguard fund you just have to have or, for that matter, one that doesn't offer a healthy selection of funds from all the major asset classes. Convenience and variety, therefore, should be your watchwords.

You'll need to sample the wares to decide which supermarket is right for you. Schwab pioneered the concept, and while we're not endorsing its product, the firm's OneSource is a fine place to begin your research. Once you have a grip on what a supermarket with lots of breadth and depth looks like, you'll be in a better position to assess the competition. To help you get started, we've listed the Web sites of some of the companies that offer fund supermarkets. Happy shopping!

http://www.schwab.com
http://www.fidelity.com
http://www.troweprice.com
http://www.etrade.com
http://www.vanguard.com
http://www.tdwaterhouse.com

13. How Can I Find a Financial Planner?

MOST OF US can benefit from working with a financial professional. Maybe we're new to investing and don't know where to start. Or we need estate-planning advice. Or we'd simply like an advisor to set our minds at ease by giving our financial lives the once-over. The question isn't whether we need an advisor, but how to find a suitable one.

"In most cases, the choice of an advisor is far more important—and potentially damaging—to a person's financial future than the choice of which mutual funds to invest in," notes Chuck Jaffe, author of *The Right Way to Hire Financial Help.* "You're not only buying expertise, you are buying trust and confidence, and trying to strike up a profitable relationship that will last a lifetime. That's not easy."[1]

To choose an advisor who suits your financial needs and personality, follow these steps.

Decide What You Want

Self-examination is the starting point. Are you looking for someone to handle one part of your financial life, such as taxes or estate planning, or are you seeking a financial advisor who can take care of it all? Do you want an advisor to pick and choose your mutual funds or stocks, or someone who'll leave that to you? Knowing the answers to these questions helps you narrow your search to candidates with skills to match your needs. Once you've set your priorities, begin your search by asking your accountant or attorney for recommendations. Query friends and professional colleagues who work with financial planners.

If you come up short, check these resources to find advisors in your area: International Association for Financial Planning, National Association for Personal Financial Advisors, or the Personal Financial Planning Division of the American Institute of Certified Public Accountants (AICPA).

Identify a handful of advisors whose services meet your needs. Then call with a few preliminary questions. Ask what their investment and income requirements are, or how much money you'll need to become a client. Also confirm their services and specialties.

After you've found a few good matches, set up initial meetings, which should be free of charge. Be sure to verify that the person you will meet with is the person who'd be your advisor. In some larger firms, that isn't always the case. You wouldn't want to find the advisor of your dreams only to discover later that he or she doesn't handle your account.

Ask the Right Questions

For that first meeting, bring a checklist of questions, concerns, or issues you want addressed. Approach your preliminary meeting as if you were interviewing someone for a job, because you are—the job of helping you with your finances.

As with any job interview, you must scrutinize the candidate's resume, known as the ADV form. To register as an investment advisor, applicants must fill out ADVs and file them with the Securities and Exchange Commission. (Note that financial planners who manage less than $25 million in assets don't need to register; request a resume nonetheless.) Ask for a copy of this form as soon as you walk in the door.

The ADVs include advisors' educational backgrounds, and the professional designations they hold, such as Certified Financial Planner (CFP), Certified Public Accountant-Personal Financial Specialist (CPA-PFS), or Chartered Financial Consultant (ChFC).

Updated in Every Issue!
The Morningstar® FundInvestor™ 500

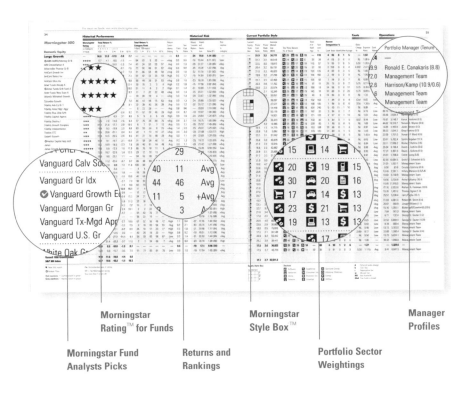

Morningstar Fund Analysts Picks

Morningstar Rating™ for Funds

Returns and Rankings

Morningstar Style Box™

Portfolio Sector Weightings

Manager Profiles

Includes funds selected by Morningstar analysts as ideal for building and maintaining a diversified portfolio.

Also includes the Morningstar Rating for Funds, returns, fund portfolio data, expenses, and much more!

Improve your portfolio with Morningstar FundInvestor — RISK-FREE!

Morningstar Guarantee: If not pleased with the first issue, cancel and receive a full refund. Keep the free reports with our compliments.

FSNIN9D1008

Build On Your Fund Know-How and Earn Better Returns with Our Monthly Newsletter!

You've made a great start in becoming an even better fund investor. *Morningstar® FundInvestor™* helps you keep up the momentum with practical guidance every month. Each issue shows you how to pick great funds, build great portfolios, and monitor the performance of your portfolio. See for yourself by asking for the next issue—completely risk-free.

Review an issue RISK-FREE!
Get 12 monthly issues for just $89

Monthly features include:

500 Top Funds. We have painstakingly handpicked the 500 best and most notable funds, on which we provide comprehensive data each month.

Morningstar FundInvestor Portfolios. Three portfolios of mutual funds for conservative, moderate, and aggressive investors.

Red Flags. Discover which funds our analysts think you should avoid.

Portfolios & Planning. Follow real-life examples of how to improve your portfolio from financial planner Sue Stevens, CFP, CFA, CPA.

Bulls vs. Bears Debate. Let our team of experts help you decide if a noeworthy fund should be booted from your portfolio.

---

3 Free Bonuses: You'll also receive three FREE reports. They cover our Wealth Portfolios, 15 picks for five-year growth, and the 5 principles of successful fund investing. You may keep them even if you decide not to continue your subscription.

The ADV has a number of sections, but the most important information is in Schedule F. In that schedule, you'll discover how advisors are compensated (more on that later), and whether they have business ties to particular insurance or mutual-fund companies. If these ties exist, they should be disclosed to you in writing.

If you'll be relying on the planner for investment suggestions—which funds or stocks to buy—be sure the two of you share the same investment philosophy. You wouldn't want someone calling you every month with buy and sell recommendations if you're the buy-and-hold type. So ask candidates to walk you through their fund- or stock-selection process, and to thoroughly explain what would make them sell a stock or fund. Request a copy of a typical financial plan.

Calculate the Cost

Don't leave an advisor's office until you completely understand what the advice will cost—and get it in writing. Advisors can be compensated in several ways.

► Fee-only advisors charge an hourly rate, a flat rate, or a percentage of your assets or income.

► Commission-based advisors receive income from the investments they use to execute your financial plan; in these cases, you foot the bill by paying charges (or loads) on the funds you buy.

► Fee-and-commission advisors will charge you for developing a financial plan and then receive commissions from the products they sell to you.

► Finally, some advisors are salaried.

Have the advisor estimate what it will cost to create your plan and manage your investments, including both fees and commissions.

On average, expect to pay at least $2,000 to have a financial plan drawn up. Most financial planners charge $100 an hour or more and include the time they spend both drawing up a plan and meeting with clients. Advisors who rely mostly on commissions may charge less, but they generally make up the difference with the commissions they earn on your investments.

The costs of managing your investments may vary. If you're working with a fee-only advisor, the typical range for annual fees is 0.5% to 1% of the value of your portfolio. The fee may be higher for smaller accounts.

Conduct a Background Check

If you're comfortable with the person you've interviewed, discover no negatives on his or her ADV, understand the investment philosophy, and deem the costs fair, then take the final step of a background check.

First, gather references from the candidate, but be specific with your request. Don't just look for references from other clients. Instead, ask for references to investment professionals (such as CPAs or CFAs) or attorneys who've seen the advisor's work before.

Further, contact professional and government regulatory organizations to verify that no disciplinary action has been taken against your candidate. Some resources: CFP Board of Standards, National Association of Insurance Commissioners, National Association of Securities Dealers Regulation, and the Securities and Exchange Commission. Check with your state regulator, too; contact the North American Securities Administrators Association for the phone number.

Although some information about disciplinary action may be included in the ADV, remember that advisors themselves fill out the form. And some may be less than honest.

Set the Ground Rules

Once you've selected your candidate, be sure to protect yourself with the following checks and balances:

▶ Don't give your advisor unlimited discretion over your money. "No matter how good your advisor, the final decisions must always be yours," says Lynn Brenner, author of *Smart Questions to Ask Your Financial Advisers*. "Nobody else knows your needs as well as you do, or cares as much about satisfying them."[2] Be sure you remain in control.

▶ Ask to receive account statements directly from a third-party custodian, such as a brokerage firm or a trust company. That way you can be sure your advisor is executing your plan, not hopping a plane to points unknown with your assets.

▶ Tell the advisor how often you'd like to meet to discuss your finances. Make your financial planner work for your business. The good ones will.

Notes

1. Charles A. Jaffe, *The Right Way to Hire Financial Help.* (Cambridge, MA: The MIT Press, 1998).
2. Lynn Brenner, *Smart Questions to Ask Your Financial Advisers.* (Princeton: Bloomberg Press, 1997).

14. How Do I Read a Fund's Prospectus?

BE WARNED: THESE documents aren't light reading. They can be packed with legal jargon, convoluted sentences, and boilerplate information to fulfill the Securities and Exchange Commission's disclosure requirements and to protect fund companies from legal liabilities. But if you're thinking about buying a fund, the prospectus is an important document. Reading it should help you understand a fund's investment policy, the amount of investment flexibility it has, what it owns, who runs it, and how it has performed.

The prospectus tells you how to open an account (including the minimum amount of money you'll need to open one), how to buy and sell shares, and how to contact shareholder services. But more important, you'll find the six things you absolutely need to know about a fund before you decide to buy shares in the first place.

Investment Objective

The investment objective is the mutual fund's purpose in life. Is the fund seeking to make money over the long term? Or is it trying to provide its shareholders regular income each month? If you're investing for a young child's education, you'll want the former. If you're retired and looking for a monthly dividend check, you'll want the latter. But investment objectives can be notoriously vague. That's why you'll want to check out the next section.

Strategy

The prospectus also describes the types of stocks, bonds, or other securities in which the fund plans to invest. (It does *not* list the exact stocks that the fund owns, though. You'll find that list in the shareholder report.) Stock funds spell out the kinds of companies they look for, such as small, fast-growing firms or big, well-established corporations. Bond funds specify what sorts of bonds they generally hold, such as Treasury or corporate bonds. If the fund can invest in foreign securities, the prospectus says so. Most (but not all) restrictions on what the fund can invest in are also mentioned. Morningstar analysts value this section because it gives them a sense of what constraints the fund manager has and can expose the possibility of unexpected investments, such as shorting stocks, down the road.

Be warned, though. It's not unusual for funds to give a laundry list in the prospectus of all the possible things they *could* invest in. You shouldn't assume that the fund *will* invest in all the types of securities mentioned. Prospectuses are written very broadly, so they don't always give you a specific idea of how the fund typically invests.

Risks

This section may be the most important one in the prospectus. Every investment has risks associated with it and a prospectus must explain these risks. A prospectus for a fund that invests in emerging markets will reveal that the fund is likely to be riskier than a fund that invests in developed countries. Bond-fund prospectuses typically discuss the credit quality of the bonds in the fund's portfolio, as well as how a change in interest rates might affect the value of its holdings. A fund should spell out all the potential risks of its strategy, even if it has a solid track record.

Expenses

It costs money to invest in a mutual fund, and different funds have different fees. A table at the front of every prospectus makes it easy to compare the cost of one fund with another. Here, you'll find the sales commission the fund charges, if any, for buying or selling shares. The prospectus also tells you, in percentage terms, the amount deducted from the fund's return each year to pay for management fees and operational costs. You'll even see the estimated cost of owning the fund over projected 1-, 3-, 5-, and 10-year periods. Those dollar amounts assume that you invested $10,000 at the beginning of the year, that the fund's underlying fee structure stayed the same, and that the fund returns 5% per year.

Note: A fund's actual expenses might be lower than the numbers in the prospectus. Be sure to check the shareholder report for the most current picture.

Past Performance

As fund companies always point out in their ads, "Past performance cannot guarantee future results." But it can suggest how consistent a fund's returns have been. A chart known as the "Financial Highlights" or "Per Share Data Table" provides the fund's total return for each of the past 10 years, along with some other useful information. It also breaks out the fund's income distributions and provides year-end NAVs. (NAV or net asset value is the price per share of the fund.)

Some prospectuses include additional return information in a bar chart that illustrates the fund's calendar returns for the past 10 years. This chart can give you a handle on the magnitude of a fund's ups and downs over time. The prospectus may also use a graph showing how $10,000 invested in a fund would have grown over time (also known as a mountain graph, because the peaks and valleys resemble a mountain range) or a table comparing the fund's performance to indexes or other benchmarks to present return information. (Unless otherwise stated, total-return numbers do not take sales charges into account.)

Be wary of comparisons between the fund and a self-selected benchmark. A fund company is motivated to present its offerings in the best possible light. There are guidelines to prevent the fund company from grossly misleading investors, but there's no guarantee that the fund will pick the most appropriate peer group against which to compare returns. Use an independent third party like Morningstar to ensure that you get appropriate comparisons.

Many fund prospectuses also provide tax-adjusted return information. (Even if the information isn't in the prospectus, it always will be in the shareholder report.) This information deserves your attention if you're going to hold the fund in a taxable account. You will see returns labeled Return before Taxes, Return after Taxes on Distributions, and Return after Taxes on Distribution and Sale of Fund Shares for 1-, 5-, and 10-year periods.

The first set of returns is just the total return discussed in Chapter 2. The next set shows what investors keep after paying taxes on any income distribution or capital gains distributions that the fund made. If a fund gets income from bonds or dividend-paying stocks that it owns, or sells a security at a profit, it is required to distribute that money to shareholders. Most shareholders choose to reinvest and get more shares instead of a check, but they still have to pay taxes on the distribution. The last set of returns is what investors would have kept after selling their shares of the fund and paying taxes on any gains they made from the fund. These calculations all assume that the investor is taxed at the highest federal rate, and they don't take state taxes into account.

Management

The Management section details the folks who will be putting your money to work. You might reasonably expect that the prospectus would actually tell you the name and experience of the fund manager or managers. However, some funds simply list "management team" or some other less-than-helpful phrase. If that's the case, consult the fund's Statement of Additional Information (more on that shortly) or annual report to see if it provides more specific information. You should feel free to call up the fund company itself and ask who's running the fund, or check out its Web site.

If the prospectus does name names, check how long the current manager has been running the fund—its past record may have been achieved under someone else. Find out whether the manager has run other funds in the past. A peek at those funds could give you some clues about the manager's investment style and past success.

15. What Do I Need to Know About the Statement of Additional Information?

WHILE THE PROSPECTUS is packed with important information, it shouldn't be your sole source of data on a fund. A fund's Statement of Additional Information (SAI) contains more useful tidbits about the fund's inner workings. Be sure to ask for this document specifically when you call for information on a fund: Fund companies routinely send out prospectuses and annual reports, but they don't treat SAIs as comparably important documents.

If fund families think SAIs are secondary, why bother requesting one? For starters, the SAI often provides far more detail than the prospectus about what the fund can and cannot invest in. For another, this document is usually the place where you can find out who represents your interests on the fund's board of directors—and how much you pay them.

Finally, you can find more details about your fund's expenses here. Shareholders in Brandywine Fund would not know they shelled out $43 million in brokerage fees in 2001 unless they had read the fund's SAIs. (Brokerage fees are the cost a fund incurs to buy and sell securities, and they're not included as part of the expense ratio.) SAIs also break down where 12b-1 fees go, if the fund charges them. (These are fees that the fund can use for marketing, rewarding brokers, and attracting more investors.) For example, Federated Kaufmann Fund spent about $2 million of the $12 million in 12b-1 fees it collected in 1999 compensating brokers for selling the fund. It's your money; you should know where it's going.

16. How Do I Read a Fund's Shareholder Report?

A MUTUAL FUND'S shareholder report is part biography, part blueprint, and part ledger book.

A good shareholder report is like a biography in that it sets out what happened to the fund over the past quarter, six months, or year, and why. It's like a blueprint because it sets before you all the investments—stocks, bonds, and other securities—that the fund has made. And it's like a ledger book because it discloses a fund's costs, profits, and many other financial facts. Mutual funds are required to release a shareholder report at least twice a year, though some fund families publish them quarterly.

Not all the items discussed here are required by law to appear in a mutual fund's report. The SEC allows some of the information to be included in other documents, such as a fund's prospectus or Statement of Additional Information. However, a good report will contain all of the following elements.

Letter from the President

Usually, the first item you'll find in a shareholder report is the letter from the president of the company that advises, or runs, your fund. The best letters will contain straightforward, useful discussions of the economic trends that have affected the markets during the past 6 or 12 months. This discussion provides some context for evaluating your fund.

Letter from the Portfolio Manager

This is similar to the president's letter, but much more specific to the fund, and therefore much more important to you as a shareholder. Well-written shareholder letters discuss individual stocks that the fund owns and industries to which it is exposed. Third Avenue Value manager Marty Whitman writes exemplary shareholder letters every three months. In these letters, he describes which stocks have been sold, bought, or left alone, and why.

A good manager letter will also explain what fueled or hindered your fund's performance. The Weitz Funds' shareholder letters are noteworthy in this regard. The June 2002 semiannual report for Weitz Value bluntly stated: "After bucking the downtrend in the market for the past two years, we 'participated' (all too fully) in the decline in the 2nd quarter of 2002." The letter goes on to explain that Adelphia's accounting fraud cost the fund about 3% of its assets. The fund also lost about 5% due to its investment in Quest.

Finally, a good shareholder letter should indicate what you can expect from the fund in the future, given the manager's strategy.

Reviewing Fund Performance

After reading your manager's comments, look to see how the fund has performed. A good report will compare your fund's performance to a benchmark, such as the S&P 500 index (the standard benchmark for large-company funds) or the Russell 2000 index (for small-company funds), as well as to the average performance of funds with similar investment strategies.

When evaluating your fund's performance, make sure that the benchmark the fund has chosen is appropriate for its style. A technology fund should not compare itself to the S&P 500 and nothing else; it should measure its performance against a technology benchmark.

In addition to benchmark comparison, a good report should give you an idea of how the fund has performed over various time frames, both short- and long-term. If you hold the fund in a taxable account, be sure to check its tax-adjusted returns. While these may also appear in the prospectus, you'll get the latest numbers here.

Reviewing Portfolio Holdings

Funds often list the portfolio's largest holdings and provide some information about what these companies do or why the manager owns them. Some reports will also indicate, in the form of a pie chart or table, how portfolio assets are distributed among market sectors. International funds will usually break out the portfolio's country exposure, too.

This general overview is complemented by a complete list of the fund's portfolio holdings—including stocks, bonds, and cash—as of the date of the report. These holdings are usually broken down by industry. (Foreign funds may break holdings down by country.) Even though you might not recognize all the names of the stocks in the portfolio, this listing is useful if you're wondering whether the fund is holding many names in a specific industry or is making a few selected bets.

Footnotes

Don't forget to read the fine print. In the footnotes, you can find out if the fund managers are practicing such strategies as shorting stocks or hedging currencies, which can significantly affect the fund's performance.

Footnotes can also provide insights into particular portfolio holdings. The footnotes of Baron Assets, March 31, 2002, report revealed that the fund held large enough stakes in some stocks that they were deemed "affiliates," meaning that the fund had a special ownership relationship with those firms. Other stocks were noted as illiquid securities and 144 A securities, which means they're more difficult to trade than common stocks. Because it's harder for the manager to get rid of these stocks if something goes wrong, they can spell greater risk for the fund.

Financial Statements

A fund's annual report concludes with its financial statements. Brace yourself: There's considerable data here, and it's not usually placed within any kind of useful context. Morningstar gets a lot of its data from this part of the report. After we enter it all into our databases, we crunch the numbers, distill the information, and put it in context to make it more use-able for you.

If you want to dig into the raw numbers, though, here's what you should focus on. First, examine what's known as the fund's Selected Per Share Data. This is usually the last page of actual information, located just before the legal discussion of accounting practices. Here you'll find the fund's NAVs (net asset value, or price per share), expense ratios, and portfolio turnover ra-tios for each of the past five years (or more). Check to see whether the fund's expense ratio has gone down over time (this should happen if the fund's as-sets under management have been increasing) and whether its turnover rate has changed much over time (if so, you may want to find out why—did the manager change her strategy?).

Cost-conscious investors can check out the breakdown of fund's ex-penses, including management fees, under the Statement of Operations. Fi-nally, find out how much unrealized or undistributed capital gains a fund has in the Statement of Assets and Liabilities. These figures can be the key to a fund's future tax efficiency.

A gain is unrealized when a stock has gone up but the fund hasn't sold it. When the fund sells the stock, that's a realized gain, which has to be distrib-uted to shareholders. This means that if a fund has a lot of unrealized or undistributed gains, you will get socked with the tax consequences when the fund realizes this gain. High unrealized capital gains don't necessarily spell trouble, though. Funds can accumulate unrealized gains precisely because the manager has been trying to limit taxable distributions. Do be cautious if a fund with a big unrealized gain has recently had a manager change or strategy change or shareholders have been cashing in. A change of strategy or manager could mean the fund will begin dumping the existing holdings and realizing the gains, which could spell a big tax hit. Likewise, if shareholder redemp-tions are large enough, the manager may be forced to sell stocks to raise cash and incur taxable gains in the process.

What to Do

You can request a prospectus, SAI, or annual report by phone, by direct mail, and sometimes by e-mail. Many fund companies have their fund lit-erature available online at their Web sites. All mutual funds have to file their prospectuses and reports (and a host of other documents) with the SEC. You can view these at the SEC's Web site: www.sec.gov.

While we suggest that you begin your fund evaluation with these documents, don't stop there. Seek out third-party sources, such as Morningstar, to help put your fund into context. Compare it with other funds that do similar things. You need to see how its costs stack up, if its performance is competitive, and if it compensates for the risks it is taking on.

Recommended Reading

THESE ARE SOME of our favorite books on investing and mutual funds.

Common Sense on Mutual Funds: New Imperatives for the Intelligent Investor
by John C. Bogle, 1999. Published by John Wiley & Sons. The best book on
funds, period.

Classics: An Investor's Anthology
by Charles D. Ellis with James R. Vertin, 1990. Published by Business One
Irwin.

Classics II: Another Investor's Anthology
by Charles D. Ellis with James R. Vertin, 1991. Published by McGraw-Hill
Professional Publishing. Two wonderful anthologies. If we only had space for
two investment books, these are the ones we would keep.

Asset Allocation: Balancing Financial Risk
by Roger C. Gibson, 2000. Published by McGraw-Hill Trade. An essential
text that has influenced a whole generation of financial advisors.

The Intelligent Investor: A Book of Practical Counsel
by Benjamin Graham, 1985. Published by HarperCollins. The wisdom in this book still resonates decades after its publication.

Security Analysis: The Classic 1934 Edition
by Benjamin Graham and David L. Dodd, 1996. Published by McGraw-Hill Trade. This book is considered the bible of investing by many top managers.

Buffett: The Making of an American Capitalist
by Roger Lowenstein, 1995. Published by Doubleday. A great biography. You cannot call yourself a serious investor and not be a student of Buffett.

One Up on Wall Street: How to Use What You Already Know to Make Money in the Market
by Peter Lynch, 1990. Published by Simon & Schuster. This classic is one of the most accessible books on picking individual stocks.

A Random Walk Down Wall Street
by Burton G. Malkiel, 2000. Published by W.W. Norton & Company. Makes the case for indexing and shows how much of what we attribute as brilliance among managers may really be random chance.

The Wall Street Journal Guide to Understanding Money & Investing
by Kenneth M. Morris, Virginia B. Morris, and Alan M. Siegel, 1999. Published by Fireside. This easily skimmed, user-friendly guide provides novices with solid money and market information.

The New Commonsense Guide to Mutual Funds
by Mary Rowland, 1998. Published by Bloomberg Press. Rowland's guide is the perfect choice if you would rather not spend a lot of time reading about funds—or want to read about them in short, digestible chunks.

The Money Game
by Adam Smith, 1976. Published by Random House. While the attitudes are dated, this remains a great history.

The Only Investment Guide You'll Ever Need
by Andrew Tobias, 2002. Published by Harvest Books. A great introduction to thinking about the key trade-offs of personal finance.

The Money Masters and The New Money Masters
by John Train, 1994. Published by HarperBusiness. Wonderful introductions to some of the best money managers ever.

Other Morningstar Resources

IN ADDITION TO this book, Morningstar publishes a number of products about mutual funds. There's something for everyone, from newsletters to sourcebooks. Most can be found at your local library, or you can call Morningstar to start your own subscriptions (800-735-0700).

Morningstar® Mutual Funds™
This twice-monthly report service features full-page financial reports and analysis of 1,600 funds specially selected for building and maintaining balanced portfolios. Our report service is favored by professionals and serious investors and carried in more than 4,000 libraries nationwide. Trial subscriptions are available.

Morningstar® FundInvestor™
Monthly newsletters offers 48 pages of fund investing help, including Morningstar model portfolios, analysis of funds, funds to avoid, the FundInvestor 500, and Morningstar Analyst Picks. Christine Benz is the editor.

Morningstar.com

Our Web site features investing information on funds, stocks, bonds, retirement planning, and more. In addition to powerful portfolio tools, you'll find daily articles by Morningstar analysts and editors, including Russel Kinnel. Much information on the site is free, and there's a reasonably priced Premium Membership service for investors requiring more in-depth information and sophisticated analytical tools, which you can try for free for 14 days.

Morningstar® Funds 500™

Annual book of full-page reports on 500 selected funds. The new edition appears in January of each year and includes complete year-end results of funds covered, as well as general fund industry performance information. Christine Benz is the editor.

Index